Zygmunt Bauman

Zygmunt Bauman

Prophet of Postmodernity

Dennis Smith

Polity Press

The right of Dennis Smith to be identified as author of this work has been asserted in accordance with the Copyright, Designs and Patents Act 1988.

First published in 1999 by Polity Press in association with Blackwell Publishers Ltd.

Editorial office:
Polity Press
65 Bridge Street
Cambridge CB2 1UR, UK

Marketing and production:
Blackwell Publishers Ltd
108 Cowley Road
Oxford OX4 1JF, UK

Published in the USA by
Blackwell Publishers Inc.
Commerce Place
350 Main Street
Malden, MA 02148, USA

ISBN 0-7456-1898-7
ISBN 0-7456-1899-5 (pbk)

A catalogue record for this book is available from the British Library.

Library of Congress Cataloging-in-Publication Data
Smith, Dennis, 1945–
    Zygmunt Bauman: prophet of postmodernity / Dennis Smith.
        p. cm. — (Key contemporary thinkers)
    Includes bibliographical references and index.
    ISBN 0-7456-1898-7 (alk. paper). — ISBN 0-7456-1899-5 (pbk.: alk. paper)
    1. Bauman, Zygmunt. 2. Postmodernism — Social aspects. 3. Civilization,
Modern — 20th century. I. Title. II. Series: Key contemporary thinkers (Cambridge,
England)
HM449. S55 2000
303.4 — dc21   99–27526
                                                                                          CIP
Typeset in 10½ on 12 pt Palatino
by Best-set Typesetter Ltd., Hong Kong
Printed in Great Britain by MPG Books, Bodmin, Cornwall

This book is printed on acid-free paper.

Key Contemporary Thinkers

Published

Jeremy Ahearne, *Michel de Certeau: Interpretation and its Other*
Peter Burke, *The French Historical Revolution: The* Annales *School 1929–1989*
Michael Caesar, *Umberto Eco: Philosophy, Semiotics and the Work of Fiction*
Colin Davis, *Levinas: An Introduction*
Simon Evnine, *Donald Davidson*
Edward Fullbrook and Kate Fullbrook, *Simone de Beauvoir: A Critical Introduction*
Andrew Gamble, *Hayek: The Iron Cage of Liberty*
Philip Hansen, *Hannah Arendt: Politics, History and Citizenship*
Sean Homer, *Fredric Jameson: Marxism, Hermeneutics, Postmodernism*
Christopher Hookway, *Quine: Language, Experience and Reality*
Christina Howells, *Derrida: Deconstruction from Phenomenology to Ethics*
Simon Jarvis, *Adorno: A Critical Introduction*
Douglas Kellner, *Jean Baudrillard: From Marxism to Post-Modernism and Beyond*
Chandran Kukathas and Philip Pettit, *Rawls: A Theory of Justice and its Critics*
James McGilvray, *Chomsky: Language, Mind, and Politics*
Lois McNay, *Foucault: A Critical Introduction*
Philip Manning, *Erving Goffman and Modern Sociology*
Michael Moriarty, *Roland Barthes*
William Outhwaite, *Habermas: A Critical Introduction*
John Preston, *Feyerabend: Philosophy, Science and Society*
Susan Sellers, *Hélène Cixous: Authorship, Autobiography and Love*
David Silverman, *Harvey Sacks: Social Science and Conversation Analysis*
Dennis Smith, *Zygmunt Bauman: Prophet of Postmodernity*
Geoffrey Stokes, *Popper: Philosophy, Politics and Scientific Method*
Georgia Warnke, *Gadamer: Hermeneutics, Tradition and Reason*
James Williams, *Lyotard: Towards a Postmodern Philosophy*
Jonathan Wolff, *Robert Nozick: Property, Justice and the Minimal State*

Forthcoming

Maria Baghramian, *Hilary Putnam*
Sara Beardsworth, *Kristeva*

James Carey, *Innis and McLuhan*
Thomas D'Andrea, *Alasdair MacIntyre*
Eric Dunning, *Norbert Elias*
Jocelyn Dunphy, *Paul Ricoeur*
Matthew Elton, *Daniel Dennett*
Nigel Gibson, *Frantz Fanon*
Graeme Gilloch, *Walter Benjamin*
Karen Green, *Dummett: Philosophy of Language*
Espen Hammer, *Stanley Cavell*
Fred Inglis, *Clifford Geertz*
Sarah Kay, *Žižek: A Critical Introduction*
Paul Kelly, *Ronald Dworkin*
Valerie Kennedy, *Edward Said*
Carl Levy, *Antonio Gramsci*
Dermot Moran, *Edmund Husserl*
Harold Noonan, *Frege*
Wes Sharrock and Rupert Read, *Kuhn*
Nick Smith, *Charles Taylor*
Nicholas Walker, *Heidegger*

Contents

Part III Dialogue

Preface

This has been a very enjoyable book to write. Zygmunt Bauman's sustained exploration of the nature of modernity and postmodernity is one of the great intellectual journeys of our times. Zygmunt Bauman was generous with his encouragement and made it clear from the beginning that he would not try to influence what I wrote, or offer approval or otherwise of the interpretations I might come up with. It cannot be a comfortable experience to be subjected to someone else's interpretation of the meaning of your life and career. I want to thank Zygmunt Bauman for putting up with my impertinent attention.

While writing the book, I kept the following quotation by my desk as a constant reminder of the limits against which I was pressing:

> The text the author has produced acquires its own life. True – the text derives its meaning from the setting in which it has been conceived. In this setting, however, the author's intentions are just a factor among others; and surely the factor of which we know least. No less significant are those other constituents of the setting which the text absorbed, and those the text could absorb but did not: the absence is as vociferous as the presence.
>
> On the other hand the reader is no more free than the author in determining the meaning of the text . . . He understands as much as his knowledge allows him . . . If the author sends his signals from an island whose interior he has not and could not explore in full, the reader is a passenger who walks the deck of a sailing ship he does not navigate. The meaning is the instant of their encounter. (Zygmunt Bauman, *Hermeneutics and Social Science*, p. 229)

I have gained a lot from conversations with Ulrich Bielefeld of the Hamburger Institut für Sozialforschung, with John Rex of the Centre for Research in Ethnic Relations at Warwick University and with Richard Kilminster and Ian Varcoe, both of the School of Sociology and Social Policy at Leeds University. I owe thanks to others also. Janina Bauman was kind and tolerant when I rang or came to call. Val Riddell suggested the theme of this book but, sadly, did not live to see it published. Evelin Lindner gave me detailed and valuable comments on several chapters and has made the book a better one. Caroline Baggaley at Keele University has been a good friend. Tanya Smith has provided insight, wit and a sense of proportion. Aston Business School has a long-standing tradition of encouraging research in the social sciences and it is a pleasure to have the support of colleagues such as Henry Miller, Reiner Grundmann, John Smith and Helen Higson. The 'invisible college' of social scientists at Aston University crosses departmental boundaries and includes Sue Wright and Dieter Haselbach of the School of Languages and European Studies.

Presentations drawing upon the book's argument at various stages of its development were given at Leeds University, Sheffield University (at the kind invitation of Sharon Macdonald), Aston Business School and the British Sociological Association's Annual Conference at Glasgow. I have benefited from the comments of many colleagues and hope they find the final result interesting and worthwhile. If not, I do not expect them to share the blame.

Part I
Setting the Agenda

1

Living Without a Guidebook

Introduction

If you are new to the hotly raging debate about modernity and post-modernity, start by reading Zygmunt Bauman. He is one of the most interesting and influential commentators on these aspects of our human condition.

Zygmunt Bauman has brilliantly described humankind's trek through modernity during the past few centuries. He has also drawn a vivid map of the new world coming into being as modernity turns postmodern.

Bauman is part of the story he tells. He can be found on the map he draws. Born in 1925 in Poland and educated in Soviet Russia, Bauman fought with the Red Army against the Germans during World War II. He emigrated from Poland to the West in 1968. Since then he has published a new book every one or two years.

Critical perspectives

This book presents an overview of Bauman's work between the 1960s and the late 1990s, and it also provides a critical perspective on that work. I have tried to get 'behind' the texts themselves in order to understand why they were produced and what they were intended to achieve.

Bauman wants to awaken people to their creative potential and to their moral responsibilities. That is not difficult to discover, since he is quite explicit about it. However, the way Bauman defines his objectives changes over the decades. So does the way he tries to achieve them. Bauman does not announce these alterations of definition and direction. They have to be reconstructed through the kind of critical analysis I have carried out in the first part of this book, where I trace the main outlines of Bauman's life and career as a young refugee, a wartime soldier, a military bureaucrat, a revisionist intellectual and an émigré.

Analysis of this kind asks 'why *this* agenda?' and 'why this *change* of agenda?' Our response to a specific text is altered if we are able to see it as part of a larger constellation of writing, especially if that larger constellation tells its own story. I say 'tells its own story' as if the process were unproblematic, a matter of simply downloading a file. In fact, it requires a concentrated effort of interpretation, in the course of which one has to keep the imagination under tight control, avoid unwarranted assumptions, try to avoid going too far beyond the evidence, but, at the same time, not ignore the evidence that exists.

These are, I assume, the working practices of a good detective, although I must say straightaway that I am not looking for a 'conviction'. I am in broad sympathy with Zygmunt Bauman's objectives. My curiosity comes out of fascination, not suspicion.

This first part of the book, 'Setting the Agenda', sets out my understanding of the long process that led from Bauman's search for a 'modern Marxism' in the 1960s (Bauman 1969: 1) to his evocation of 'postmodernity and its discontents' in the 1990s (Bauman 1997). In the second part of the book, entitled 'The Road to Postmodernity', I show how Bauman's major works in English can be understood in the light of the interpretation developed in part I. In particular, I trace the genealogy of Bauman's vision of modernity and postmodernity, and explore its intellectual content.

In the final part of the book, 'Dialogue', I appraise Bauman's work from two other directions. I locate Bauman in the field of play occupied by critical theory and post-structuralism, examining the points of convergence and tension. In this context, I pay particular attention to Adorno, Habermas, Foucault and Lyotard. Finally, I debate the nature of modernity and postmodernity with Zygmunt Bauman in a correspondence that appears as the last chapter in the book.

This book exemplifies one of the methodological principles explored by Bauman. To borrow a passage from his *Thinking Sociologically*, my narrative goes in circles rather than developing in a straight line. Some topics return later, to be looked upon once again in the light of what we have discussed in the meantime. This is how all effort of understanding works. Each step in understanding makes a return to previous stages necessary. What we thought we understood in full reveals new question marks we previously failed to notice. The process may never end; but much may be gained in its course. (Bauman 1990b: 19)

So it is with this book about Bauman.

Sociology plus

Bauman is a sociologist. That means he is in the business of 'viewing human actions as *elements of wider figurations*' and seeing human actors as 'locked together in a web of *mutual dependency*'. As a sociologist, he wants to 'defamiliarize the familiar' and make the world more amenable to individual and collective freedom. He realises very well that, when people are free to think and act for themselves, this 'may be seen as having a destabilizing effect on the existing power relations' (Bauman 1990b: 7, 15, 17; emphases in original).

Bauman's sociology is intrinsically critical, dedicated to testing 'common sense' (p. 8): in other words, the unsystematic mixture of conventions and prejudices in terms of which we typically manage the routines of daily life. However, when Bauman has breached the barricade of 'common sense', which way does he march? This question could be asked of any critical sociologist – and most sociologists would say that their discipline is intrinsically critical.

At this point, it becomes relevant that Bauman is more than 'just' a sociologist. He is also a highly competent social philosopher, well versed in, for example, Hegel, Husserl, Heidegger, Wittgenstein and Lévinas. More than that, Bauman has been a socialist for most of his life. In the late 1980s, his wife wrote that he was still 'a sincere socialist . . . deep in his heart' (J. Bauman 1988: 115). He retains a very strong commitment to equality, freedom and justice, although he now prefers to describe these as 'western, Enlightenment values' (Bauman 1992a: 225).

Finally, Bauman is not only a sociologist, a social philosopher and (in some sense, at least) a socialist. He is also an accomplished storyteller, a maker of historical narratives. A significant part of the power of Bauman's work comes from the stories he relates. The structure and dynamic of these narratives tell readers where they are located in time and space. They also tell them the direction in which they are moving, or perhaps should be.[1]

Two narratives are central to Bauman's early and later work, respectively: the narrative of progress towards a socialist utopia; and the narrative of the transition from modernity to post-modernity. They both begin with the breakdown of a 'traditional' social order, have heroes or pioneers, and end by challenging the reader to take some action or make some choice.

I imagine that some readers will come to this book feeling rather puzzled about the meaning of the terms 'modernity' and 'post-modernity'. If their meaning is not problematic for you, then you would do well to skip the next two sections. However, if you remain puzzled, or if you are simply curious about the way I understand these ideas, then read on, aware that I am aiming these passages at 'beginners'.

What is modernity?

Everyone knows that if something is 'modern' it is up to date, in tune with the latest ideas, more advanced than previous versions. That applies, most obviously, to things like cameras, cars and high-tech kitchen equipment. These modern items are desired and bought by modern people. They are made and distributed by modern organizations, most of which are trying to design something even more modern for next year or the year after that.

The modern world is permanently on fast forward. Modernity means constant change. Many terms in this paragraph would have made no sense to anyone in 1975. Go to your lap-top or palm-top computer. Use it to get on to the Internet. Access a search engine. Now find some web-sites dealing with the idea of modernity. Surf between them. Follow the links. Find out when in history men and women started describing themselves as modern people living in a modern age.

You will discover that the idea of modernity, of living in the 'modern age', began in Europe sometime during the late sixteenth century. It implied a contrast with other 'ages' that were not modern, epochs that had gone before, that were out of date, whose moment had passed. Europeans began to see history as divided into three epochs: ancient, medieval and modern. The Greeks and

Romans did not know they were 'ancient'. Medieval knights did not realize they were in the 'middle' of history. But we, like our sixteenth-century ancestors, 'know' we are modern.

In the modern age, three powerful forces have come into play. The first is the modern national state. The state has dug its roots deep into the soil of society and sucked up resources in the form of tax revenues. States have used tax income to build up their muscle power (more soldiers, more bureaucrats, more display) and used that muscle power to defend, develop and, in some cases, terrorize the populations they control.

The second powerful force is modern science. Scientists and engineers have explored the properties of the environment and tried to discover the operating principles of matter. They have developed tools for manipulating the natural world, asserting greater human influence over it. Weapons have become more deadly, medicines more effective, engines more powerful. Systems of transport and communications have penetrated into the world's furthest recesses.

The third great force is capitalism – the systematic pursuit of profit. Traders and manufacturers have pushed and shoved local communities into producing for the market. They have cut their way through the thicket of habit and custom to bring labour, skills, energy sources and raw materials into new money-making relationships. Capitalism has drawn the whole population into activities that feed into the creation of mobile wealth – resources that can be used to engineer still further change.

At the heart of modernity is a struggle for betterment: being better, doing better, getting better. The competition takes place at several levels: between individuals, families, cities, empires, governments and companies, for example. Any group prevented from taking part in the contest on equal terms (due to discrimination, disability, oppression or imprisonment) feels extremely discontented.

The 'modern' assumption is that everybody has a right to take part in the struggle for betterment. Or, rather, every group claims that right for its own members. They may wish to deny the same right to certain other groups whom they regard as 'inhuman' or 'uncivilized'.

An aspect of the struggle within modernity is the contest between ideologies. These idea-systems compete to justify the different demands and restrictions imposed upon the masses by bureaucrats, bosses and experts. At the heart of all these ideologies of modernity is the promise of a better earthly existence to come.

One powerful ideology inspired by the progress of science is the ethos of planning: the idea that experts can manipulate the world to produce desirable outcomes by using their scientific knowledge in a rational way. Another, opposing, ideology also draws inspiration from a scientific source. This is social Darwinism, the notion that social competition, however nasty, tends to favour those fittest to survive. The assumption is that we all benefit from this in the long run.

Social Darwinism is sometimes interwoven with the *laissez-faire* ideology of the market. This approach argues that an invisible hand ensures that, even though people pursue their own selfish interests as buyers and sellers, the total amount of useful wealth within society tends to increase and, again, we all benefit from this in the fullness of time.

Both *laissez-faire* and social Darwinism were powerful in the nineteenth century, although their influence remained powerful in the twentieth. During the past seventy-five years, other ideologies have become prominent. Democracy gained a powerful global advocate when the United States came out of its long period of isolation, especially during and after World War II.

Democracy has often been interlinked with Keynesian welfarism. This is the idea that the state can manage capitalism in such a way that the people enjoy full employment as well as social rights such as education, health care and pensions.[2] The modern national state has also been the focus of other ideologies, notably fascism and communism. Each of these two systems claims that state power can be used to make society perfect.

Every ideology assigns a particular role to each of the 'big players': in other words, the state, science, capitalism and the people themselves. For example, communism and fascism both give leading roles to the state and science, while *laissez-faire* emphasizes the capitalist market. In all cases, the 'winners' are, supposedly, the people. This entity is presented sometimes as a hive of busily interacting individuals (workers, consumers or citizens), sometimes as a united body (a *Volk*, a 'nation' or a proletariat).

During the past century, men and women have been trained to see modernity through the rose-coloured spectacles provided by ideologies of this kind. The job of making these spectacles, keeping them well polished and ensuring that they are worn properly has fallen to the ranks of the intellectuals, in government, in education and in the media. They have been the priests of modernity.

What is postmodernity?

One of the notable features of Western culture *in the present phase of modernity* is the widespread use of the idea of postmodernity by intellectuals. Talk about postmodernity does not mean that modernity has ended. It is more accurate to say that postmodernity is a key idea employed by intellectuals trying to cope with the impact of four massive changes in the 'big picture' of modernity during the last three decades of the twentieth century.

Firstly, national states have been cut down to size. They have become much less ambitious in the claims they make about their capacity to reshape society. During the 1980s, the US federal government and many European governments abandoned Keynesian welfare strategies. When the Soviet Union broke up during the early 1990s, this brought the twentieth century's most sustained and ambitious experiment in state-sponsored modernization to an end. Opponents of the ethos of planning argued that this finally destroyed the claims of that ideology.

Secondly, awareness of risk has increased. People in the West are being forced to stop expecting that a caring state will protect them from cradle to grave. They must live with a high level of risk and make what arrangements they can to cope. The old safety nets have been torn to bits. The family is an increasingly unstable institution. The welfare state cannot meet the demands placed upon it. Most frightening of all, science has shown its dangerous side.

We use science and technology to drive the world faster, to squeeze more out of nature, to give us a better life. But we do not feel in control. The level of risk is spiralling upward. The explosion in the Soviet nuclear plant at Chernobyl, the discovery of the hole in the ozone layer, the scare over British beef and BSE, the shock of AIDS and our failure to find a cure for this disease: all these happenings have combined to popularize a very pessimistic thesis. This has three parts. Science is just as likely to produce bad outcomes as good outcomes. The risk of science threatening life and health is high and difficult to predict. Finally, bureaucrats and officials are likely to disguise or underestimate the level of risk.

Thirdly, capitalism has become global. Large-scale businesses have cut themselves free from the close links with national states that Keynesian welfarism required. Multinational companies conduct their operations across national borders. They can shift their investments from country to country depending on which government offers them the best deal. They are intrinsically unreliable as long-term partners for states trying to manage particular national economies. In fact, the very idea of a 'national economy' has become an anachronism.

Fourthly, European imperialism has come to an end. In 1900, cities such as London, Paris, Brussels, Amsterdam, Vienna and Moscow were not just political or commercial capitals of their respective countries. They were all the headquarters of vast multinational or multiethnic empires, both within Europe and beyond. This vast imperial structure has sunk like the *Titanic*. The iceberg it struck was the United States, an ex-colony of the British empire which grew more powerful than its old master. America's interventions in World War I and World War II were decisive and had fatal results for European imperialism.

The European empires sank below the waves in an uneven way. Some were more buoyant than others and broke surface again, briefly. World War I swept away the Austrio-Hungarian empire of the Hapsburgs and its arch rival the Ottoman empire. The Russian and German empires were also broken up. However, by the early 1940s a multiethnic German empire had been re-established under Hitler.

Further decline was precipitated by World War II. The Allied victory destroyed Hitler's German empire. The war also led to the final disintegration of the British and French empires. However, after the war Stalin rebuilt the Russian empire in Eastern Europe. The final phase began in 1989. The break-up of the Soviet bloc was the last great decolonization movement in modern European history.

These four changes – the shrinking of the national state, the spiralling of risk, the globalization of capital and the collapse of European imperialism – add up to a large-scale restructuring of the architecture of modernity. New rules and conventions are taking shape only very gradually. We are still adapting our expectations, learning appropriate strategies for survival.

The key 'load-bearing' structures are no longer national states. Institution building is going on at a higher level, the level of multinational and transnational corporations, international agreements such as the North American Free Trade Area, and supra-state bodies such as the European Union.

The ideological repertoire cultivated by intellectuals during the twentieth century has lost its power to convince or energize the population. This applies above all to ideologies that gave a large role to the planning function of the national state. People do not want to lose their democratic right to vote, but they do not have very high expectations of government.

Europe is the big loser in this game of global restructuring. Five hundred years of European global pre-eminence have come to an end. It was over by 1945. The cost of American military support for the United Kingdom and France was the dismantling of the old empires, making room for 'Coca-Cola capitalism'. This was an offer the European allies could not refuse. During the quarter of a century following the end of World War II, the United States enjoyed global near-hegemony.

It was only very slowly that the profound implications of the loss of empire began to penetrate the European consciousness. Europeans lived in a kind of imperial afterglow until the early 1970s. Then the oil shock came. It showed that the days were over when cheap energy would be delivered without fail to the West by subordinate Third World governments. The 1970s delivered a series of humiliations to the West, culminating in President Carter's deep embarrassment over the American hostages taken by the new revolutionary government of Iran.

Ironically, by helping to end European imperialism, the United Staets has made itself the chief target of African and Asian politicians who need a hate figure to blame for the misery and discontent of their people. Much of the fury directed against the United States in the Third World is the discharge of centuries of frustration brewed up under European rule. With so much attention directed at 'American imperialism', it has been easy to forget the much longer period of European rule that preceded it; even easier to forget that European culture and politics have themselves been deeply influenced by Europe's long centuries of privileged existence.

For centuries, Europeans were 'the masters'. It has not been easy for them to cope with their dethronement and adjust to their loss. Acknowledging the sense of loss is difficult to do. Guilt and embarrassment swamp all other feelings. Nostalgia for the old days is Europe's 'love that dare not speak its name'.

During the past three decades, intellectual life in Europe has registered an intense, subterranean feeling of bereavement and emptiness. The prefix 'post' has become a much used syllable: postmodern, postindustrial, postcolonial, post-Enlightenment, poststructural and so on. The repeated use of this word expresses a deep sense that a momentous change has occurred. Whenever 'post' is employed in this way it carries a hidden force drawn from the West's biblical tradition, either a negative force, as in Adam and Eve's loss of innocence *after* the Fall, or a positive force as in humankind's redemption *after* the Messiah's arrival on earth.

The idea of the 'postmodern' has been floating around the cultural ether on both sides of the Atlantic since the 1970s and can be traced back even earlier.[3] The term is sometimes applied to exciting experimental work in the arts, using the fragmentation of old forms as an opportunity to make daring experiments. However, it is from the distinctive European experience that the word 'postmodernity' gets its strong connotations of disillusionment, disappointment and even despair.

The logic is simple, powerful and devastating. Europe played the leading role in making the modern world. However, that continent no longer has the leading part in running that world. As a result, West Europeans experience a 'postmodern' existence at the end of the millennium. The world is still modern, but 'their' modern world has gone.

Europe's intellectuals have certainly experienced a decline in their circumstances as a social group. The shrinking of the state has reduced their employment opportunities and weakened their job rights. The discrediting of experts has undermined their prestige. For some, the European Union has provided a new focus. It is a project with reassuring overtones of the nation-state.

However, Europe's public sphere, the arena of political debate, is weak and fragmented. Furthermore, Europe is multicultural and multilingual. Intellectuals have no stable base within this polity. There is no pan-European education system that will transmit their ideas to a pan-European public. Intellectual debates do not cross national boundaries very easily. Habermas, Foucault and a few others may be read throughout Europe, but do their commentators (in French, English, German, Spanish, Italian, Polish, Czech and so on) ever read each other?[4]

The crumbling of Europe's empires and the collapse of belief in socialism and Keynesian welfarism created a large political and ideological vacuum. The European Union, post-Maastricht treaty, now occupies some of that space, both political and ideological. A large share has also been taken by ethnic nationalism. Privatization has cut away large chunks of the remaining political space, taking major services out of government's hands. Intellectuals, especially in Europe, have been traumatized by these changes. In large measure, they are being pushed aside. Governments pay less attention to them. So do citizens and consumers.

These changes have been felt less intensely by intellectuals in the United States for several reasons. Ideologies that gave a large planning function to the state made fewer inroads there in the early and mid-twentieth century, so their decline is less disturbing. American intellectuals are much more used to surviving in a social climate dominated by the interests of business. Veblen's *The Higher Learning in America* (1918) still provides valuable insights on this question. Liberal critics of capitalism such as Robert Park, Louis Wirth and other members of the Chicago school of sociology were more familiar than their European counterparts with the need to cultivate public opinion.[5]

Finally, the emergence of global capitalism has confirmed, not undermined, the position of American business as the leading force in world affairs. Indirectly, this sustains the authority and prestige of the American government and its 'think tanks' staffed by university professors. In the long term, the United States' position of leadership will probably be challenged by Asian capitalism, but at the turn of the millennium this time had not yet arrived.

However, let us return to the troubled plight of European intellectuals. What is their function in these new conditions of restructured modernity at the turn of the millennium? Who is their audience? If they do not wish to become business consultants, television entertainers, nationalist spokespersons, feminist campaigners or Eurocrats – all plausible strategies – whom will they seek to influence? What will they tell them? There is no clear answer, no consensus on the main outlines of a critical perspective that challenges the prevailing political mood and offers a viable alternative. There is a deep uncertainty about which way to turn. All this has been poured into the debate on postmodernity.

The outpouring of scholarly work on postmodernity and the whole 'post' family (post-Fordism, postindustrialism, postemotionalism, poststructuralism, postcolonialism, postpositivism and so on) is like a loud chorus of distress coming from birds forced out of their nests by the uprooting of a giant tree. There is no dominant melody within the cacophony. It is difficult for anyone listening to these discordant outpourings to work out an overall message. Charles Lemert catches the mood of general confusion in the title of his recent book: *Postmodernism Is Not What You Think* (1997).

Two dispassionate reviews of the literature published in the early 1990s both found the air thick with contention. Margaret Rose (1991) observed 'very wide differences of philosophy between many of those now using the same term'. The following year, Barry Smart reported 'major differences over the conceptualisation of the post-modern, and the associated question of its relationship to the project of modernity' (1992: 180). He warned against 'an unqualified endorsement of the polymorphous perversities sometimes associated with manifestations of the postmodern' (p. 182).

Rose tried to find order in the field. However, the kind of order she found is mind-boggling in its complexity. In a typical passage, Rose argued that

> many of the more recent concepts of post-modernism may be placed in the . . . categories of 'deconstructionist', 'double-coded' and 'ideal' post-modernisms. Within these categories, deconstructionist post-modernism may be said to have criticised modernist value systems of various kinds (for Hassan, the old canons of modernism; for Lyotard, the 'metanarratives' of modernity – of capitalism, progress and consensus; for Jameson the 'culture of capital'; for Burgin, Greenberg's valorisation of high modernist art; or for Fekete that which he terms the 'modern' 'fact-value' distinction), as well as other rival forms of post-modernism which they have seen to be antipathetic to theirs. Further to this, and in opposition to many of the deconstructionist theories outlined above, Charles Jencks's theory of post-modernism as a double-coding of modernism with other codes has presented the post-modern as both incorporating and transforming modernism, while ideal post-modernisms such as Fuller's have expressed dissatisfaction with both the above sets of theories and looked to the future establishment of values which are both 'post' the 'modern' and all earlier theories dubbed post-modern. (1991: 176)[6]

This summary reads like a report filed by a war correspondent in the Balkans. In that respect, it gives the right impression. There is no consensus on the nature of postmodernity.

Before moving on, I should emphasize that the last two sections have described my own understanding of modernity and post-modernity as distinct from Zygmunt Bauman's views on this matter. However, it is now time to turn to Bauman.

Why Bauman is worth reading

To recapitulate, the centre of gravity within modernity shifted in the twentieth century. In Europe this felt like an earthquake, one that gave massive jolts to the continent during the first and second world wars, then delivered a series of aftershocks. One of these aftershocks swept away the Soviet bloc, the last of the great European empires, which collapsed in the years after 1989. This twentieth-century earthquake in Europe has set off the great debate about postmodernity – a debate that has become louder and more difficult to decipher with every passing decade.

Within this debate, the voice of Zygmunt Bauman is distinctive. It is clear and understandable. There is no undertone of panic. Nor is there despair. I believe the reason for this is that Bauman assimilated the 'postmodern' experience at an individual level many years before it became a fashionable topic.

We need to understand the following key facts about Bauman. He has believed in the promise of socialist modernity with great intensity. He has been painfully disillusioned about the capacity of existing institutions in Poland and Eastern Europe to fulfil this promise. He has suffered the shock of displacement: from the communist establishment, from Poland, from direct involvement in the state socialist experiment. He and his family were confronted with the disorienting challenge of adapting to Western capitalism.

All this happened to Bauman before 1970. Bauman is certainly not the only person to whom it happened. However, not many people have been able to survive and assimilate the experience as well as Bauman. Nor have many others been so effective in turning that experience into insightful sociology, challenging social philosophy and provocative historical narratives.

When postmodernity rose up the agenda during the 1980s, Bauman was able to watch as his fellow intellectuals in the West caught up with him, so to speak, in terms of their own experience of disillusionment, displacement and disorientation. The value of Bauman is that he has had more time to reorient himself. His situation is a little like the archetypal early-twentieth-century immigrant to the United States who arrived 'the day before yesterday'. He is able to give advice to today's arrivals – men and women still shaky from the voyage to postmodernity, people still finding their land legs.

Bauman is worth listening to. His project is tremendously ambitious. He believes we are entering a new epoch, one brought about by the restructuring of modernity and our changed attitude towards it. Postmodernity is the human condition that arrives *after* people stop believing in the big promises made by modern ideologies: *after* they refuse to accept any longer, for example, that socialism will bring equality and freedom, or that fascism will purify society, or that democracy will give power to the people, or that science gives humankind the power to bend nature to its will.

Bauman wants to grasp the essential features of postmodern men and women as thinking, feeling, choosing beings. He wants to make sense of the social worlds in which they, increasingly, find themselves. He wants to understand how inhabitants of the postmodern habitat may try to construct meaningful lives for themselves.

The myth of the cage-dwellers

The quickest way to give you the essence of Bauman's approach to modernity and postmodernity is to tell you a story. It has echoes of Plato's myth of the cave. You will recall that Plato thought human beings live out their lives like people held in chains within a darkened cave. These cave-dwellers are prevented from seeing the real life that is being led outside the cave in glorious light. They can only look at the shadows of that reality flickering on the walls of their cave. In fact, as far as they are concerned, the shadows *are* reality. Only the few people who manage to become released from their chains are able to escape from the cave. They discover reality in its shining essence outside. They realize that the shadows on the wall are not real, but just the dim outlines of a copy of reality.

I am going to modernize, or postmodernize, Plato's myth. According to my myth, Modernity is a city whose happy inhabitants are confined not within caves, but within ergonomically designed cages. Here is the myth of the cage-dwellers.

In Modernity City, people live in cages. Inside every modern cage, fastened by a high-tech chain to the high-tech bars, is a modern guidebook explaining how to live a good life as a modern cage-dweller. The guidebook is fully illustrated with wonderful pictures. It is a reassuring book and reading it makes every cage-dweller feel content. Its soothing messages are reinforced by sounds and images produced by the cage-dweller's television set, video-recorder and CD-ROM player. These are the cage-dweller's 'shadows on the wall'. Within their familiar cages, the cage-dwellers of Modernity City are well adjusted to their reality. The vibes are good. Life is kind.

However, this earthly paradise has a serpent. Its name is Postmodernity. The serpent slithers into the city every night and unlocks a few of the cage doors. Each night a few more cage doors are unlocked. Imagine the scene. The inhabitants of the unlocked cages are startled from sleep by the sound of the key turning. Frightened but curious, they step outside their cages. Stumbling about in half-light, they quickly lose their bearings.

They find themselves in an ambiguous world of half-recognized shapes and shadows. Swirling mist obscures the vision. Nothing is clearly defined. The road signs are difficult to read and seem to conflict with one another. This confusing terrain stretches far into the distance in all directions.

The released inmates desperately miss their precious guide-books, left inside their familiar cages. But what use would they be? They only give instruction about how to be a good cage-dweller. They do not tell you what to do when you are outside the cage. Some people manage to scramble back into their cages. They desperately hold the doors shut from the inside. But for them it is difficult to be as content as they were before. They now know there are vast tracts of human existence not explained in the guidebook.

Other ex-inmates stay outside their cages. Perhaps they cannot find the way back in, perhaps they do not wish to return. Either way they are in a state of confusion. The iron bars that structure modern life no longer confine them, but they no longer have guidebooks telling them who they are, what to do, how to feel, how to relate to one another. They are postmodern men and women.

Postmodernity coexists with modernity. The two are always related. At any one time, some cages are locked, some are open and empty, and some are unlocked with their occupants holding them shut from the inside.

In terms of my metaphor, Bauman has been imagining what 'life on the outside' will be like when most people have left their cages and lost their guidebooks: in other words, when postmodernity has successfully upstaged modernity and established itself as the dominant partner in the relationship.

The postmodern world, Bauman believes, is a world of rootless strangers – a world in which men and women try to survive and create meaning by drawing on whatever personal resources they happen to have. It is a world where people do not have the reassuring guidance of moral absolutes enforced by higher powers. When inhabitants of this world are confronted with ethical dilem-mas, they can no longer refer them 'upwards' to bureaucrats, professionals, politicians, scientists or 'experts' acting as a kind of moral priesthood. They can – in fact, they have to – choose for themselves which rules of behaviour to follow in particular life situations.

This is not a simple matter. How do they judge which rules are 'best'? Do they follow the customs of the group they happen to be amongst at that moment ('when in Rome . . .') or do they apply their own rules and standards? If the latter, are they, for example, attempting to be 'fair', seeking to be 'humane' or just trying to be 'themselves'?

If they are attempting to be 'fair', how do they decide what others 'deserve'? If they are seeking to be 'humane', how do they judge another's best interests? If they are trying to be 'themselves', how do they decide who 'they' are? They have to figure it out on their own without a teacher to correct their homework. Bauman certainly does not have answers to such questions. Or rather, he does not have answers for others. He says that in the new postmodern world coming into being, the responsibility for trying to answer them belongs to each one of us. We cannot forward these queries to any other address.

The rest of this book

In the next chapter, I introduce Bauman's vision of how societies are and could be. In the following chapter, 'Who is Zygmunt Bauman?', I identify a number of key transitions during his career that have shaped Bauman's evolving intellectual agenda. In chapter 4, I explore the way the intellectual *modus operandi* that Bauman acquired in his early career continued to shape his work in the West, even after his discovery of postmodernity in the mid-1980s.

Part II, entitled 'The Road to Postmodernity', contains five chapters. 'The Road to the West' looks at Bauman's analyses of social processes in Polish society and British society before the mid-1970s. 'The Road to Utopia' focuses upon Bauman's theoretical explorations of culture, sociology and socialism during the mid- and late 1970s. 'The Road to the Berlin Wall' returns to the theme of British and Polish society. It looks at Bauman's responses to developments in the United Kingdom and Poland, and more generally in state socialist and capitalist societies, during the 1980s.

'The Trilogy' is an exposition of *Legislators and Interpreters* (Bauman 1987), *Modernity and the Holocaust* (Bauman 1989) and

Modernity and Ambivalence (Bauman 1991). I show that in writing this trilogy, Bauman reoriented his work. He shifted his focus away from the distinction between socialism and capitalism, and towards the distinction between modernity and postmodernity. Finally, 'Bauman's Vision of Modernity and Postmodernity' examines the central themes of Bauman's writings during the 1990s.

Part III, entitled 'Dialogue', contains two chapters. As already noted, the first, 'Between Critical Theory and Poststructuralism', contrasts Bauman with Adorno, Habermas, Foucault and Lyotard. The correspondence between Bauman and myself is in the concluding chapter.

2

No Easy Choices

Culture, choice and sociology

At the centre of Bauman's work are three closely related ideas: culture, choice and sociology. According to Bauman, *culture* is what happens when human beings create order and meaning for themselves. It is an active process of 'making' the world. Societies are shaped by human *choices*. The task for *sociology* is to interpret the nature of culture and explain the part played by choice.

Bauman argues that human beings make their lives coherent by searching for pattern and significance within them. Day by day, hour by hour, they shape the world through their imaginations, intellects and social behaviour. Culture is the medium and expression of this human capacity to 'structurize' (Bauman 1973a: 62) society. However, most societies are unequal. In other words, some people's behaviour, imaginations and intellects count for more than others. The perceptions of those with the best access to knowledge, wealth and other means of power have the greatest influence.

In modern societies, intellectuals – people who think for a living – play a leading role in creating order and meaning. In Bauman's view, intellectuals have a special responsibility to think systematically about the nature of culture, the variety of meanings embedded within different cultures, and the different forms of orderliness that are possible. The influence of intellectuals depends upon several things. They need an institutional or social base, such as the universities, and it helps if those with political power tolerate them and, perhaps, employ them. Intellectuals need access to the media of mass communication. Above all, they must be able to provide interpretations and explanations of the world that relate to the experiences, needs and wishes of their audience.

Turning to the second idea (that societies are shaped by human choices), it is obvious that people do not always get what they wish for; nor do they always believe they are in a position to choose freely. Some people may persuade others to do their bidding because they have more wealth, knowledge or means of force. In other words, the powerful may override the needs or wishes of the weak and choose 'for' them. However, Bauman believes that everyone should be given the chance to think through their own interests and responsibilities as individuals within societies. They should also be encouraged to make autonomous choices in the light of those interests and responsibilities and in full knowledge of what is possible.

Bauman's point is that human beings are able to make several aspects of society different and better by acts of choice. Their capacity and responsibility to do this are much greater than they would like to acknowledge. People like to avoid difficult choices and so may make the comfortable choice of believing they have no choice. This is self-delusion, in Bauman's view. It is a sort of unspoken collective conspiracy to imagine that society is more unequal than it actually is. (People say, 'What can *we* do about it?' Bauman answers, 'More than you think.')

If people think that no realistic alternatives exist, then this very belief has the effect of incapacitating them. It leaves effective control over society in the hands of political, professional and bureaucratic elites. Belief in their own powerlessness disenfranchises ordinary men and women. It is a force for inequality. Intellectuals can make the balance of power resources less unequal by dissolving this belief. They should make relevant knowledge and understanding more available throughout society. (People say, 'What do *we* know about such matters?' Bauman answers, 'You could and should know more.')

This is where the third idea (that sociology's task is to interpret and explain the nature of culture and the part played by choice) comes into play. The sociologists' main responsibility is to work out the scope for choice that now exists within society. They should make people aware of alternative strategies and techniques for organizing their lives at work, in the home and elsewhere, politically, socially and economically. They should indicate as accurately as they can the costs, benefits and risks associated with each of these alternatives, including the alternative of doing nothing.

Sociologists should be ruthlessly honest about the limitations of their own knowledge and understanding. However, they should also demonstrate, where relevant, the misleading, inaccurate or unfounded nature of the 'truths' built into popular discourse, including 'official' pronouncements. The result of this work should be to expand the range of strategies for organizing society and their own lives that people consider possible and realistic. Where this is indeed the result, it increases the number of choices that people are aware of and, as a result, increases their freedom.

The reward for all these efforts, if successful, would be a world in which more people made more autonomous choices. It would be a world in which men and women had more accurate and informed understanding of their individual and shared interests – a world where they had more knowledge about the possible consequences of their actions. Such a world would conceivably have more freedom, less inequality and less injustice. However, this outcome is by no means guaranteed.

As Bauman realizes perfectly well, the greater the number of actors (people, organizations, businesses, governments and so on) making autonomous choices, the more difficult it is to predict the outcome when the effects of their choices interact with each other. Under these conditions, making choices is rather like trying to pick your way in a vehicle through heavy traffic. The eventual result of one driver's choices (turn left? turn right? slow down? speed up?) depends on what several other drivers decide. The outcome might be something no one wants: for example, a crash or a traffic jam.

It is true that, in principle, drivers may be persuaded that it is in their interests to proceed more slowly and carefully, with more consideration and forethought. They may agree to abide by specific conventions. Jams and accidents may be reduced as a result. But how are these moves to be coordinated? Within national societies, governments carry out this task of coordination. They impose speed limits, issue codes for behaviour on the highways, put traffic police on the roads, test motorists for alcohol and drugs and, generally, provide a stable framework of enforceable rules which mean that most people can get from A to B with the minimum possible inconvenience.

However, governments have been reducing the number of social activities that they regulate in this way. The 'nanny state' is very busy on the roads, but it is giving up its responsibilities in many other areas. Very big problems arise when national governments deregulate large areas of social and economic life. An increase in autonomy of choice coincides with a decrease in the ability to control or predict the outcome of any particular choice. For example, if the labour market is deregulated, it becomes easier to enter certain occupations, but it also becomes much more difficult to guarantee how long you will be working with any particular organization. You are at the mercy of the choices yet to be made by several other people.

The challenges posed by deregulation are similar to those encountered at the transnational or global level of social interactions. The difference is that regulation at this level has always been weakly institutionalized, although a degree of informal coordination is provided by diplomacy and other contacts between the most powerful national states. At the global level, there is no equivalent of the national state coordinating international economic and political traffic. Bodies such as the United Nations, the European Union and the World Trade Organization partly fill this gap, but only in the rather patchy way that the US Cavalry policed the frontier in mid-nineteenth-century America.

Bauman has explored these issues, especially in books written during the 1990s. He recognizes that deregulation or lack of regulation produces uncertainty in two ways: there is no framework of rules to guide the actor's choice; and it is very difficult indeed to anticipate the future effects of choices. Freedom becomes a burden. Faced with choices, people do not know what they 'should' do. This 'should' has two meanings. Firstly, there is the pragmatic 'should': what should I do to make sure I get maximim benefits and do not suffer too many costs? Secondly, there is the ethical 'should': what is the morally right or good way to behave?

As Bauman points out repeatedly, the fundamental problem – an insoluble one – is that maximum freedom and maximum security do not come in the same parcel. High levels of freedom usually mean low levels of security. High levels of security usually mean low levels of freedom.

Bauman's vision

Ever since he became a writer, Bauman has been exploring the implications of the three tenets mentioned: that culture is the order-creating and meaning-creating activity of human beings; that societies are shaped by human choices; and that sociology's task is to interpret and explain the nature of culture and the part played by choice. Bauman's explorations have been guided by a strong sense of 'vision'. By 'vision' I mean an intuitive grasp of 'how the world really is': the way it fits together, how human beings fit into it, and what scope there is for making sense of it, acting within it and so on. Schumpeter, for one, recognized the importance of vision. He wrote:

> In every scientific venture, the thing that comes first is Vision. That is to say, before embarking upon analytical work of any kind we must first single out the set of phenomena we wish to investigate, and acquire 'intuitively' a preliminary notion of how they hang together or, in other words, of what appear from our standpoint to be their fundamental properties. (Schumpeter 1986: 561–2)

Between the 1960s and the early 1980s, Bauman's vision was dominated by a powerful sense of how things could be if human beings actively struggled to bring about the free, equal and just society envisaged in the socialist utopia. Not the utopia of material abundance promised in some unspecified future by the state socialist regimes, but the utopia of rational beings enjoying fulfilled lives envisaged by Marx.

Bauman's analyses of capitalist and communist societies focus on three things: the extent to which progress had been made in the direction of equality, freedom and social justice; the need for practical measures to make society still 'better'; and the obstacles that such measures would face.

In Bauman's view, the main obstacle was the way social control operated in capitalist and state socialist societies. He believed the best way to transform these social control systems was to understand and act upon the forms of consciousness (the values, objectives and habits of thought) that predominated among the people as a whole and within leadership groups.

Bauman refuses to predict the future, but he is very alert to signs in the present that show what 'might' happen. For example, in 1981 he believed that Polish Solidarity was an indication that socialism might be maturing in the direction he favoured (Bauman 1981). He made it clear that there were strong forces resisting this outcome. Nevertheless, the evidence of the Polish movement fed his hope.

Up until the early 1980s, Bauman's perspective was, broadly speaking, that of the committed socialist intellectual who feels a strong responsibility to deploy his knowledge and understanding in ways that would help societies move towards the 'utopian' horizon.

In the mid-1980s, the focus of Bauman's vision shifted significantly. He began to see a different kind of future than before. He developed a different analysis of human choice. Finally, he changed the way he saw his own role – his own relationship to the human situation that he was investigating.

The future that Bauman began to envisage after the mid-1980s was no longer the socialist utopia, but the postmodern human condition. Bauman saw a world taking shape in which the challenge facing humankind was not how to awaken hope, but how to cope with foreboding. The culture of postmodernity, in Bauman's view, is drenched with anxiety. People feel ambivalent about themselves and the world they live in. They try not to think or care too much. They are uncertain about the present and lack trust in the future.

As Bauman puts it, 'Postmodernity has its own utopias', but 'one may be excused for failing to recognise in them what one has been trained to seek and find in the utopias that spurred and whipped the modern impatience with the forever imperfect realities of the present'. In postmodernity, men and women enjoy a pleasure-seeking spontaneity that 'makes nonsense of all concern with the future except the concern with being free from concern with the future – and able to act, accordingly, in an unconcerned fashion' (Bauman 1993: 27).

Just over a decade after his hopeful response to Polish Solidarity, Bauman was discovering very different tendencies within society, indicating a type of future on the cards quite unlike his hoped-for socialist utopia. He reported these 'intimations of postmodernity' (Bauman 1992a) and set out in ideal-type form the principles that they expressed.

He saw a world taking shape where some people would enjoy the one-dimensional freedom of the consumer market place, while their capacity to act as citizens withered and died. Meanwhile, the poor would be denied all freedom. The main task of governments would be to repress those who could not join in the consumer carnival. Global capitalism would run increasingly out of control. Everybody's chances would depend on how they happened to be affected by its hazardous fortunes.

There are several important differences between the glimpses of a possible socialist future that Bauman saw in 1981 and his 'intimations' about postmodernity in 1992. In 1981 he was *enthusiastic* about tendencies that he believed would, if unchecked, lead towards *the kind of society he wanted*; at the same time, he recognized that *the forces opposing these tendencies were strong*. By contrast, in 1992 he was *dismayed* about tendencies that he believed would, if unchecked, lead towards *the kind of society he did not want*; at the same time, he recognized that *the forces opposing these tendencies were weak*.

Bauman's approach to human choice changed. In work inspired by his earlier vision of a socialist utopia, he was very interested in refining a methodology for drawing a wide variety of social interests into mutual dialogue. He hoped this would enable those groups to understand that they had choice about how their society was structured. Discovering this possibility and debating its implications would be the first steps in the process of choosing to move towards the utopian horizon in a coordinated way.

By contrast, in work inspired by his later vision of postmodernity, Bauman approaches choice in a different way. He argues that fundamental decisions about values and purposes face all individuals. Responsibility for these choices cannot be avoided. Their outcome is highly unpredictable. The risk of getting it wrong is very high. Bauman's own role is to explain that these unavoidable choices are the deep-seated source of our contemporary malaise. He has no methodology to offer for making 'good' choices in postmodern society. In fact, as he points out, external guidance about how to make these choices is not available.

There is a large contrast between Bauman's mission in the 1970s and his objectives two decades later. In the 1970s Bauman was doing theoretical work that would clarify and help overcome the difficulties of bringing about a structured dialogue among diverse social interests – one that would, hopefully, lead them to become oriented towards a single utopian outcome. By the 1990s, Bauman was exploring the theoretical implications of a human condition in which, as he saw it, isolated individuals confront unavoidable moral dilemmas in ways that lead to diverse social outcomes, many of them highly unsatisfactory.

In this later period, Bauman has placed himself in a different relationship to the social processes he is examining. During the 1970s he took the stance of the concerned and responsible 'legislating' intellectual, who wants to develop a blueprint or methodology for the process of achieving a good society – a methodology that draws the elite closer to the people at large. By the 1990s he had turned away from blueprints and methodologies. Instead, he became an interpreter, a perceptive 'outsider' able to penetrate meanings hidden from others. In his guise as the insightful 'stranger', Bauman has taken on the task of explaining to his fellow men and women what their situation as human beings is in a postmodern world where they, too, are strangers to each other.

In the early part of his academic career, Bauman tried to drive his version of the socialist project forward, acting as a kind of navigator-surveyor-engineer. When that project foundered, when 'road ahead closed' signs appeared on his chosen route to the socialist utopia, Bauman abandoned the vehicle, but not his values and ideals, and joined the crowd of refugees shivering on the mountainside.

Bauman found himself among people who were disoriented by the failure of modernity's ambitious programmes, whether socialist, social democrat, liberal or whatever. He transformed himself from a navigator into a weather forecaster – a role more immediately useful to the refugee who has lost confidence in all destinations.

Bauman's career and intellectual influences: a brief overview[1]

One way to get a glimpse inside Bauman's head during these successive phases of his career is to see what intellectual company he keeps. In the early decades, up to the early 1980s, Bauman was especially influenced by three writers: Karl Marx, Antonio Gramsci and Jürgen Habermas.

The central idea that Bauman takes from Marx is that, in order to understand the world, human beings have to regain control over it. Within capitalism, most men and women are dominated, required to live and work under conditions of exploitation and estrangement. They exist in a distorted world. As a result, their knowledge of it is distorted. In order to see it clearly, they have to overcome alienation and make the world their own again.

When human beings try to remake the world and reshape themselves, the very activity of doing this gives them a fuller grasp of the nature of things. They begin to know reality more clearly and more completely in the same breath that they work to change it. As Bauman puts it, 'Marx turns epistemology into sociology' (Bauman 1978: 58).

The second important influence is Gramsci. He understood 'capitalism's vitality and resilience' and realized that its stability had a 'cultural foundation' (Bauman 1976b: 102–3). According to Gramsci, capitalism was strong because its ruling ideas had thoroughly infiltrated civil society. Capitalist ideology was promoted and sustained by the intellectuals. They provided a total world-view that explained and justified the inequalities, oppressions and injustices of capitalism, partly by presenting them as beneficial and inevitable, partly by drawing attention away from them.

When this world-view has become established, domination is replaced by hegemony, by people's unreflecting acceptance of habits and values that take capitalism for granted. Capitalism becomes common sense, a part of everyday life, the 'right' way to do things. It embeds itself deep within civil society, in homes and offices, schools and churches, bars and music halls. The state does not visibly impose the interests of the capitalist bourgeoisie. Instead, the norms and practices of civil society express 'the cultural hegemony of a specific social group' and 'the ethical content of a class-dominated state' (p. 66).

Gramsci's work shows that 'culture is . . . the field of the most decisive battle'. The task of socialist intellectuals is to establish socialism as 'a new cultural idiom which remoulds common sense'. To do this they have to 'establish a strong link between [themselves] . . . and the subordinate classes' (p. 68).

The third major influence is Habermas. He argues that 'cultural sciences' such as sociology are 'hermeneutic': in other words, concerned with understanding the meanings (values, goals, sensitivities, world-views) embodied in specific forms of life such as classes, nations and ethnic groups. However, they want to do more than just give a coherent account of those meanings. They also want to test those understandings against the standard of 'truth'.

The strategy used to search for truth is 'sociological hermeneutics' (Bauman 1978: 241). This involves putting the different forms of life with their different understandings of the world into communication with each other. For example, members of different social classes, nations and ethnic groups might be invited to sit around a table and discuss their understandings about violence, authority, justice and so on.

Habermas pays great attention to the conditions under which such a discourse would take place. All participants must be committed to searching for the truth in a cooperative manner. Their communication must be rational, honest and unconstrained. Everyone must have access to all relevant knowledge. It must be agreed that issues will be determined on the basis of the strength of the arguments put and not on any other factor. When these 'ideal' conditions for 'undistorted' communication are met, there is a much greater chance of truth emerging from discourse.

Bauman drew the lesson that the socialist intellectual's task was to work towards bringing the social and political conditions for undistorted communication into being. Those conditions were, in fact, very similar to the conditions of equality, freedom and just treatment that were basic to the socialist utopia.

However, by the mid-1990s, Marx, Gramsci and Habermas had faded into the background. Their place had been taken by Michel Foucault, Theodor Adorno and Emmanuel Lévinas. How can this be explained?

Undistorted communication requires a reaching-out towards other people, a readiness to listen, receptivity to their interests and a willingness to take those interests into account. It needs some semblance of a democratic community with a tradition of caring and sharing. For several decades during the mid-twentieth century, the socialist experiment in the Soviet Union and Eastern Europe had applied pressure on the West to pay lip service at least to those values. However, during the 1980s that particular experiment came to an end.

By the late 1980s, there seemed to be no viable alternative to the capitalist model of society. When Bauman analysed this type of society in *Freedom* (1988), he concluded that most of its members were unable to perceive the world clearly. They were hypnotized by the delights of consumerism and unwilling to look beyond their own narrowly defined interests.

Since the late 1980s, Bauman's strategy has been to break through this complacency and expose the anxiety beneath. It is worth recalling for a moment the myth of the cage-dwellers that I invented to convey Bauman's central message. In terms of that myth, Bauman has been showing his readers the bars on their cages, pointing out the doors swinging open, and indicating the confusion waiting for those who step outside. Bauman has made it clear that modernity is a trap, postmodernity is a minefield and most of us are caught between the two.

During the late 1980s, Bauman became more pessimistic about the chances of restructuring modernity by subverting capitalist hegemony. Foucault became more prominent in Bauman's work at this time. He repeatedly draws upon Foucault's interpretation of the Panopticon, Bentham's plan for an 'Inspection House' (Bauman 1988: 10; Foucault 1977; Bentham 1843). This was a prison or asylum specially designed to allow total surveillance and control over the inmates by hidden guards. In the Panopticon, rigorous discipline is imposed to make people follow the detailed rules imposed by those with power over them. The ultimate goal is to make the inmates conform even when they are not being watched, even after they leave. The Panopticon penetrates and shapes the consciousness of its victims. It places a spy inside each heart. Bauman thinks that capitalist modernity operates on those same principles.

During the 1980s, Foucault took the place of Gramsci in Bauman's work. The idea of 'hegemony' was replaced by the idea of 'discipline' – doing the proper thing because it has been drilled into you. Bauman saw that discipline in the capitalist market place was so effective that people did not even recognize it was happening. He was reluctantly impressed by the slick way in which consumers were seduced into brightly lit shopping malls and manipulated into playing their roles as happy consumers in the advertisers' wonderland. He noted the effective information and control systems embedded in computerized credit card records and video recording systems.

In a similar way, Habermas was displaced by Adorno. Like Bauman, Adorno learned to make the condition of exile useful intellectually. He adopted the role of the stranger and used this role to penetrate the deceptions of ideology that comforted other people. By embracing the stranger's role, Adorno placed himself in opposition to the main thrust of modernity since the seventeenth century. His enemy was the Enlightenment – the great intellectual movement promoting rationality as a means to defeat ignorance and superstition.

Adorno believed that the Enlightenment was driven by fear of the void and fear of the stranger, the outsider. Belief in God declined and religion no longer provided a foundation for belief. Science was installed as the new basis for truth. Rather than face the void, intellectuals insisted that scientific laws and methods provided the guidance that human beings needed to organize societies and run their lives.

Outsiders upset the tidy categories that scientific theory and bureaucratic reason liked so much. They did not fit in. That made them a threat. Science and bureaucracy had all the tools they needed to protect their own interests. Scientists and bureaucrats became adept at deploying their knowledge and skills to exercise arbitrary power over their clients and victims. Outsiders were pulled into shape, thrown out or destroyed.

With bitter realism, Adorno accepted that the naivety of human beings gives them psychological protection from the riskiness and nastiness of life. The protection is flimsy, but people cling tight to it. They fiercely resist having their naivety disturbed and exposed. This leaves the intellectual with two choices: *either* accept the uncomfortable situation of being a hated, feared or neglected outsider, telling people uncomfortable truths that they do not want to hear, *or* get involved with the power structures and fight to impose your ideas. Adorno did not place any hopes in a third option: the strategy of free and open dialogue that Bauman had found so attractive in the 1970s. As Bauman put it when accepting the Adorno prize at Frankfurt in 1998:

> Adorno knew – unlike so many others who for the sake of clear conscience and mental equilibrium do not know or would not admit that they know or would not wish to know – that there are not, nor should there be, straight answers to convoluted questions, neither are there *eindeutig* [clear – DS] solutions to ambivalent predicaments. He knew that whoever thinks and cares is doomed to navigate between the Scylla of pure yet impotent thought and the Charybdis of effective yet polluted bid for domination. *Tertium non datur.* (Bauman 1998a: 7)

Finally, Bauman turned to the work of the ethical philosopher Emmanuel Lévinas, especially in *Postmodern Ethics* (1993) and *Life in Fragments* (1995). Neither book has Marx's name in the index. This does not mean that Bauman has ceased to admire the work of Marx. In fact, on the one hundred and fiftieth anniversary of *The Communist Manifesto* in 1998, Bauman wrote in *Enlightenment 2*, an electronic journal published on the Internet, that it stood out as 'one of those few hard and immovable rocks against which we measure the velocity, the force, the direction and the undulation of the waves of history' (Bauman 1998c: 1).

However, in one sense Lévinas does provide a substitute for Marx or, better perhaps, a catalyst for the mechanisms that Marx was focusing upon. Bauman took from Marx the insight that human beings would not achieve clear knowledge of reality until they began to cooperate with each other in order to transform that reality – to alter the state of their social being. However, Bauman realized that there could be no cooperative endeavours while men and women lived selfish lives in the consumer society. Where would the elementary urge to reach out to others come from?

Lévinas poses a challenge that, if met successfully, would help build bridges between isolated selves. Instead of directing his exhortations towards an alienated class, the exploited proletariat, as

Marx and Engels did in *The Communist Manifesto*, Lévinas is exhorting the anomic individual, facing psychic emptiness. The challenge is to make morality 'the *absolute beginning*' (Bauman 1993: 74; emphasis in original), putting ethics before ontology. This means being-for the Other, having responsibility for your fellow human beings, even before you 'exist'. To put it another way, it means experiencing yourself as being 'pre-installed' with the moral propensity to care for others. It means having a sort of awakening to your 'true' self.

Lévinas points towards a moral self that we can become if we accept its high standards. Marx had offered Bauman a utopia on the distant horizon. Lévinas offered an equivalent target within the self – an inner horizon. As Lévinas put it, 'There is a utopian moment in what I say; it is the recognition of something which cannot be realised but which, ultimately, guides all moral action . . . There is no moral life without utopianism – utopianism in this exact sense that saintliness is goodness' (Lévinas 1988: 178; Bauman 1993: 76).

In the next chapter, I look at the way Bauman's intellectual agenda has developed in the course of his career. I also suggest some reasons why Bauman has been transformed from a 'priest' of modernity into a 'prophet' of postmodernity.

3

Who is Zygmunt Bauman?

'And now abideth faith, hope and charity, these three; but the greatest of these is charity.' (1 Corinthians, 13, 13)

Faith, hope and charity

This chapter begins with the celebrated words of St Paul about faith, hope and charity. That is because they provide a preliminary guide to three phases in Bauman's life and work.

Faith – Bauman grew up in Poland and was educated in the Soviet Union. As a young adult, he became a devout and active communist – a man who was, in his wife's words, 'a blind worshipper of the party line' (J. Bauman 1988: 115).

Hope – Bauman suffered disappointment with state socialism as a political system. In fact, the system rejected him twice: once in 1953 and again in 1968. However, for over three decades, from the early 1950s to the mid-1980s, he retained the ideal of a socialist utopia founded on the platform of modernity. He aspired to help bring this utopia nearer through his writing. These were decades of hope – a hope that survived bitter setbacks.

Charity – Bauman felt the platform of modernity give way below his feet during the late 1980s and 1990s. State socialism in Eastern Europe and the Soviet Union collapsed with astonishing rapidity. Bauman saw that his aspirations for a socialist utopia would be extremely difficult to fulfil. Disappointed in his faith, disillusioned in his hope, Bauman decided that the most substantial resource left to humankind was our innate moral impulse to care for others. Modernity had kept this impulse buried below thick slabs of concrete. As the hold of modernity weakened, the concrete began to crack and fragment. Beneath the concrete lay charity, *caritas*, the urge to be-for-others. This hidden treasure was exposed by the slow earthquake of postmodernity. Bauman began to assay this treasure and to weigh up the chances for turning it to effective use. He is still engaged in this task.

The roots of wisdom

My first answer to the question posed in the title of this chapter is that Zygmunt Bauman is the possessor of the very distinctive 'voice' that can be heard in the following typical extracts from his writing over the past few years:

> It has been said that sociology is the power of the powerless. This is not always the case, though. There is no guarantee that having acquired sociological understanding one can dissolve and disempower the resistance put up by the 'tough realities of life'; the power of understanding is no match for the pressures of coercion allied with resigned and submissive common sense. And yet were it not for that understanding, the chance of successful management of one's life and the collective management of shared life conditions would be slimmer still. (Bauman 1990b: 18)

> People sunk up to their ears in the daily struggle for survival were never able, nor felt a need, to codify their understanding of good and evil in the form of an ethical code. After all, principles are about the future – about how much that future should differ from the present . . . Survival, on the contrary, is essentially conservative. Its horizon is drawn with yesterday's paints: to stay alive today means not losing whatever it was that secured one's livelihood yesterday – and not much more than that. Survival is about things not getting worse than before. (Bauman 1995: 41)

> Great crimes often start from great ideas. Few great ideas prove completely innocent when their inspired followers try to make the word flesh – but some can hardly ever be embraced without the teeth being bared and daggers sharpened. Among this class of ideas, pride of place belongs to the vision of purity. (Bauman 1997: 5)

> There are many ways of being human, but each society makes a choice of the way it prefers or tolerates. If we call a certain assembly of people a 'society', implying that these people 'belong together' and 'make a totality', it is because of their choice. (Though seldom a 'deliberate' choice

. . . the choice cannot easily be abandoned.) It is this choice, or the lasting sediments of it, that makes one assembly of people look different from another. (Bauman 1998e: 83)

All vogue words tend to share a similar fate: the more experience they pretend to make transparent, the more they themselves become opaque. The more numerous are the orthodox truths they elbow out and supplant, the faster they turn into no-questions-asked canons. (Bauman 1998b: 1)

These extracts come from five recent books by Bauman. They show the kind of generalization that Bauman uses to develop his arguments. They are big statements about life and culture, often with a sardonic, worldly edge to them. Each statement is a major signpost in the text, pointing with authority in a particular direction.

Statements of this kind make an implicit claim to knowledge in the form of 'wisdom'. But what is the basis of Bauman's claim to wisdom? My response to this question is that Bauman's wisdom is rooted in experience. His life has been a long process of searching and learning – a process that can be 'read' in his books. I believe the distinctiveness of Bauman's wisdom comes out of the distinctiveness of his personal experience. So, in order to understand and appreciate Bauman properly, we need to know something about his background.

Bauman's agenda

When I ask the question 'who is Zygmunt Bauman?', I am trying to discover enough information to account for Bauman's writing agenda. This is relevant because Bauman's agenda sets out the key topics on which he wishes to influence the way we think. I always prefer to know why someone else is trying to influence me in a particular direction, especially if they are gifted with a silver tongue. It is impossible to get certain knowledge on this point, but vital to raise the issue.

This is a practical matter. There are several philosophical reasons why we can never be sure we have identified the 'truth' about another person's intentions and motivations.[1] However, such considerations do not prevent the detective from asking the 'suspect' where he was on Saturday night (hidden question: 'what were you up to?'); nor do they stop the wary householder from asking the 'market researcher' what she is trying to sell (hidden question: 'what's your game?').

Bauman is neither a 'suspect' nor an 'unwanted caller'. On the contrary, he is a brilliant analyst of the human condition. His books are in great demand. When customers buy them, they are inviting him into their homes and their minds. They want to learn from him. He is a teacher. When readers open his books, especially his later works, they receive an immediate fix of adrenalin. Anyone who plunges into *Legislators and Interpreters* (1987), *Modernity and the Holocaust* (1989) or *Modernity and Ambivalence* (1991) will find themselves beguiled by the seductive mixture of empathy, rationality and literary grace.

All the more reason to ask of Bauman's agenda: why are *these* items there and not others? Why does *this* item appear on the agenda and this *other* item disappear at this point in time? Another relevant question is: why has Bauman pursued these issues by writing about them rather than by undertaking *other* forms of action?

The point is that a published text is an act of communication. It is, almost always, an intervention in a debate or an attempt to get a debate under way. A text is intended to change the world, at least a little. However, texts are not the only way to work for change. In fact, Bauman did not begin his adult life as a writer. During World War II, he was a soldier fighting in a Polish division with the Red Army – a man of action committed to the communist cause. After the war, Bauman remained in the Polish army and became a senior officer – a dedicated bureaucrat working for a better society. Only later did he turn himself into a writer.

It is important to ask 'who is Zygmunt Bauman?' in the sense of 'who is setting this agenda and why is he doing it this way?' Notice that the suspicious detective and the quizzical householder both try to get confessions: 'what were you up to? what's your game?' However, Bauman is not in the confessing business. In fact, he is very eloquent on this point. When he received the Adorno prize at Frankfurt in July 1998, he gave the grounds of his self-imposed silence. Bauman cited Carl Jung who, when pressed to reminisce about his own work,

responded that he had no wish nor ability to take a distance big enough to view his own predicament objectively. [Jung] . . . warned about the common error of 'auto-biography': they either spin a net of illusions about themselves, writing of what should have been the case rather than what has been, or produce an apology *pro domo sua*. I fully sympathise with Jung on this point. And I agree with Marcel Reich-Ranitzki, who, when asked by the *Le Monde* journalist why, in stark opposition to his French counterpart Bernard Pivot, he never invites the authors to his *Literarische Stunden*, replied that the authors are the last persons he would ask about the meaning of their books. (Bauman 1998a, 1)

This is a pretty solid defence. Bauman warns, in effect, that his autobiographical account would be thoroughly unreliable. There is no point in replying that it would, nevertheless, be 'interesting'. Bauman is all too familiar with the way words can be twisted, motives misrepresented and character blackened. To show this, we can quote the account that Bauman's wife, Janina, gives of what life was like for them in Poland thirty years before:

> The following days brought more threatening phone calls. Five bulky strangers chose a bench in our courtyard and sat there for hours, keeping an eye on the entrance to our staircase and staring up into our windows. Lena came running home, frightened to death: a gang of hooligans had attacked her in the park. The TV screen was choking with hatred, and spat out [Zygmunt's] name time after time. A scholarly article appeared in a respectable magazine. It attacked [Zygmunt] and others for their dangerous influence on Polish youth. It was signed by a close friend. (J. Bauman 1988: 195)[2]

That happened in April 1968, shortly before Bauman and his family moved to the West. Details like this suggest that there are biographical reasons for Bauman's silence on his own biography. Perhaps the biggest reason is that too much pain is hidden there.

Fortunately, enough has been written – for example, by Janina Bauman (1988) and Stefan Morawski (1998) – to tell us how and why Bauman's personal situation turned him into a writer. We also know, broadly speaking, the objective circumstances in which Bauman's books were written: the points in historical and biographical time when they took shape; their locations in social, cutural and geographical space. Knowledge of these circumstances provides a context in which to place Bauman's explicit statements about his ideals and objectives in the books themselves.

In this book, then, I have brought together two sets of factors: a sense of the author's ideals and objectives on the one hand and, on the other hand, information about his personal circumstances – or, at least, the points in time and space from which he has looked at the world. When these two sets of factors are taken together and interpreted with as much empathy and insight as possible, it helps make sense of the writer's agenda. It helps us to understand what Bauman thought was problematic, and why.

I treat the texts as instrumental rather than expressive, as means to produce change in the world rather than emanations of the writer's personality and socio-cultural background. The latter factors are relevant and interesting. However, the main critical task is not to treat the books as a hall of mirrors in which the real image of the author is hidden. It is, rather, to explore the texts as instruments of analysis and persuasion, as attempts to reshape the understanding and consciousness of their readers, to explode their commonsense assumptions. The Bauman opus is not so much a hall of mirrors as a collection of guided missiles. My object is to understand the strategic context in which the texts have been constructed and deployed by Zygmunt Bauman. An important part of that strategic context is Bauman's own life and career.

A brief biography

A valuable source for information about Bauman's life is the autobiography written by his wife, Janina Bauman, entitled *A Dream of Belonging: my years in postwar Poland* (1988). Her husband appears in the guise of 'Konrad'. From Janina Bauman's book we learn that Bauman was born into a poor Jewish family living at Poznan in western Poland. The family suffered badly not only from poverty, but also from anti-Semitism. When World War II broke out in 1939, the family fled to the Soviet Union. Four years later, at the age of eighteen, Bauman joined the Polish army in Russia. He became a junior officer and served in an artillery unit that advanced against the Germans all the way to the Baltic.

Bauman was wounded, but recovered in time to take part in the battle for Berlin in 1945. In the postwar years, Bauman rose to the rank of captain and became a political officer stationed in a large military unit at Warsaw. During these years, he was a communist and a member of the Polish Workers' Party.

Why did Bauman become a communist? He has been almost completely silent on this subject, but he gives us a clue about his reasons in the review he once wrote of a book about Jewish communists in Poland. Bauman recalls that many Jews were 'brought into the ranks of revolutionary radicalism by the unbearable pressure to resolve in their personal lives the contradictions produced societally and resolvable (if at all) only by societal means' (1990a: 175). I would translate this as meaning, in Bauman's own case, that as a Jew from a poor household confronting racial smears and facing the threat of Hitler's SS, he was strongly attracted by communism's promises. In Soviet Russia, he had felt Polish, not Jewish.[3]

Bauman's views during the late 1940s were later recalled by his wife:

> Unflinching in his faith, yet sound and clear in his reasoning, [he] . . . explained that there would be no room for anti-Semitism, or any other racial hatred, under Communism – this fairest of social systems, which would guarantee full equality between human beings regardless of language, race or creed. We were particularly lucky, he stressed, to have been born at the right time and in the right place to become active fighters for this noblest cause. The greatest of historical changes was happening before our eyes, here and now . . . I listened enthralled. Here was the voice of an honest Communist; his arguments seemed sound and he truly believed what he was saying. (J. Bauman 1988: 45)

Bauman knew perfectly well that nasty things happened inside the Communist Party: for example, that office chiefs made their underlings spy on each other. His reported comment on this was that, although 'the Party ranks were still full of untrustworthy individuals, ruthlessly ambitious climbers and ideologically immature members', this was 'a transitory weakness'. People often committed 'grave mistakes' in the Party's name. However, it was the 'most powerful agent of social justice and had to be implicitly trusted. You cannot make an omelette, he said, without breaking eggs' (p. 77).

This is, I suspect, the voice of a man who did not expect to be one of the eggs that was broken. If so, he had good reason to be self-confident. In fact, Bauman achieved very rapid promotion and by the early 1950s he was one of the youngest majors in the Polish army. At about this time, he began his graduate studies in philosophy and the social sciences.

However, at the age of twenty-eight, Bauman was summarily dismissed from his post in the army. He was one of the victims of an anti-Semitic purge. Bauman's father, he was told, had been seen making enquiries at the Israeli Embassy about the possibility of emigration.

Bauman's dismissal destroyed a very promising career as a professional soldier. Just how promising can be seen from the judgement made later by a friend who knew him in Poland. According to Stefan Morawski, Bauman's 'extraordinary intelligence, ideological equipment and political capacities, provided him with capacities which could easily have led him from being a major to being a general' (1998: 30–1). Janina Bauman tells us that Bauman was absolutely devastated.

> [It was] a terrible shock, a bolt from the blue. It knocked [Zygmunt] off his feet . . . Every morning I left [him] staring blankly at his books and on my return in the evening would find him in the same position. A week passed before he pulled himself together and went to the university . . . All of a sudden we found ourselves in an empty world. No friends called to cheer us up . . . The officers with whom we had spent [a] hilarious night a few days before crossed the street to avoid meeting us face to face. Neighbours on the staircase turned their faces away. (J. Bauman 1988: 105–6).

After the initial shock, Bauman showed great powers of recovery and adaptation. He dyed two of his military uniforms a civilian brown and began a second career.[4] By 1954 he was a junior lecturer in the Faculty of Philosophy and Social Sciences at Warsaw University. Already by that time

> he had changed a great deal. Ever since he had left the army he seemed to see things more clearly. Though still a sincere socialist – which deep in his heart he has remained to this day – he now began to see that all was not right in this world of his . . . Perhaps Marxist theory . . . needed a new interpretation in our modern times and changed society? . . . He was no longer a blind worshipper of the Party line. (p. 115)

Bauman began to make visits abroad: for example, to the London School of Economics, where he spent a year in the late 1950s. By 1961 he had become an assistant professor working in the Sociology of Political Relations section. He was also head of the Editorial Committee of *Studia Socjologiczne* (Sociological Studies), one of Poland's two general sociology journals.

He published several books in Polish, including a treatise on Marxist sociology that went into a second edition and was translated into Serb and Italian.[5] By the mid-1960s, Bauman held the Chair of General Sociology at Warsaw University. In 1966 he was elected president of the Executive Committee of the Polish Sociological Association.[6]

Bauman took an independent line in his work. He could not bear the idea of intellectuals being nothing more than intelligent puppets presenting the party line. He wanted to think for himself and that sometimes meant disagreeing with the regime.[7] There was a price to pay for this: '[He] was now branded as one of the most active revisionists and fell into disgrace with the Party bosses. His books and articles were censored, his public statements condemned by official spokesmen, his behaviour closely watched' (p. 163).[8]

In 1967, the Six Day War between Israel and Egypt was followed by a virulent anti-Zionist campaign in Poland. The Party leadership compared Polish Jews to a 'fifth column': in other words, to spies working for a foreign power. Many Jews were sacked or forced to resign. In January 1968, Bauman handed in his Party card.

Then, at the end of March 1968, Bauman was dismissed from his academic post along with five other professors at Warsaw University. This was announced on national radio. The sacked professors were accused of being a dangerous influence on Polish youth. As Bauman sardonically remarked years later, he was spared the agonies of the male menopause since the Polish authorities kindly gave him something else to worry about.

Bauman emigrated from Poland shortly afterwards. He has built a third career, this time in the West. After travelling with his young family to Israel in 1968, he made his way, via jobs in Canada, the United States and Australia, to the United Kingdom, where he became Professor of Sociology at Leeds University in 1971. Bauman published five books during the 1970s and four in the 1980s. He won the Amalfi prize for *Modernity and the Holocaust* (1989). He retired from Leeds in 1990. Since then he has published on average at least one book a year. In 1998 he received the Adorno prize. He has recently been made an emeritus professor of the University of Warsaw.

Transitions

What does this tell us about the experience from which Bauman draws his wisdom – his way of seeing the world? I think it shows that he has been forced to come to terms with several radical changes in his personal circumstances. One major transition was the change from a military environment to a civilian one. As a major in the Polish army, Bauman had bureaucratic command of people and resources and was used to having his orders obeyed by subordinates. As a civilian, especially one surrounded by other intellectuals, he had to win in other ways the right to be listened to and the capacity to exercise influence, not least through skilful persuasion.

What is doubly impressive is that Bauman has now succeeded in developing a seductive prose style, artful and gracious, in English – a language not his own. In this respect, he is now able to teach his colleagues, English speakers from the cradle, many lessons in what used to be called 'civility'.

This change in Bauman's situation coincided with a further transition, from being a successful member of the Party establishment to being outside the establishment. We will return to this shortly. Both these shifts contributed to a third transition: from a life of intense military or political activism to one of intense sociological or philosophical reflection.

Activism and reflection have always overlapped in Bauman's life. However, the balance has shifted. The young soldier on active service in the mid-1940s gave way to the ambitious political officer in the late 1940s and early 1950s. By the 1960s, the baton had been passed to the busy revisionist writer, who was dangerous enough to merit public condemnation. This persona gave way to, first, the Western academic of the 1970s and early 1980s, carefully deploying his thoughts in learned texts, and, more recently, the internationally celebrated guru publishing his reflections in book after book.

Bauman has also undergone the painful metamorphosis from ideological certainty to intellectual doubt. Again, the balance between certainty and doubt has shifted over a long period of time. The man of 1948 was confident that he, or at least the Party, had all the right answers. Half a century later, in *Globalization: the human consequences*, Bauman claimed to be unsure whether his book was even 'asking the right questions' (1998b: 5). In 1948 he believed that 'The greatest of historical changes was happening before our eyes, here and now.' By 1998 he accepted that 'History is . . . a playground of the contingent, the unexpected, the fortuitous, the capricious, the under-determined and the unpredictable' (1998c: 5).

Another change that Bauman has undergone is the transition from relative poverty to relative affluence. This occurred not only through his rise within the military and academic bureaucracies, but also, later, with his move from a socialist to a capitalist society.

Bauman's move from East to West is the most widely known fact about him. However, the implications of this transition are inseparable from the others just mentioned: from civilian to military; from established to outsider; from activist to reflective guru; from dedicated ideologist to systematic doubter; and from poverty to relative comfort. It is this *particular mixture* of involvements, ruptures and transitions, and their *complex interweaving* through three careers, that makes Bauman's own perceptions, his particular 'take' on the world, so fascinating.

Puzzles

At first sight, there are two puzzles about Zygmunt Bauman's career. Firstly, the evidence of his early work suggests that his very serious intention was to reconstruct Marxism. How then did he become so identified with postmodernity? I will look at this question shortly.

Secondly, there is the question of anti-Semitism. This played a significant role in Bauman's life at several key points between 1925 and 1968. Anti-Semitism haunted his childhood. In 1939 the advance of the Nazis triggered migration to the Soviet Union. In 1953 it was anti-Semitism that cost Bauman his first career as a soldier. Then, in 1968, it destroyed his second career as an academic at Warsaw University. His first home when he came to the West was in Israel.

Why did Bauman wait for two decades after he had travelled west before dealing with the theme of anti-Semitism and, more generally, the plight of the outsider or stranger in his books? Why did something so central to his life remain, for so long, so marginal to his writing? I should emphasize that I do not think there was any special moral 'requirement' for Bauman or anyone else to write about this theme at any particular time or, indeed, at all. However, I am curious about the mechanisms that initially kept it off the agenda and later put it on the agenda.

Anti-Semitism and Bauman

In trying to solve this puzzle, it helps to remember that Bauman was schooled in Soviet Russia, a place of sanctuary for his family, at a time when the communist cause was fighting for its life.

Bauman was soon in soldier's uniform, fighting for a system which proclaimed that ethnic prejudice was abhorrent and that being Jewish made no difference.[9]

As Morawski points out, Bauman did not change his Jewish-sounding name when he returned to Poland after the war: 'He wanted to be himself, to challenge and test the new system which promised brotherhood rather than parochial xenophobia' (1998: 30). This suggests that between 1943 and 1953 there were strong links between Bauman's belief in freedom and equality, his commitment to socialism as an ideal, his service to the Communist Party, his desire to understand Marxism, and the sheer excitement and satisfaction of his personal success as a military officer and a valued Party member.

I believe that this helps to explain why Bauman did not explore the situation of the outsider, especially the Jew, much earlier than he did. It seems likely that what bothered Bauman about his experiences in 1953 and 1968 was not the existence of anti-Semitism as such, but *the fact that a socialist regime could submit to its appeal.* If this is correct, the persona through which he experienced his suffering was not that of the victimized Jew, but that of the disappointed true socialist.

Such a response is very different from that of someone like Hannah Arendt, whose reaction to Nazism was to become intensely Zionist – to emphasize her Jewish identity more than previously. However, Bauman's response is not an isolated one. Others have reacted in a similar way, responding in terms of a persona or self-understanding that did not give priority to their identity as Jews.[10]

Neither insider nor outsider

Returning to Bauman, why was he so late to adopt the role of the stranger or outsider – the role that is suggested by strong self-identification as a Jew? I think it is because, during the period between the early 1950s and the late 1980s, Bauman was neither an established insider nor a thoroughly marginalized outsider. He was somewhere in between. His position was in some ways like that of an unfrocked heretic priest: in other words, a member of the priesthood who has been deprived of his right to exercise authority because of his unorthodox views.

Bauman was no ordinary 'priest'. To continue the metaphor, he might have gone on to become a cardinal or even better. We can only guess how his intellectual and political development might have proceeded if he had remained within the communist hierarchy – if the party had truly behaved as if it believed in equality, freedom and justice. Would he have still discovered postmodernity and bent it to his intellectual will? Perhaps not.

So far, I have given a provisional explanation for why Bauman's 'turn to Jewishness' was so delayed.[11] The question of why he finally made that 'turn' when he did is one I deal with later. For the moment, I am going to pay attention to the other puzzle: how did Bauman make the transition from Marxism to postmodernity?

Marx and the art of motorcycle maintenance[12]

In the event, during the late 1950s Bauman began a comprehensive re-evaluation of the intellectual and moral heritage that he had acquired in his youth as an 'honest communist'. For over three decades, his writing focused on a range of issues that fed into his overriding objective of helping to construct the intellectual basis for a 'better' socialism – a more modern Marxism.

For example, in one series of articles and books, most notably *Socialism: the active utopia* (1976a), Bauman focused upon the nature of communism and capitalism. At the same time, in a complementary series of publications that included *Towards a Critical Sociology* (1976b), Bauman concentrated upon the complex relationships between culture and sociology. This sustained inquiry was well under way by the time Bauman came to the West, and it continued during the 1970s and early 1980s.

I believe this has been much more than a fanciful game in an academic ivory tower. A dedicated intellectual exploration of this kind requires a very powerful motivation. When I attempt to imagine what the mainsprings of this motivation might have been in Bauman's case, I find the following reasoning plausible.

In the postwar years, Marxist socialism as an 'actually existing' system failed the people. It also failed Bauman. The system gave him a glimpse of success, then brutally snatched it away. Bauman, I believe, almost certainly wanted to know why this had happened and how matters could be improved.

It seems to me that Bauman has taken Marxist socialism apart with the same urgency that someone might inspect the workings of a powerful motorcycle that has thrown them into a ditch halfway through a thrilling journey to an exciting destination. The fallen rider would want to know what was wrong with the machine, especially if, like Bauman, they knew they had good road skills.

Bauman has stripped down the machine, laid the components out on the ground, checked how well they fit together, tested different settings, compared them with the manufacturer's blueprint and introduced other items cannibalized from other types of machine.

Bauman has deconstructed the Marxist socialism with which he became familiar as a young man. He has deconstructed it as intellectual theory, political regime and social order. He has unravelled the strands of Marxism, separated out the constituent elements of history, sociology and philosophy, and worked out his own approach to each of these disciplines. He has also carefully inspected the *modus operandi* of state socialism, looking in particular at the role of culture and intellectuals, and the part played by power, especially bureaucratic power.

If this interpretation is correct, then by the early 1980s, the deconstruction process was practically complete. In intellectual terms, Bauman had completely disassembled the Marxist vehicle that had thrown him. The ground was covered with piles of components, each pile containing bits of the faulty machine along with components taken from elsewhere that had some family resemblance to them. Bauman had enough knowledge as a result of his forensic investigation to explain why the machine had failed.

However, knowing why the old Marxism had failed was not enough. The whole point of the exercise was to find a way to make a new, more modern Marxism that could propel humankind towards socialism. In fact, Bauman made significant intellectual progress towards designing an improved model, drawing in particular on the ideas of Habermas and Gramsci.

Bauman's objective was a social existence in which rational and emancipated human beings exercised their freedom in a creative fashion. He wanted to encourage a process of dialogue within civil society. His hope was that intellectuals such as himself would encourage ordinary people to take an informed, rational and active part in making society freer, more equal and more just.

During the early 1980s, there were indications in both East and West that major social changes were under way. In 1980 Polish

Soldarity demonstrated to Bauman that the working class could undergo 'True collective learning' in the course of 'collective action' (Bauman 1981: 50). Meanwhile, the British political system was being placed under intense strain by the reforms imposed under Margaret Thatcher's Conservative government. There were riots in many British cities during 1981.

By the time Bauman published *Memories of Class* (1982), he believed that 'a time of transition' had arrived within capitalist societies: 'the whole system of social production and satisfaction of needs seems to be in an acute crisis'. In his view, solving the crisis depended on 're-negotiation of the problems of unfreedom and emancipation' (p. 198). The time was ripe, it seemed, for bringing into being a thoroughly democratic society, in which citizens played a much more active part in running their own affairs. However, the 1980s brought disappointment, as the next chapter shows.

4

The Power of the Past

Discovering postmodernity

The early 1980s were a time of hope for Zygmunt Bauman. His writings from this period were optimistic. However, Bauman's programme of creative dialogue and action depended on a reconstruction of the political sphere. The idea was that, as society became more democratic, the central state would take less responsibility for regulating the details of social life. Instead, local assemblies of various kinds would become more powerful. The everyday lives of most people would become more 'political'. Men and women would make more decisions collectively as citizens in their localities.

In the event, things did not work out like that. Only one half of this hoped-for process of reconstruction occurred during the 1980s. National governments certainly became less ambitious. They went into retreat and intervened less frequently in the daily lives of citizens. However, the space vacated by the 'nanny state' was filled not by the citizen but by the consumer. The 1980s were indeed a 'time of transition'. However, the beneficiary was not local democracy but global capitalism.

The discovery that active citizenship and participatory democracy were easily swamped by consumerism and the power of global capitalism presented serious difficulties for Bauman's intellectual strategy. The point is that Bauman had learned his socialism, both old-style and new-style, in the context of a highly developed public sphere headed by a powerful central state. This had been the case in prewar Soviet Russia, postwar socialist Poland and also, to a lesser degree, in West European societies before the 1980s during the period of corporatist management of the Keynesian welfare state.

To oversimplify, the 'map' in terms of which Bauman oriented himself during these decades had three major landmarks. Two of these were the state and the people. Bauman identified himself with a third force, the progressive socialist intellectuals, who might, he hoped, be able to mediate between the state and the people. As we have seen, he was interested in how to mobilize the population so that it subjected the state to effective criticism and became politically active within a dynamic civil society: discussing vital issues, organizing for change, enjoying a rich cultural life.

This strategic perspective depended upon the existence of a state that had powerful leverage within society, and citizens who were interested in exercising influence over the state and being politically involved. Neither condition applied by the mid-1980s, in Bauman's view. The people were hooked on consumption and cared little for politics. Meanwhile, governments had less control than before over their own national economies and, as a result, less capacity to control unemployment levels, price levels and so on.

By the time he published *Freedom* (1988), Bauman diagnosed the condition of the people, both East and West, as being a form of captivity or disablement, although he does not use these terms. In the East, the people were repressed by the state. In the West, they were seduced by consumerism. Either way, the obstacles to creative socialist praxis were enormous.

To revert briefly to the motorcycle metaphor introduced in the previous chapter, the question was no longer whether Bauman could construct a roadworthy vehicle: in other words, a viable modern Marxism. The point was that the road had disappeared. The political landscape was being transformed in a fundamental way. The shape of societies was being altered from 'outside' and 'above' by large forces that seemed impossible to control.

As he approached retiring age, Bauman had tested social reality against the standard set by his utopia, and he had found reality wanting. However, Bauman was not alone in his disappointment. Consider the situation in Europe during the 1980s. In Eastern Europe and the Soviet Union, the socialist experiments were approaching their terminal crisis. In the West, levels of welfare provision were falling considerably below people's expectations, while unemployment rose in a way not experienced for half a century.

Everywhere, the state was helping people less, the market hurting them more.

Disappointment and frustration were prospects faced by many, not just among the ranks of factory and office workers, but also among highly educated managerial and professional circles. Utopias were collapsing or deflating, East and West.

The world was full of half-finished or disintegrating 'modern' projects. Many occupants of this disconnected world were in a thoroughly confused state, not understanding what was going on. At some point in the mid-1980s, Bauman placed these facts at the centre of his vision. In other words, he discovered postmodernity.

From priest to prophet

Having discovered this new territory, Bauman proceeded to occupy it and set himself up as its cartographer. Bauman was certainly not the first to discover postmodernity, but he rapidly made it his own.[1]

Bauman has stopped trying to find ways of making modernity 'work'. He thinks that great schemes of modernity are most harmful when they are most effective. Bauman has come to the conclusion that legislators of all kinds, people with 'modernizing' blueprints in their hands or heads, are likely to be self-deluded and dangerous. At their worst, they become like Hitler or Stalin. Both men claimed they could make a more 'perfect' world. Both men created Hell on earth.

In practice, Bauman believes, the amount of harm that legislators can do has been diminished since the state has gone into semi-retirement. In any case, national governments have been forced to bow to the power of multinational and transnational corporations as these institutions have grown larger, more powerful and more demanding.

Bauman believes that, in this new globalized world, no one is in control, neither governments nor big business. In fact, the whole planet is in a state of high risk. However, consumers can buy short-term comfort in the market place. Consumerism seduces us into accepting the deeply unsettling condition of postmodernity. It does not stop us being anxious, but it offers us a range of pre-packaged short-term solutions for our sense of dissatisfaction.

This is a view of modernity from the outside, through the eyes of someone no longer committed to modernity's projects or taken in by modernity's promises. It is a view that appeals to an increasing proportion of the population. It strikes a chord with the ever-growing ranks of the disillusioned, disappointed, estranged and bewildered.

In recent years, Bauman has embraced the role of outsider with open arms. The secular 'priest' of the early 1950s has transformed himself, nearly half a century later, into a prophet. In this guise, Bauman looks towards the future, towards the postmodern world taking shape in the interstices of modernity. He reports his 'intimations of postmodernity' (Bauman 1992a).

Bauman has given his own account of the distinction between the priest and the prophet. The traditional function of the priest, in his view, is 'the interpretation of the supra-individual order, modelling the inscrutable into intelligibility, imposing an iron-clad logic upon seemingly irrational, chance events, lending meaning to apparently nonsensical human fate' (Bauman 1976b: 31).

By contrast, 'the religion of the prophets . . . contains no easy promises of releasing the tormented individual from the burden of his responsibility. It demystifies rather than interprets the mystery of human existence . . . The prophets, therefore, unlike priests, offer little comfort [but] . . . point their accusing fingers at the self, now left alone on the suddenly empty stage' (p. 58). This is the Bauman of the 1990s except in one respect. Bauman's finger points at us in a challenging rather than an 'accusing' way. He tends to write about individual responsibility rather than blame.

When I say that Bauman has adopted the prophet's role, I do not mean that he claims to know what key events will happen in the future or when such events will occur. Prophecy is different from prediction. It is less precise but more profound. Prophecy means using a powerful imagination to define the human condition in a new epoch not yet fully unfolded. It means catching early sight of moral dilemmas, emotional torments, social pressures and political choices that are due to plague us in the future. Prophecy is being able to catch straws in the wind and read incipient trends long before they become massive facts obvious to all.

In fact, prophecy is more than that. It makes a bid not just to visualize the future, but also to influence that future by shaping our attitudes here and now. Prophecy tries to mould our perceptions of ourselves and the world. If it is successful in doing this, it cannot help but also influence how we feel and what we want. It is when

we act upon our inclinations and pursue our preferences that we
make our own contribution, however limited, to how the future
unfolds.

In other words, prophecy can affect action (or 'praxis') in the
real world. Of course, exercising influence through action is a
long way short of exercising control. In fact, the unpredictability
of the future is one of Bauman's cardinal principles. Unanticipated
events and unexpected consequences are rife. However, the more
people a prophet influences, the more persuasive the message, the
greater is the chance that, whenever men and women have
the opportunity to give the world a push in one direction rather
than another, they will do it in the way the prophet would have
wished.

Bauman believes that prophetic figures such as Marx were able
to influence future events, even though they could hardly control
them. Here is what Bauman wrote in the late 1960s:

> It is . . . nonsensical to ask whether Marx was able to 'predict' the
> triumph of the Marxist revolution in Tsarist Russia, since he was one of
> its main causes, one part of the 'historical block' which made the social-
> ist upheaval really inevitable precisely in these 'praxis-like' terms. This
> is, indeed, the only way one can make predictions in the realm of the
> social sciences; providing one does not keep them secret, one 'ploughs
> in' predictions, thus making them a new and significant part of an his-
> torical situation, in which conscious human beings are the only actors.
> (1969: 16–17)

Bauman has been very actively 'ploughing' his views on postmodernity into our consciousness. By doing this, he has been following the strategy he described two decades earlier, in the 1970s.
As he put it then, intellectuals may act 'not just in the role of interpreters of the experience, but as *makers of experience* which may lead
to an alternative society via criticism of the *status quo*' (Bauman
1976a: 118; emphasis added).

Out of Poland

Bauman's views on the function of prophecy were formed before
he left Poland and have persisted throughout his career. It is worth
asking what other intellectual legacies have been left by Bauman's
early career in his Polish homeland. A related question, to be
pursued in the following section, concerns how the subsequent

trauma of moving to the West has affected Bauman in respect of both his methodology and his agenda.

One aspect of his early experience, the poverty around him, has embedded itself deep in Bauman's consciousness. Despite his increasing propensity to doubt, he remains absolutely certain that poverty is a fundamental evil. The themes of poverty and the need for radical action to prevent repression of the poor broke surface once again in Bauman's *Work, Consumerism and the New Poor* (1998a) after a decade of relative neglect. This work demonstrates the continuing importance of Bauman's basic commitment to freedom and justice. In 1990 Bauman was asked about his commitment to these values. He answered:

> These principles stay with me all the time – if you call them socialist, fine; but I don't think they are particularly socialist, anyway. They are much wider than that. I really believe that communism was just the stupidly condensed and concentrated effort to push it through; but the values were never invented by the communists. The values were there, much wider; they were western, Enlightenment values. I can't imagine a society which could dispose completely of these two values, ever . . . Once the ideas of justice and self-assertion were invented, it is impossible to forget them. They will haunt and pester us to the end of the world. (Bauman 1992a: 225)[2]

One source of normative control within society had been the type of peasant village still remembered in the Poland of his youth. The way of life in these rural settlements expressed a powerful idea of collective responsibility: individuals recognized their shared interest as members of the village; the community had authority over individuals; and neighbours shared the burden of providing welfare and maintaining security. As will be seen, Bauman emphasizes the importance of the peasant village in shaping the aspirations and character structure of the urbanized peasants who staffed the factories and offices of postwar socialist Poland.

Bauman himself cannot have been untouched by these influences and the values they instilled. To someone from such a background, the passing of the peasant village posed the challenge: how is moral vigour to be pumped back into society now the old source has dried up? Bauman is deeply aware of the extent to which moral impulses are rooted in interpersonal solidarity.

Bauman is far from being a rural sentimentalist. However, he has paid a lot of attention to the consequences flowing from the breakdown of traditional rural communities.[3] As he sees it, this process dissolves forms of social solidarity, collective identity and cultural authority that took many generations to build up. He attacks communitarians for believing that they can recreate these features artificially.

There is another legacy from Bauman's early years: a dialectical habit of mind that may, perhaps, come from his grounding in Marxism. The 'inner rhythm' of his intellectual procedures has remained remarkably consistent. There is a repeated pattern in the way Bauman presents his theories and models of the world. This pattern has three phases. It begins with a duality of some kind that harbours strong inner tensions. This duality tends to dissolve into unity. Finally, another type of duality emerges from this unity.

This unity/duality pattern can be quickly illustrated. During the 1970s, Bauman was making large generalizations about two opposed intellectual systems, positivism (which claimed to produce scientific truth) and existentialism (which offered human emancipation), while arguing that a third approach, sociological hermeneutics, combined the pursuit of both truth and emancipation.

At that time, Bauman was focusing his attention upon what he saw as two competing social systems: state socialism in the East (including the Soviet Union and the East European societies in the Soviet bloc) and capitalism in the West (that is, Western Europe and the United States). However, by the 1980s he was treating East and West as two sub-types of one basic kind of social order that is modernity. More recently, Bauman has argued that modernity produces a sort of precipitate that is postmodernity. Modernity and postmodernity are, so to speak, like positive and negative charges in the same atom: again, two elements in tension with each other.

The two key players in Bauman's model of postmodernity are capitalism and the isolated individual. While capitalism encompasses the whole globe, people are discovering that they are strangers, each belonging to a constituency of one, the self. So, while the globe is *unified* by the universal influence of capitalism, the sphere of empathy among humans shrinks to the individual *unit* – the stranger among strangers. On the one hand, the unity of the whole; on the other hand, the unity of the individual. Both arenas, the self and the global whole, are, as Bauman sees it, likely to be zones where irresponsibility rules, since it is increasingly difficult to hold either capital or the individual to account. Two kinds of unity: another version of the unity/duality pattern.

There are further nuances. In *Postmodern Ethics* (1993), Bauman points out that even though postmodern men and women feel alone, they are still challenged to act in some way by the needs of others, especially the poor, the weak and the suffering. In other words, each of us is forced into a relationship with others, even if it is a relationship of rejection, one where we hold them away from us.

The 'I' and the 'Other' are yet another case of positive and negative charges in the same atom, another instance of unity/duality. Finally, in *Work, Consumerism and the New Poor* (1998e) and in *Globalization: the human consequences* (1998b), Bauman focuses upon the opposition between the rich and the poor – a duality that threatens to collapse into unity through a 'holocaust' of the poor.

Continuing this last theme, it seems probable that Bauman's sensitivities about consumerism and poverty were sharpened by the process of discovering the West. I have a good source for this observation. The shock of transition to a consumer society is beautifully crystallized in Janina Bauman's diary of her visit to see her husband Zygmunt in 1958, when he was spending a year in London.

Janina saw extreme wealth and utter poverty. When Zygmunt took her to Stepney, 'a truly squalid part of London', she was 'immediately reminded of the Warsaw ghetto just after the war'. However, she was proud to know that in Poland by the late 1950s there were 'neither tattered old women sleeping in the streets, nor idle fur-coated ladies driving their luxury cars along the same streets. Everything is drab in our country, but everyone shares the drabness to more or less the same extent' (J. Bauman 1988: 137–8).

After a few weeks, Janina was 'fed up with luxury, with the abundance of goods for sale' (p. 139). She describes the day her husband took her round Harrods:

> [Zygmunt] only wanted to show me this place, knowing that he wouldn't be able to buy anything there. Indeed . . . Those fur coats, those porcelain sets, those leather armchairs . . . Precious jewellery . . . I was stunned, but not out of greed. In the end [Zygmunt] couldn't bear being just a window shopper and suddenly decided we would buy something after all. What? A piece of cheese.

At the immense circular cheese counter, the man in charge 'gave a scornful glance when [Zygmunt] asked for Camembert'. The man held the open box of cheese towards Janina.

I was so frightened that my legs began to tremble. I had no idea what
was expected of me. But [Zygmunt] knew and whispered in Polish:
'Touch it,' which I did. 'Say it's all right.' I said it was all right. 'Thank
you, Madam,' said the formidable man with a malicious grin and
wrapped the damned Camembert in a beautiful sheet of paper. Never,
never again. (p. 140)

This diary extract says a great deal between the lines. Firstly, it
shows that the glitter of Western consumerism hit visitors from
Eastern Europe full in the face. Secondly, feelings of bedazzlement
were quickly followed by disgust at the greed and selfishness
encouraged by consumerism. Thirdly, the passage shows that shopping in a consumer culture was experienced as a way of defining
yourself, of saying who you were. It challenged your sense of identity, but at the same time it offered you the chance to adopt a new
identity if you could buy the right things and behave in the right
way. Consumerism gave you disturbing choices.

To someone displaced, even temporarily, from a familiar social
environment, sudden immersion in the consumer market place was
a deeply unsettling experience. It epitomized the transformation of
consciousness that takes place, in Bauman's view, when people feel
displaced within modernity, when they stop feeling comfortably at
home in the modern world. In this postmodern condition, ambivalence rules. Life is experienced in a fragmented way. Consumerism
seeps in between the fragments and offers us products and services
that will, supposedly, put us together again.

This episode has already introduced the question of how
Bauman's approach was affected by his emigration from Poland
to the West. As the next section will argue, the effect has been a
considerable one.

A sociology for strangers

In books such as *Towards a Critical Sociology* (1976b) and *Hermeneutics and Social Science* (1978), Bauman concentrated on developing
a methodology for promoting dialogue among social groups as
the basis for action leading in the direction of a socialist utopia.
However, there was an underlying problem with Bauman's
espousal of this particular approach in the West.

Anyone trying to encourage and influence dialogue among social
groups (workers, professionals, politicians and so on) needs to have
detailed knowledge about the history, experience, culture and

attitudes of the different groups involved. They also have to be able to communicate with those groups, understanding their various points of view while at the same time showing them other perspectives.

There is no doubt that Bauman's best chance for enacting such a strategy with reasonable effectiveness would have been in Poland, where he had intimate knowledge of the interests involved and understood the complex historical roots of the contemporary political situation. In that context, his writings during the mid-1960s were political acts that sent ripples through the power structure. They had an effect. Indeed, the effect was sufficient to draw answering attacks from the regime.

The situation was quite different for Bauman in his voluntary exile. He was a stranger without intimate 'inside knowledge' of Western societies comparable to his deep understanding of Central and Eastern Europe, including Russia. Bauman was, in practical terms, ill-equipped to take part in his own preferred programme of promoting dialogue between social groups.

When he came west, Bauman must have felt very much a fish out of water – a little like Dorothy transported by a whirlwind to the Land of Oz. He had lost close contact with a society whose workings he understood intimately and found himself in a world that paid little attention to him. It was a world whose principles he found alien – a world where he could earn a living but had little influence beyond the university. We can only guess at Bauman's sense of powerlessness and his frustration at being out of the game.[4]

The experience of migration and exile fundamentally changed Bauman's relationship with the societies he studies and writes about. When he wrote about Poland in the early 1970s, it was like someone describing a house so familiar that he could find his way around it in the dark. In Bauman's early writings, the different groups in Polish society – the factory workers, the middle-level bureaucrats, the first-generation revolutionaries, technocrats and so on – come over vividly as people with distinct instincts, prejudices, interests and collective mannerisms, so to speak. One can almost see and hear them arguing, joking and conspiring.

In Bauman's later work, centre stage is taken not by specific human groups but by the consumer market and modern bureaucracies, especially the state. In Bauman's writings from the early 1970s, systemic features like 'the market' and 'bureaucracy' were abstract parameters rather like lines of longitude and latitude. By the 1990s, these systemic features have become leading actors in

Bauman's story, much more than abstract parameters. In this later work, it is the market and bureaucracy, not particular social groups, that display strong and distinct personalities.

As described by Bauman, the market is like a tantalizing seductress who entraps us in an enchanted garden while telling us that we are free. Similarly, modern bureaucracies are sinister asylums, whose inmates are injected with a drug that dulls the conscience and numbs the capacity for feeling care. In Bauman's later work, market and bureaucracy are no longer merely rules based on partially conflicting principles, which sometimes facilitate and sometimes frustrate human purposes. Instead, they are monsters who rule the world, carving it up between them, living off human weakness.

Bauman's later work is not filled with concrete social groups who live in specific ways in particular places. Instead, it is populated with archetypes: tourists and vagabonds, strollers and players, consumers and flawed consumers, rich and poor. These are abstract entities, personifications of different perspectives, plights and strategies. In his hands, the Jews become the prototypes of the archetypes. He presents their situation as being a microcosm or condensation of the situation of *all* men and women in postmodernity: rootless strangers in an ambivalent world.

These strangers – that is to say, all human beings – are Bauman's constituency. He does not show us their faces. He does not sort these strangers into groups for us and show them interacting with each other, as he did when writing about Poland. Instead Bauman takes us 'behind the eyes' of the universal stranger and shows us the world that this stranger sees. It is, one might conclude, the world that Bauman sees.

Bauman has approached the challenge of being an 'outsider' in the West by seeking to persuade his Western audience that they, too, are 'outsiders'. Insofar as he is successful in doing this, Bauman creates a bond of shared identity between himself and his readers. Paradoxically, by teaching his readers to be outsiders, he makes himself an insider, no different from the rest.

Part II

The Road to Postmodernity

5

The Road to the West

Keeping on the road

Zygmunt Bauman's analyses of modernity and postmodernity did not suddenly spring into existence during the late 1980s. They matured slowly, the outcome of sustained intellectual effort over the preceding three decades. During this time, Bauman was not 'looking for' postmodernity. He was preoccupied instead with the challenges he faced as a revisionist intellectual in communist Poland and, later, as a socialist émigré living in the capitalist West.

This chapter deals with the years leading up to the mid-1970s. During this period, Bauman was very busy keeping himself firmly on the road leading towards his chosen utopia of socialism. This itself was quite an achievement, since he had to cope with two potentially devastating life changes. I am referring, of course, to his dismissal from the Polish army in 1953, an event that turned him into an academic rather than a professional soldier, and his emigration to the West in 1968 after being hounded by the regime.

Bauman did more than just survive these personal crises. He assimilated the new experiences they forced upon him into his thinking and fed the results into his work. In this chapter, I investigate some of the writing that Bauman produced analysing the situation of socialist intellectuals and devising the theoretical guidelines for a modern Marxism. I also consider his early empirical analyses of the British labour movement and state socialist regimes in Eastern Europe.

An unexpected discovery

When I opened the pages of the *Polish Sociological Bulletin*, published in communist Poland during the early and mid-1960s, I was not expecting to find anything very exciting there. Bauman had a couple of pieces in the 1962 volume: one on the values of Warsaw youth (1962c) and another on Party organization in an industrial works (1962a).

Both pieces were written in a very impersonal manner. They were obviously based on very thorough and professional research and were full of statistical tables. They contained data useful to anyone interested in suggesting reform of the system, but there was very little critical discussion in the articles themselves. It was all between the lines. The articles themselves were precise, careful and as dry as dust.

None of this was surprising. I thought: 'What do you expect? This is communist Poland.' But then I moved forward down the volumes to 1965 and 1966. I opened them at the articles by Bauman. There was a radical change of style. Instead of a cautious and heavily coded presentation, I encountered a clear and independent mind developing an overtly critical perspective on the society's institutions.

There was a further surprise when I read through one of Bauman's articles from 1966 entitled 'Three remarks on contemporary educational problems' (1966c). In the article, I found the central themes from three of Bauman's books on modernity and postmodernity that did not appear until two decades or more later. The terms 'modernity' and 'postmodernity' were not mentioned in the 1966 article. Instead, the ideas are presented as observations on the difficulties of getting Polish state socialism to work well.

In the article, Bauman accuses the Polish schools of failing to prepare young people for the complexities of life in an industrial society. He points out that, at school, pupils are given a very strong feeling of ideological certainty about the nature of their society and the direction of their own lives. In his view, this type of education is very harmful because it makes the pupils blind to the fact that life presents difficult moral challenges and that it is by no means always clear how these challenges should be dealt with. As Bauman puts it:

> the teachers obstinately try to convince their pupils that there is only one accepted pattern of behaviour, whose rightness is absolute and

unwavering . . . The only thing that the pupils have to do is study this pattern intellectually and diligently suit themselves to it, for them to acquire a feeling of indomitable power backing their own actions, for them to save themselves from the feeling that they are responsible for their own actions, for them to be able to treat themselves not as an agency but as an instrument, as a tool in the hands of some supra-individual cause. (p. 87)

However, in real life, when they leave school, young Poles soon discover that society is much more complex than orthodox communist ideology tells them. They struggle with this situation and cope with it in different ways. Some become emotionally insecure. Others retreat into a private world. Many become very cynical.

Bauman argues that the people running social institutions (government officials, industrial managers and so on) must pay much more attention to the effect that their own attitudes and behaviour have upon the feelings, expectations and motivations of the people they employ or deal with. At the same time, the schools should try much harder to prepare pupils for the realities of life. According to Bauman: 'not only must the educationist be a planner, but the planner must also be an educationist' (p. 85). The educator-planner or intellectual – in other words, someone like Bauman himself – is, in fact, the central figure in Bauman's own scheme for improving socialism.

One of the big problems facing the 'planning' intellectual is how to help people come to terms with the complexity of industrial society. This is more than a matter of coordinating different bureaucracies – making the bits fit together, so to speak. It is also a question of helping people to find meaning in their lives. People need to be able to organize their lives in a decent way, avoiding despair and cynicism.

However, this is difficult to achieve in a complex industrial society. Children are told one thing by their parents, another thing by their friends. On vital issues of conduct, factory workers have different ideas from bureaucrats, who in turn disagree with experts and intellectuals, and so on. In other words, 'The behaviour demanded by one group in a given situation is often denounced by another group, and differs again from the code demanded by still another group' (p. 86).

In view of the 'chronic state of structural and cultural disintegration of contemporary society' (p. 86), teachers should encourage young people to make their own choices, rationally and sensibly, thinking through the consequences of how they behave. School children should learn that they need to work out their own rules and criteria for dealing with difficult life situations: 'rules for choosing between different patterns . . . [and] criteria enabling [them] to choose between alternatives'. Above all, every young person should be 'prepared . . . for the fact that his life will consist of a whole series of individual decisions and choices, and that no one and nothing, neither divine providence nor historic necessity, will free him of the responsibility for his deeds' (p. 89).

There are three ways in which this article published in 1966 anticipates arguments that Bauman was to develop later:

- In 1966 Bauman makes the point that ideology reinforced by bureaucracy encourages conformity and neutralizes the sense of personal moral responsibility: over two decades later, this argument was central to *Modernity and the Holocaust* (1989).
- In 1966 Bauman points out that legislating intellectuals find it a very challenging task to plan society effectively when cultural homogeneity has been undermined by subcultural heterogeneity: over two decades later, this idea was central to *Legislators and Interpreters* (1987).
- Finally, in 1966 Bauman's view is that everyone must take responsibility for their own moral choices: nearly three decades later, this idea was central to *Postmodern Ethics* (1993).

Intellectuals and innovation

Bauman's overall stance during the mid-1960s was positive and optimistic. This is clear from two other articles he wrote: 'Social structure and innovational personality' (1965) and 'Two notes on mass culture' (1966d). In these articles, Bauman again focused on subcultural diversity – the fact that different groups hold different moral views and follow different ways of life. He sees this as an opportunity, not a threat. The point is that intellectuals such as himself respond positively as societies become more complex. By contrast, increased complexity poses a threat to the kind of small-minded bureaucrat he dislikes.

You can hear the undertones of contempt for routine-driven Party hacks in Bauman's comment that 'human behaviour in a multi-dimensional society, instead of being a culturally pre-determined chain of systematically arranged acts, becomes a series of choices . . . That is why acts of human behaviour more and more often include elements of creativity, of innovation, of something which was not in its entirety pre-determined by the preceding events' (1965: 57). Another way of saying this is: when societies become complex, you need some creativity and imagination to operate effectively within them. You cannot just turn to the appropriate page of the rulebook issued by Party headquarters.

In Bauman's view, socialism needs people with an 'innovational personality' (p. 54), in which category Bauman clearly includes himself. The conflicts and tensions found within a society with diverse subcultures produce a very stimulating environment for innovators. Such people have both the capacity and the right to engage in constructive criticism, he suggests.

This is fighting talk. I doubt if Party high-ups were pleased to read Bauman's opinions. He thought that intellectual critics were entitled 'to submit the prevalent cultural system to critical analysis and to come forward with a counter-proposal' that might stimulate or serve human needs better. If this alternative analysis proved to be 'historically rational and accurate', argues Bauman, it might rally enough 'social forces . . . for it to become a major factor shaping social reality' (1966d: 69). The clear implication was that intellectual critics should be critical of official policies if they thought it necessary. They should seek support from within the society, and with such popular backing they might actually win their arguments with the regime.

When Bauman looked about him in Poland, he saw two main forces for social conformity. One was the ideological orthodoxy transmitted by the Party bureaucracy and the educational system. The other was mass culture with its levelling effect. However, there was a factor that worked against these two forces for social conformity. This was the tendency towards subcultural diversification, which meant that as people moved about in society, they found different standards of behaviour being followed at different times and in different places. Bauman believed that subcultural diversity was a good thing, especially if it provided the means to satisfy all the needs, and even the preferences, of all the people.

However, 'within mass culture, one subculture plays a role of special importance . . . This is the subculture of the culture-makers': in other words, those who are 'professionally engaged in the creation of cultural values. I have in mind the intellectuals' (p. 73). It is the intellectuals who keep culture dynamic. They have the task of 'creative experiment'. This task is carried out 'in the interest of society' because the culture they produce is 'the raw material for the future culture of the entire society' (p. 74).

Bauman, Galbraith and Mill

In 1966 Bauman was writing as an avowed socialist. In his later years, he has sometimes denied that his ideas are particularly socialist. He did this, for example, in the interview carried out in 1990 that I quoted in the previous chapter. It is not worth spending much time on terminology, since the essential point is Bauman's continuing commitment to equality, freedom and social justice. These commitments are not a socialist monopoly.

For example, Bauman's views on the intellectuals' role are similar to those of John K. Galbraith – surprisingly similar, considering that one was responding to the excesses of corporate capitalism and the other to the inadequacies of state socialism. Galbraith wants the 'educational and scientific estate' (1974: 375) – in other words, academics, intellectuals and experts of various kinds – to take the lead in civilizing society.

Galbraith argues that intellectuals should be fighting mediocrity, conservatism and corruption, especially in government and the business sector. They should do this by giving ordinary people a clear idea of what a better society could be like, standing up for high ideals and showing practical ways to put them into practice. Bauman was making similar points in Poland during the late 1960s.

Compare also John Stuart Mill. Like Galbraith and Bauman, Mill thinks intellectuals have a large public role: one of raising standards and educating the people. As a matter of fact, Bauman's situation in postwar Poland has some intriguing similarities to Mill's situation in mid-nineteenth-century Britain. Mill disliked the conformism and mediocrity of the petty-bourgeois shopkeeper culture that threatened to dominate Britain's incipient democracy. For his part, Bauman had little sympathy with the small-minded conservatism of the middle- and low-level Party bureaucrats who administered the socialist state in Poland. Mill and Bauman were both intellectuals fighting their corner, determined to maintain their right to be creative and different.

For Bauman and for Mill, defending diversity as a general principle, protecting the right to be different, was the best way to throw a barricade around society's intellectuals – the surest means of giving them freedom to think new thoughts. I am certainly not suggesting that Bauman wanted to make intellectuals into an isolated elite. Far from it; in fact, just the opposite. Nor did Mill.

Mill thought that one of the main tasks of intellectuals was to get involved in educating the people and helping them learn the skills of self-government. So did Bauman. As we have seen, he wanted intellectuals to be spreading their influence, actively rallying social forces. He wanted planners to be educators as well.[1]

Bauman is aware of this overlap between Mill's views and his own. In 1959 he published a book about British socialism based on a study of Bentham, Mill and Spencer (Bauman 1959). He later recalled: 'I was struck by the fact that J. S. Mill, starting from some very straightforward liberal individualistic assumptions ... ended up, following the logic of utilitarianism, with becoming in fact a socialist' (Bauman 1992b: 218).

Modern times, modern Marxism

Bauman did not stop at Mill in his search for theoretical constructs that could be used to supercharge the 'modern Marxism' that 'modern times' required (Bauman 1969: 1). He tapped into recent American sociology, including C. Wright Mills. He also drew upon French structuralist anthropology, the Frankfurt School of critical theory, and the revisionist Marxism of Gramsci and Lukács. All these influences are evident in the paper that Bauman contributed to Peter Berger's *Marxism and Sociology: views from Eastern Europe* (1969).[2]

In this paper, Bauman investigates 'what is and what is not Marxist human science in modern times' (Bauman 1969: 11). When Bauman writes about the 'modern' in the late 1960s, he is not condemning modernity; nor is he contrasting it with 'postmodernity'. Instead, he presents the 'modern' as something highly desirable and praiseworthy. Bauman is proud to be modern – a declared opponent of the Marxist orthodoxy that tradition sanctifies.

He contrasts the theoretical programme of 'modern Marxists, at least in Poland' (p. 14) with Marxism's 'time-honoured tradition' (p. 3) dominated by Plekhanov, Kautsky and Bukharin. This 'popular variety of Marxism' had focused on economic determinism so as 'to bring the guiding philosophical doctrine closer to the natural cognitive set of the mass following' (p. 15). Hungry peasants were quite ready to believe that material wants and necessities drove human beings and history.

Bauman objects to single-factor explanations of any kind. Economic factors are just one part of a total structure – an integral part of the 'unified life-process' (p. 1).[3] He supports 'the entirely modern demand to understand-through-allocating-in-a-structure . . . , not the traditional search for *the* efficient cause' (p. 2; emphasis in original).

Bauman's battle with tradition is linked with another struggle: against managerialism. He argues that the social sciences have, unfortunately, adapted to the 'technical thinking' demanded by managers of large-scale organizations. The main problem confronting such organizations is the manageability of their units. Managers want knowledge of 'laws of "cause and effect"' (p. 4), so that they can manipulate and predict human behaviour efficiently.

In response, most men and women frame their own personal problems in managerial terms, each person asking, 'How to adjust my dreams and cravings to the environment I can neither change nor even influence?' The result is a form of false consciousness shaped by 'the managerial pragmatistic world-outlook'. The 'ideal state in which "people want to do what they must" (Eric Fromm) is nearly achieved' (p. 6). People treat the here-and-now as the 'real' and assume that this reality is 'reasonable' (p. 11).[4]

Bauman supports an opposing approach, which shows ordinary men and women that 'our world is one of many possible worlds' (p. 11). Large organizations are hostile to publicizing facts that suggest alternative social arrangements are possible. Bauman wants to challenge the 'constant managerial pressure towards secrecy in scientific investigations' (p. 9). He wants to open up choice and give people more opportunities to express themselves, in the market and elsewhere.

In Bauman's view, people should not be too ready to adjust their dreams and desires to what the managerial ideology says they can have. From the point of view of 'man as a pure and simple human being' (p. 5) what is 'really maladjusted is the society' (p. 6). Marxism should provide the kind of knowledge and understanding that people need in the life-process. In this spirit, the sociologists should serve not the managerial function but the 'anthropological' function (p. 7).

Bauman argues that Marxist human science should be holistic and structuralist. It should be interested in the structure of knowledge-seeking processes, including procedures for ascertaining 'truth'. Also relevant are the relationship between science, ideology and social structure, the role of theories, values and cultural biases, and the sociologist's role in society. Above all, Marxist sociologists should be 'in permanent dialogue with the most modern of [their] . . . scientific contemporaries' (p. 14).

In opposition to economic determinism, Bauman 'puts to the forefront the active, motivating role of mental structuralization of the human world'. Ideas count. What men and women think and believe shapes their action and, in turn, their action shapes the world. To put it another way, 'The truth is . . . a process, the very pronouncement of an idea being a powerful factor in making its content true through the praxis it initiates' (p. 14).

This does not mean that idle dreaming is enough to guide action. Praxis is effective only when 'the set of opportunities involved "objectively" in a historical situation finds the adequate ideology which in its turn is relevant enough to the private experience of the masses to gain their support and to stimulate their action' (p. 16). The challenge facing intellectuals such as Bauman was twofold: to assess the opportunities within historical situations accurately as a result of rigorous investigation of 'macro-social problems and issues' (p. 13); and to provide ideologies that were adequate, relevant and stimulating. In that way, new realities could be created through creative praxis.

So far, we have seen Bauman's analysis of the role of intellectuals and the nature of culture within civil society in the particular case of Poland. The next two sections of the chapter look at two other analyses carried out by Bauman in the early part of his career. These are his study of the British labour movement and his exploration of postwar East European state socialism, with special reference to Poland.

Between Class and Elite

In 1960 Bauman published *Between Class and Elite: the evolution of the British labour movement – a sociological survey* (Bauman 1972). The book was based on research carried out at the London School of Economics under the supervision of Bob Mackenzie. It was translated into English twelve years later, soon after Bauman took up his appointment at Leeds.

In this book, Bauman divides the evolution of the British labour movement into four periods. Between 1750 and 1850 the movement was 'embryonic'. It 'came of age' between 1850 and 1890. A 'mass' movement evolved between 1890 and 1924. Finally, in the years between 1924 and 1955 a process of 'consolidation' occurred.

Bauman distinguishes between three 'subsystems' that interact with each other in a flexible way. These are the working class, the organized labour movement and the elite leadership of that movement. He divides up the working class into its different strata and identifies competing tendencies within the labour movement. Within the labour elite he identifies two main groups: heroic agitators and conservative bureaucrats. Bauman then argues that the working class, the labour movement and the labour elite were each able to respond to changing circumstances in a creative manner. None of them alone, and certainly not the working class, was the decisive factor in bringing about historical change.

Within this framework, Bauman tells a story of the breakdown of traditional rural structures and the emergence of a new skilled stratum keen to make its way into respectable bourgeois society. He shows that tensions developed between old and new models of trade union organization and also between skilled and unskilled workers. However, the workforce became homogenized as the semi-skilled stratum grew in size. Meanwhile, the labour movement became increasingly bureaucratic, increasingly conservative, and more thoroughly embedded in the structures of British capitalism.

I am not going to discuss Bauman's argument in detail. It was almost certainly a major achievement in the context of Polish sociology in 1960. However, twelve years later, when it appeared in English, it obviously made no reference to the ideas and methodologies developed by English labour and social historians such as E. P. Thompson during the 1960s. This is ironic, since Bauman was deeply interested in issues such as working-class culture.

Bauman is evidently a very keen admirer of the bravery and determination shown by the first generation of labour leaders in Britain. He lets his sympathies show clearly. These leaders had the charisma needed to sway large crowds. They were far more 'heroic' than the respectable, status-seeking bureaucrats who succeeded them (Bauman 1972: 113). (Is Bauman, perhaps, having a quiet dig at middle-level Polish administrators here?)

In a later generation, the 'heroic leaders' of the Independent Labour Party were true 'martyrs', displaying 'monastic fanaticism'. The biographies of these 'Ascetic' and 'very learned' men made 'fascinating and edifying reading' (pp. 174, 198). Bauman employs enthusiastic language when discussing these figures. His comments on them stand out from the surrounding text, which is measured and uniform in tone. This suggests that these men represent a character type that he had learned to respect and perhaps even wanted to emulate.

In 1960 Bauman is already distancing himself from Marxist orthodoxy. Although he retains a broadly evolutionary and dialectical approach to social change, he insists that 'Human history is notorious for its insidious defiance of possibilities' (p. 322). Nobody knows the script in advance. Bauman's analysis breaks away from the idea that history has to be written according to an ideological script, which assigns the working class a historical role that it 'should' fulfil. He dismisses 'politically loaded cognitive formulae' and argues strongly for a much more 'detached' approach (pp. x–xi).

Polish peasants and politics

Ten years later, Bauman was out of Poland. He took the chance to write directly about the kind of conflicts and tensions in which he had been involved. However, Bauman remained proud of many things that state socialism had achieved and was deeply interested in whether there were any prospects for its eventual improvement and success.

Reading 'Social dissent in the East European political system' (Bauman 1971b) is like being taken on a tour of someone's old home. You get the feeling that, even though your guide has moved on to new accommodation, he still has a sneaking affection for this place he used to live in, despite its ugly side. He knows some nooks and crannies you were not aware of and now and again smacks his fist against the wall, murmuring 'pretty solid, eh?'

Bauman argues that the peasantry is the key to making sense of socialism in Eastern Europe. It is vital 'to demonstrate an empathetic understanding of this group's sense of achievement and personal indebtedness to the victorious revolution' (p. 39). The system was profoundly shaped by its 'extremely intensive and massive upward mobility' (p. 34). Bauman has no doubt that 'many a "Kremlinologist" lacking in sociological interests' completely fails to grasp just how important the peasantry is.

After the revolutions in Russia and Eastern Europe, enormous numbers of peasants left the land. They flocked into industry and staffed the lower and middle rungs of the political hierarchy. Their children filled the urban classrooms. For the 'young and ambitious', city life offered 'quite real and attractive assets, and opportunities to reach values more tempting than a sheer improvement of living standards' (p. 36). There was no 'desperate flight' from rural poverty. By the early 1960s, people in the countryside were eating much better than before the war.[5] Towns appealed to the imagination and the mind rather than just the stomach.

The new ex-rural industrial workforce had to be disciplined very rapidly – much more quickly than in the West during the nineteenth century. The socialist societies were engaged in a 'desperate last-chance attempt' to catch up with the industrialized West. As a result, 'abundance of compulsion and forcible mobilization methods were unavoidable' (pp. 36–7).

The factory workforce generally accepted the regime's authoritarian style. This was partly because of the secret police, partly because the workers' way of thinking was formed by the traditional pre-industrial village. Within the village, the whole community had authority over its members and took responsibility for their welfare and security. In the city and the factory, the Party took over the paternal role of the old village community.

The industrial workforce did not form independent trade unions on the Western model. Such institutions were the product of a class formula and form of struggle 'made to measure in a very different socio-political setting'. In any case, the Polish factory workers enjoyed a 'genuine improvement' in their living standards without trade unions. High job security, 'the fresh experience of urban shopping' (p. 38) and the chance to buy durable goods all gave them a vested interest in political stability under the new regime. It was 'much more "natural" and in some ways also "rational" to act in accordance with the state's monopoly of the distribution of goods and of welfare measures' (p. 37).

Not all peasant families turned towards the factory. The children of better-off peasants went into white-collar jobs – work outside the grasp of the illiterate poorer peasantry, but too badly paid to attract the more skilled elements of the industrial workforce. These upwardly mobile offspring of the middling peasantry worked their way up the hierarchies of Party, police, local government and security services, acquiring 'unheard-of power and influence'. Once in power, they adapted smoothly to their urban-industrial environment. They took the chance to 'secure the now fashionable academic certificates and degrees'. This was a pattern followed by Bauman himself. He had registered for an MA at Warsaw while serving as an army officer.

The ex-peasants of Eastern Europe were not hungry for freedom or democracy. Instead, they wanted security. Intellectual freedom was a threat to them. It made life uncertain and unsafe. It suited the interests of factory workers and bureaucrats if the state, 'their' state, kept responsibility for production, distribution and justice, however inadequately these functions were actually carried out. They wanted the new opportunity structure created by the communist regimes in Eastern Europe to stay in place.

Despite the social contract between the peasantry and the system, state socialism experienced several forms of social dissent. One group of malcontents included old-time revolutionaries who did the dirty work of overthrowing the pre-revolutionary government. They settled into local administration, but later found themselves being outflanked by central government planners who took decisions without consulting them. The old guard resisted by attacking the modernizing experts' 'morally blind efficiency'. They also appealed to 'local xenophobia' (p. 43), winning grassroots support by mobilizing anti-Semitic feelings, for example.

As the post-revolutionary elite became a gerontocracy, promotion blockages caused resentment. In the middle ranks, colonels were often no more than a very few years older than the lieutenants who were after their jobs. Meanwhile, there were functional conflicts at the top within the political elite, especially between experts with a vested interest in 'adventure and experiment' and bureaucratic rulers who were 'naturally interested in routine' (p. 46).

Inequality caused resentment. The communist elite made sure that their sons and daughters got the best educational opportunities, the best jobs, the best houses and the best consumer goods. Leading Party members benefited from two types of inequality. They dominated 'officialdom' and, at the same time, enjoyed class privilege in the realm of the market.[6]

One type of dissent that Bauman dismissed as insignificant was the demand made by a few isolated, dissident intellectuals for more freedom of expression. The ideal of freedom was likely to appeal only to a working class that had a long experience of trade union organization and a tradition of demanding the right to organize, hold meetings and so forth. This was a Western rather an Eastern experience, with the partial exception of Czechoslovakia. Only where it had occurred could there be an alliance between intellectuals and workers dedicated to following 'an alternative way, leading to bread, security and freedom at the same time' (p. 50).

Nor did Bauman think that the slackening of Russian control over its satellites in the early 1970s would lead to fundamental upheavals *within* socialist societies: 'As a matter of fact we know no single fact that would support such a conclusion' (p. 48). In a footnote, he added the comment: 'Unfortunately, the matter is not open to experimental checking [and so] . . . there is no hope that the final proof will be provided in the not-too-distant future' (p. 31). In fact, as everybody now knows, in the not-too-distant future of the 1980s the weakening of the Soviet grip on Eastern Europe did in fact allow fundamental upheavals within socialist societies to take place, beginning with the Solidarity movement in Bauman's native Poland.

Above all, Bauman was determined to draw attention to the achievements of socialism. He argued that the socialist system had supplied the central element in a paradigm that was becoming dominant in East and West. This 'paradigm so far unshattered in any irreparable way is the ever increasing satisfaction of the ever increasing needs of the ever increasing number of people, striven for by the ever increasing power and competence of the state' (p. 51). Because the revolutionary regimes in Russia and Eastern Europe had survived, the West had been forced to introduce measures such as the welfare state and to keep unemployment as low as possible.

Bauman even went so far as to claim that the state, East and West, had become so thoroughly entrenched in everyday socioeconomic life that political revolutions were a thing of the past. His point was that, if the state was no longer isolated from society, as it had been in the bourgeois societies of the nineteenth and early twentieth centuries, it could no longer be captured by revolutionaries and used as an active agent remoulding society.

Bauman did not take into account the possibility that government might substantially disentangle itself from society, making way for the penetration of market forces into spheres previously regulated by the 'power and competence of the state'. Nor did he anticipate the political revolutions of 1989–90. But, as Bauman had pointed out nearly thirty years before, 'Human history is notorious for its insidious defiance of possibilities' (1972: 322).

Conclusion

During the 1960s and early 1970s, Bauman explored the dynamics of the triangular relationships among the state bureaucracy, the people and the intellectuals. He hoped that bureaucratic planners would acquire the skills of enlightened teachers. If this were to happen, it would both acknowledge and increase the authority and influence of intellectuals such as Bauman. This would, in turn, increase the capacity of socialist intellectuals to mobilize the population at large, working towards a freer society in which people could express themselves more creatively.

In fact, the social contract between the peasantry and the bureaucracy was so strong and so central to Polish society that Bauman and those who shared his aspirations were unable to act as an effective third force. Neither the peasantry nor the bureaucrats felt any enthusiasm for progressive intellectuals who spoke about freedom and seemed to relish uncertainty.

Bauman's analysis of the way forward for Polish socialism was not given a sympathetic hearing by those with power. He decided to make a career in the West. However, Bauman retained his commitment to the goal of socialism. Along with this commitment went a strategy and a critique, both initially developed in Poland. The strategy was to continue exploring the opportunities involved 'objectively' in unfolding historical situations, East and West, in the hope that a progressive analysis might be heard at the right time. This analysis would include a positive vision of the better society offered by socialism – a vision to inspire praxis.

The critique was directed against the sociopolitical order created in Poland during the 1960s by an unenlightened bureaucracy and a highly conformist population. Bauman pointed out that socialism had so far failed to confront three challenges: preventing moral anaesthesia, coping with subcultural heterogeneity and encouraging a sense of personal moral responsibility.

As we have seen, Bauman mounted the same critique against Western capitalist societies during the 1980s and 1990s. However, the context was very different. In the 1960s, Bauman argued that the deficiencies just listed were *practical matters that could be dealt with* as long as the correct strategies were adopted by leaders who were competent and clear-sighted. By contrast, during the late 1980s and early 1990s, Bauman took a much more absolutist line: the prevalence of moral anaesthesia made modernity unacceptable;

subcultural heterogenity contributed to a climate of ambivalence that fatally undermined belief in modernity; the challenge of assuming personal moral responsibility was too daunting for modern men and women to confront as a matter of course. In other words, these issues were no longer practical matters that could be handled within the context of socialist modernity; rather they were *fundamental flaws that made modernity unacceptable.*

What changed between 1966 and the late 1980s? Basically, Bauman lost his confidence that the kind of socialism he wanted could be brought into existence. However, that is a story for later.

6

The Road to Utopia

Mechanisms of social change

During the 1960s, Zygmunt Bauman was mainly concerned with what he thought were the principal agents of social change: the state, the people and the intellectuals. During the 1970s, he paid more attention to what he hoped would be the key mechanisms of social change. As a socialist intellectual committed to the idea of working for a better society, Bauman devoted himself to a careful search for points of leverage, tools to use and blueprints to work from.

He cultivated his understanding in three key areas. He investigated the dynamics of culture. He explored the potential of sociology. Finally, he elaborated his vision of a socialist utopia. In this chapter, I examine Bauman's exploration of culture, sociology and the socialist utopia in four books: *Culture as Praxis* (1973a), *Socialism: the active utopia* (1976a), *Towards a Critical Sociology* (1976b) and *Hermeneutics and Social Science* (1978).

Culture as Praxis

The basic proposition on which Bauman builds his argument in *Culture as Praxis* (1973a) is that society is not possible without culture. At first sight, this is startling. We are much more used to hearing the opposite, that culture depends upon society.

In fact, Bauman accepts that society shapes us – makes us what we are. However, he also believes that we have a 'society-making' capacity pre-installed, so to speak, when we are born. Within limits we can make societies the way we want them to be. Bauman believes that we are 'structured beings' who are also 'capable of structuring' (p. 51). Indeed, 'the peculiarity of man consists in his being a structure-generating and structure-orienting creature' (p. 52). In other words, it is in our nature to create structures and to look for order. We want to have a consistent pattern in our individual and shared lives. We need clear coordinates for our existence.[1]

Bauman distinguishes three concepts. The 'hierarchical' concept of culture is particularly concerned with 'the opposition between "refined" and "coarse" ways of life as well as the educational bridge between them'. The 'differential' concept of culture pays attention to the 'countless and endlessly multipliable oppositions between the ways of life of various human groups'. The 'generic' concept of culture is about the unique characteristics of humankind (p. 39).

In fact, Bauman says, we should think in terms of 'the cultural process' (p. 55). By this he means the process by which human beings adapt to their environment. People do this by taking in two things from the world of which they are a part. These two things are energy and information. They are closely related.

The sources of energy that human beings need include, for example, food and heat. The information they need includes knowing where food and heat can be found or how they can be created.[2] In order to satisfy the need for energy and information, human beings adapt themselves and they adapt the world. For example, they spend time learning the best places to hunt animals or gather fuel, and they build animal traps and storehouses so as to make it easier to catch food and keep it safe.

That is an example from a society with a simple technology. To take a more modern example: in order to survive and prosper, people may take university degrees, buy computers, open bank accounts, go to supermarkets and fill their refrigerators. In doing so, they are adapting themselves and their environment so as to acquire and use energy and information as effectively as they know how.

So the cultural process, the process of adaptation, involves both making human beings fit to live in the world and making the world fit for human beings to live in. There are basically two ways in which this cultural process is handled: firstly, by using tools and, more generally, technology (ploughs, hydroelectric schemes, computers and so on); secondly, by using language – by putting into use our human capacity to create and manipulate symbols of various kinds. Language and tools are crucial elements in human praxis: our active and creative engagement with nature, each other and ourselves. Through praxis we 'structurize' the world (p. 62).

Many years later, in *Mortality, Immortality and Other Life Strategies* (1992b), Bauman identified another dimension to culture. The purpose of culture, he pointed out in this later work, was not only to facilitate life. It was also to escape from death. In fact, 'awareness of mortality . . . is the ultimate condition of cultural creativity as such'. It drives us to engage in tasks that 'are capable of giving life meaning that *transcends* life's biological limitations' (pp. 4–5; emphasis in original).

In Bauman's view, communities are structured through the cultural process. Each community draws a tight boundary around itself, defining who is included by the idea of 'we' and who are the outsiders. In medieval Europe, for example, different ethnic groups, different occupations and different villages lived side by side, each with its own distinct and separate culture, all 'hermetically sealed [and] without the slightest tendency to osmosis' (Bauman 1973a: 134).

This situation did not last. When people started moving out and mixing with each other, when new occupations developed, when new towns burgeoned – in other words, when societies became more industrial, more urban, more fluid and more modern – then a disturbing situation developed. The old categories broke down and the old boundary lines became useless. People no longer knew who they were and where they belonged. Order could no longer be taken for granted as a sort of natural fact.

In modern societies, creating order is a large task that has to be carried out actively: for example, by bureaucrats and planners. Order cannot be taken for granted the way it was in medieval Europe when people stayed inside their group compounds, so to speak. We want to push everything and everyone into tidy categories, even if this means stereotyping whole sections of the human population – treating them as being 'all the same'. We dislike anything that cuts across categories; anything that is viscous, 'slimy' (p. 137), not cut and dried.

In 1973 Bauman sensed a new cultural trend, in favour of 'bridging the unbridgeable, transcending the impassable, welding the unmixable' (p. 156). This trend was largely restricted to the avant-garde. One of its representatives was Herbert Marcuse, an iconic figure for the student movement in that period.[3] However, Bauman mused, was the avant-garde signalling a trend that would become universal? Was the modern rage for order going into retreat? As Bauman put it:

> What seems to be emerging slowly and perhaps erratically is a new level of tolerance towards sliminess and, indeed, towards trespassing of vital frontiers of meaning. It is still unclear . . . whether the current turmoil presages a total revision of the past patterns of praxis . . . It is still far too early to pass final judgement. If the chance materializes, human culture will face a revolution unmatched by the most dramatic upheavals of the past. (p. 157)

Bauman did not say more than this in 1973, but here, nearly two decades before *Intimations of Postmodernity* (1992a), we catch him already sniffing the wind.

In the meantime, there were other urgent items on Bauman's agenda. He gave himself the task of clarifying the nature of socialism, his ultimate objective, and sociology, his favoured means of getting there. He set about this in *Socialism: the active utopia* (1976a) and *Towards a Critical Sociology* (1976b). These two books have a similar design. They both compare two opposing systems and then look for something better. One book looks at two conflicting approaches to running societies. The other looks at two conflicting approaches to analysing societies.

In *Socialism: the active utopia*, Bauman contrasts capitalism with state socialism. He shows how each of these competing systems adopted certain characteristics of its rival. Then he presents his own prescription for 'utopian' socialism. In *Towards a Critical Sociology*, Bauman contrasts existentialist and positivistic approaches to making sense of human societies. He shows how the discipline of sociology has been influenced by both of these competing approaches. Then he presents his own prescription for a critical sociology.

Towards a Critical Sociology

In *Towards a Critical Sociology*, Bauman argues that sociology is an attempt to make sense of the fact that, when human beings set out to pursue their various projects in the world, they come up against all kinds of limitations and constraints. They cannot do just what they want. To illustrate this general point, take the project of building a house. Some of the constraints on a project like this are a product of nature: for example, how strong, tall, intelligent or determined the people involved are, what the climate is like, what kind of building materials are available in the district, and so on. However, other constraints derive from society: for example, laws about property rights, the price of materials and labour in the local area, building regulations, planning permission, and whether or not neighbours are used to cooperating with each other in carrying out tasks of this kind.

Social constraints seem to be a kind of 'second nature' (Bauman 1976b: 1). Their precise content may change (for example, laws may alter, prices may fluctuate, technologies may be improved), but at any one time, social restraints restrict our freedom to do exactly what we want just as effectively as the facts of geography, physics, biology and so on. Bauman distinguishes two responses to our experience of these social constraints.

One response, associated with positivism, is to assume that these social constraints are not only facts we must learn to accept, but also wise or rational arrangements. Emile Durkheim is one representative of this tradition. According to the positivist tradition, the job of sociology is to become as familiar as possible with the 'recurrent, monotonous uniformities' (p. 36) in social reality. This approach to studying society is heavily influenced by natural science. Positivism aims to produce impartial, unproblematic knowledge.

The positivist approach assumes that, if sociologists study the routines of social life, they will become adept at seeing its repeated patterns, and the way these patterns interweave with each other. They will develop a capacity to predict social patterns – to make statements such as 'A is almost invariably followed by (perhaps even "causes") B'. They may even eventually be able to carry out tasks like calculating the extra amount of physical effort that is produced for a given additional quantum of pay in specific industries: 'if we pay X amount more, we get Y amount of additional work', etc.

Planners and bureaucrats use this knowledge of social patterns as a means of social manipulation. They treat people as if they are factors to be controlled by 'scientific' intervention 'from above', in the way a laboratory technician might deliberately engineer a particular chemical reaction. However, as Bauman indicates, there are difficulties with this approach.

Positivistic manipulation of social behaviour has the undesirable effect of polarizing human beings into 'those who think and act, and those who are acted upon' (p. 41). Furthermore, the kind of sociology just described cannot account for how those people who *do* get the chance to think and act are able to make choices on their own account. At some point in the 'system' someone has to make a choice, to assert his or her will. In other words, they have the experience of exercising freedom.

This leads to the other tradition, one fundamentally opposed to positivism, that 'science of unfreedom' (p. 1). The rival approach stems from the insights of existentialism and can be traced back to the work of Heidegger and Husserl. According to this approach, the idea of social institutions constraining us 'from outside' is illusory. We have much more freedom than we imagine. Existentialism does not treat society as a kind of second 'nature', whose laws must be discovered. Instead, it emphasizes the creativity of human beings – their capacity to bring the world into existence.

Bauman pays particular attention to the work of Alfred Schutz and his followers, who argue that 'social reality' consists of implicit agreements between different people to interpret bits of the world in particular ways: for example, to say that there is a 'God' who has power over us, or there is something called the 'nation' to which we 'belong'. In other words, our knowledge of society is no more than the aggregate of these 'typifications' (p. 64).

Bauman argues that this development of existentialism, especially when elaborated by writers such as Berger and Luckman (1967), has 'a genuinely emancipating effect' (Bauman 1976b: 68). It supports the proposition that social reality is a human product – something that we make for ourselves. However, there is one drawback. Berger and Luckman reduce reality to human consciousness: 'One is inclined to conclude that, were the reflective consciousness of individuals . . . abruptly stopped or turned the other way, social reality itself would dissipate or change its content' (p. 69).

Bauman is not happy with this outcome. He wants an approach to sociology which recognizes that social reality extends outside consciousness. He also wants to find a way of assessing the authenticity and 'truth' (p. 102) of the claims that people make about social reality.

Bauman finds a way forward by exploring two ideas: history and dialogue. He accepts that positivism was originally a way of combating prejudice, ignorance and superstition. In the eighteenth century, enlightened philosophers like Voltaire and Diderot thought Reason would empower human beings. It would give them knowledge and allow them to make intelligent choices. Positivistic science would be critical of the existing social order. It would emancipate human beings from their subjection to it.

However, as the scientific approach became successful it helped bring about industrial growth, the expansion of commerce and the building of powerful military machines. The supporters of positivism – the scientists, bureaucrats and managers – developed a large vested interest in these impressive achievements. Positivist reason stopped being critical and became conservative. The task of science was redefined as the responsibility to get technical solutions that made the existing order run more smoothly. Ordinary men and women found themselves trapped and dominated by these industrial, commercial and military institutions, which planned and controlled their lives to a great extent. Positivist reason stopped being emancipatory.

Following Marx, Bauman argues that modern societies have polarized into the dominating and the dominated. The latter came to accept their 'unfreedom' as natural and inevitable. People are alienated. They have lost touch with the liberating idea that they can make the world better for themselves. They bow down to the misleading 'commonsense' view that things cannot be different from how they are.

One way people can reclaim their freedom is by challenging positivism's right to define reality. However, Bauman sees that, if we challenge positivism, we have to provide an alternative route to the goal of 'truth'. If positivistic science does not tell us what is 'real' and 'true', then who or what is to perform this function?

At this point, Bauman turns to Jürgen Habermas. According to Habermas, the task of pronouncing on what is 'real', what is 'true' and what 'should be done' is far too important to be left to 'experts' working away in their laboratories, workshops and libraries. The job of evaluating competing claims about the nature of social reality and the best way to influence it should be shared out. The 'dominated' majority, the people at large, must be brought into the act. At the moment, ordinary men and women are at a disadvantage: they know less, they are less powerful, they expect less. As a result, communication between 'experts' and the people is 'distorted'.[4]

The experts should take on a new role. They should enter into an open and equal dialogue with other members of society. The experts must stop monopolistically controlling the communication process.

Ordinary people should organize themselves to push aside the institutional barriers that deprive them of knowledge, power and high aspirations. They should emancipate themselves by acquiring these things. This requires praxis – creative action.

Dialogue and praxis go together. If dialogue gets under way, if ordinary people are treated as though their views are important, then they will see the need for more knowledge and power, and will set out to achieve them. The more effective ordinary people are in achieving these things, the more competent and productive they will be in the dialogue among themselves and with the experts.

'Critical sociology' encourages dialogue and praxis of this kind. When they occur, communication becomes less distorted. The chances of genuine consensus emerging through creative negotiation among informed, interested parties then become greater. This consensus will be grounded in a high level of shared knowledge.

Dialogue and undistorted communication are means of moving towards 'truth' or 'authentic' knowledge about social reality. However, there are complications. Truth is an ideal that is difficult to achieve in practice. Furthermore, as far as Bauman is concerned, dialogue is only one form of praxis. Other kinds of action are also needed. There are institutions to be reformed, structures to transform, battles to fight, enemies to defeat.

So when does dialogue break off and action based on the dialogue's outcome take place? Even more difficult, what if dialogue does not, in fact, lead to agreement? What if 'communication has broken down definitely' and is 'beyond all chances of repair'? Bauman replies: 'It is on this decisive threshold where courage and the decision to take risk become indispensable vehicles; and, to be sure, where the gravest and most costly mistakes can be made, more often than not confounding the very emancipatory intent of action' (p. 110).

Bauman the political animal knows that, once dialogue is broken off, your partner in dialogue may become an 'implacable enemy'. The 'pragmatics of persuasion' are then replaced by 'the pragmatics of struggle'.[5] But risks of this kind are the price of emancipation, since 'freedom means uncertainty as much as certitude means resignation' (p. 112).

This final comment on Habermas's prescription sounds like an insight learned the hard way. More generally, Bauman's views on how experts ought to behave were certainly influenced by his analysis of the mistakes committed and the wrong turnings taken by the builders of socialism, a matter to which I now turn.

Socialism: the active utopia

Compare the following two sentences:

'A spectre is haunting Europe – the spectre of communism.' (Marx and Engels 1935: 33)

'Socialism descended upon nineteenth-century Europe as utopia.' (Bauman 1976a: 9)

The first sentence is, of course, the opening of *The Communist Manifesto*. The second is the first line of Bauman's *Socialism: the active utopia*. They are both one-line paragraphs. They both introduce books that analyse the past, investigate the present and offer a vision of the future. *Socialism: the active utopia* is Bauman's personal manifesto.

Bauman describes socialism as '*the* utopia of the modern epoch' (p. 36; emphasis in original). Socialism offers a vision of the future that puts the present into perspective. Socialism is 'the counter-culture of capitalism'. It provides the intellectual and moral basis for 'emancipatory criticism-through-relativisation of . . . current reality' (p. 36). Its function is to inspire people and make them realize that things could be made better. The socialist utopia should encourage people to criticize the ways things are. It should stir them into working for a better society.

As Bauman argues, socialism took its core ideals of equality and freedom from liberalism, the philosophy of capitalist society. However, liberals defined these ideals more narrowly than socialists did. For liberals, life is a competition. Freedom means having the right to enter the competition. For liberals, equality means everyone has this right, guaranteed in law. This does not mean that there should be equality in wealth or income, or equal chances to enjoy good health or good education.

The main arena of competition within capitalist societies is the market. There everyone is bound by the same rules of exchange. Liberalism means that nobody is protected from suffering intense deprivation if they do badly in the competition, just as nobody is prevented from getting very rich if they do well. Liberalism means *equal freedom to be unequal*. How did liberal capitalism contain the envy of the poor and the resentment of angry losers in the nineteenth century? The rights of those with property were protected by the police. Employers imposed strict factory discipline on the working class.

In opposition to liberal capitalism, socialists argued that capitalism was oppressive and alienating. By contrast, the utopia of socialism offered the people a fuller version of equality and freedom, which included the right to be well fed, well educated, well housed and healthy. The idea was that it would be possible to provide these benefits for everybody because under socialism resources would be spread more evenly through the society. Furthermore, those resources would not be wasted on unnecessary things such as satisfying superfluous 'needs', artificially created by capitalism in order to keep consumer demand high.

However, as Bauman points out, this strategy depended on getting the historical timing right. Socialism would come into play only when capitalism had completed its own necessary work. Capitalism's allotted task was to develop modern technology, releasing the productive powers of nature. At the same time, it would sweep away the old, irrational, pre-industrial world with its superstitious and ignorant peasants. At this point, socialism would arrive on the scene, so to speak.

Implementing socialism meant abolishing private property. Without private property there would be no bourgeoisie. The proletariat would be the whole of society and alienation would be a thing of the past. Society's material and cultural riches could then be supplied in ample amounts to all communities. All inhabitants of these communities would be able to express and develop themselves in the ways that they wanted. Instead of everybody being free to become unequal, as under capitalism, the socialist utopia would give everybody full and equal access to resources that would enable them to be truly and freely themselves. Civil society, that arena of social life beyond the margins of the state bureaucracy, would flourish, producing a rich culture and a lively intellectual environment. That was the programme embodied in the socialist utopia.

However, as Bauman recognizes, things did not work out like that. The new revolutionary elite in Russia after 1917 found that the socialist utopia of equality and freedom could not be put into practice. Most of the population consisted of peasants. Industrialization was still in its early stages. Capitalism had not developed its technological base sufficiently to generate large supplies of material resources. The productive forces and relations were not 'mature'.

The Soviet state concentrated on building up the economic infrastructure as quickly as possible. Its goal was to catch up with the capitalist West – to match its rival's productive capacity. The socialist utopia just described was, for all practical purposes, abandoned. The Soviet goal became not socialism but industrialization: in effect, capitalism without capitalists. Industrial society in the Soviet Union and Eastern Europe was managed through the domination of the Party bureaucracy. It lagged far behind its Western rivals.

Bauman points out that the Communist Party did not encourage the growth of civil society, since that might have led to the growth of political criticism. Instead, it atomized civil society where it could. Instead of driving towards the socialist utopia of freedom and equality, state socialism was founded upon repression and inequality. The Party became a self-perpetuating establishment guarding its privileges.

The prevailing spirit in society was a dull petty-bourgeois conservatism, clinging to the status quo. State socialism promoted an ideology that justified the present rather than a utopian vision offering the prospect of human emancipation. Socialism had begun 'as an idea in search of a constituency'. It ended up as 'a constituency without an idea' (p. 109).

However, the socialist utopia did make a large impact upon Western capitalism. The idea of spreading material wealth more evenly through society was put into effect, to some extent at least, by government and business in the West. The welfare state was a silent tribute to the powerful moral pressure exerted by the utopia of socialism. So was the spread of mass consumption that brought the fruits of capitalism into millions of homes.

Mass consumption brought a major change in capitalism. It gave it a new way to remain powerful and secure. Instead of beating the people into submission, so to speak, as it had during the nineteenth century, capitalism learned the art of wooing the people – of persuading them that capitalism was good for them.

At this point, Bauman's analysis draws explicitly upon the 'remarkable insight' (p. 102) of Antonio Gramsci, who showed the vital part played by 'civil society' – the sphere of cultural and political activity. In Gramsci's view, civil society was not just a reflection of a more 'basic' structure of economic relations, as many more orthodox Marxists believed. In the classroom, in the cinema, through the popular press and in many other ways, people picked up their ideas about how society worked. In civil society, people acquired a basic grasp of how things should be and learned what was possible and what was impossible. They were taught how to think and how to behave. Gramsci argued that, in civil society, people acquired the ideology and 'everyday, habitual behaviour' (p. 64) that supported the existing system of class rule.

People's ideas about the good life, proper ways of behaving, what they 'needed', how society works and the natural way of running things all tended to 'sustain and perpetuate the totality of capitalist relations with little or no interference by the political state' (pp. 102–3). The police were needed less often once advertising copywriters had done their work of selling capitalism to the people. Intellectuals played a key role in maintaining this pattern of cultural 'hegemony' (p. 67). Civil society was their domain.

In Bauman's words, 'The stability of capitalism acquired a cultural foundation', which has made it stronger. Capitalism is also strengthened by the fact that socialists can no longer criticize capitalism for failing to deliver material prosperity to a high proportion of the Western population. That aspect of its utopia has been realized. It is part of commonsense everyday reality. Now socialism has to take up new challenges.

Socialism must point towards a future society in which alienation is overcome. It should demonstrate that many of the prohibitions built into contemporary capitalist culture are unnecessary. These include the habitual repression of dissent and stifling of disagreement in everyday life, so as to 'guard the routine monotony of human conduct and disguise obedience as rationality' (p. 123).

A further task is to subvert 'Positivism, this common-sense of modern society' (p. 125) that imposes intellectual order by pushing everything it can into tidy categories, subject to clear scientific laws. Anything that will not fit the accepted categories or follow the recognized laws is liable to be marginalized or destroyed. Socialism should encourage people to challenge the commonsense view of the world embodied in capitalist culture. It should work for a change of consciousness, allowing people to see that they can organize society differently if they choose to do so.

State socialism and capitalism both had to be criticized for their 'dream of a rationally organised society'. This dream is 'a contrivance to release men and women from the self-control and responsibility which render them human'. Capitalism and state socialism both want people to be predictable and not make choices that challenge what they have been told. In fact, 'the monotonous predictability of the rationally programmed society . . . turns out to be a recipe for totalitarianism' (p. 132). The best antidote would be an increase in human emancipation 'brought about . . . in a free and unconstrained dialogue between all the actors of the historical process' (p. 140).

Socialism: the active utopia and *Towards a Critical Sociology* both try to find a way through the obstacle of positivism in order to recover the original emancipatory spirit of the Enlightenment. They both end on a note of hope. As Bauman writes at the very end of *Towards a Critical Sociology*, 'before he may be a thinker, a symbol-maker, a homo faber – man has to be he-who-hopes' (1976b: 112). The object of hope should be a high ideal, whose achievement is way beyond the distant horizon. This is because, as Bauman puts it in the last sentence of *Socialism: the active utopia*, quoting St Paul, ' "hope that is seen is not hope. For who hopes for what he sees?" ' (1976a: 141).

Hermeneutics and Social Science

By the late 1970s, Bauman was investing a great deal of hope in the strategy of creating new meanings and a new sense of purpose through democratic dialogue. To make this strategy work, people would have to overcome their alienation and develop a new form of consciousness. They would have to explore their disagreements peacefully and openly, redefining their sense of themselves and their own potential. Above all, they would have to *understand* themselves and each other.

Bauman was fascinated by both the practical and philosophical implications of the methodology he was developing to help society along the road towards a socialist utopia. He wanted, so to speak, to understand understanding. This meant returning to the enquiry begun in *Culture as Praxis* (1973a). His second foray into this territory was entitled *Hermeneutics and Social Science* (1978).

In the latter book, as in *Culture and Praxis*, Bauman tells a story about society. In each work, he builds a historical narrative into his analysis. In *Culture and Praxis*, Bauman wrote about what happened when, as he sees it, the barriers between local communities with very different cultures broke down at the end of the Middle Ages. This increase in human volatility presented a challenge to humankind's structurizing capacity – its capacity to create order. As Europe became modern, the population became increasingly mobile, the old cultural boundaries ceased to be self-policing, and people no longer knew how they 'fitted in' to society.

In *Hermeneutics and Social Science*, Bauman pays more attention to another historical process. This is the challenge to the rule of the feudal aristocracy that was under way in Europe by the sixteenth century. Before that time, the hierarchical nature of aristocratic society sustained a hierarchical model of culture. Aristocratic culture had its own idea of perfection: the perfect knight, the perfect gentleman and so on. Aristocratic values permeated downwards through society.[6]

Educated Europeans had no interest in the different ideas of perfection pursued in other cultures: 'Hence the trained blindness to the alien way of life, so striking in medieval pilgrims to the Holy Land, and the tardiness with which Europe came to consider freshly discovered civilizations and cultures as a challenge to its own smugly assumed righteousness' (Bauman 1978: 198).

All this changed when assertive bourgeois interests confronted aristocratic rule, and when labourers became more independent, fleeing their lords' landed estates to try their luck in the city. The dilution of aristocratic authority and prestige helped to overcome Europe's blindness to other cultures. Montaigne, 'the first of modern thinkers' (p. 201), saw that all cultural styles were relative. As he put it: '"every city and every profession has its own form of civility".'

Montaigne in the sixteenth century and Pascal in the seventeenth century were both detached enough to respect other people's customs – to see them as the expression of 'autonomous beings, allowed the sovereign right to select, and to hold to, their own concepts of right and wrong, the desirable and the undesirable' (p. 202). Bauman points out that, once respect for the autonomy of the 'Other' had been achieved, the challenge of understanding the Other came on to the agenda.

Bauman raises the question of how 'I' will respond to the Other, given that we have different attitudes and values. At one 'analytical extreme', I may decide to allow the Other's objectives or wishes to guide my own conduct. This is, in Bauman's terms, 'the recognition that the other side has the authority to guide the subject's action: the acceptance of the "in-order-to" motives of the alter as the "because" motives of the ego' (p. 203).

However, there is another response at the other extreme. Ego (I) may approach alter (the Other) with the intention of changing alter's mind. Ego may try to 'transform his own "in-order-to" motives into the "because" motives of the alter'. In this case, alter has to be persuaded to accept ego's authority as 'legitimate and unquestionable' (p. 204).

So far, Bauman has imagined two cases. In the first case, the Other has authority over me. In the second case, I have authority over the Other. In both these cases, understanding and control are closely linked: either I seek to understand the Other's intentions and wishes so that they can guide my own conduct, or I seek to make my own intentions and wishes control the Other's conduct.

However, there is also a third case. When 'one "form of life" encounters another one', mutual understanding can be achieved by all concerned. This happens if people from each form of life cooperate to construct a ' *"higher order"* ' (pp. 216–17; emphasis in original) form of life that incorporates the original life forms as sub-types. In effect, this is what happens within a stable marriage or similar partnership. The two partners do not need to feel and think each other's feelings and thoughts in order to achieve understanding. Instead, this is achieved by constructing something new – their partnership.

We understand what we create. We understand it *because* we have created it. Understanding is based upon the experience of sharing a form of life that has been constructed by the partners. Shared understandings rooted in shared life experiences and a shared language may well lead to 'unproblematic, unreflective agreement' (p. 223) among all participants.

However, there is a problem. Partners may have a shared understanding, but this does not mean that they have true knowledge. Just because two or more people agree with each other does not mean that they are right. The 'rules of achieving agreement (or communal consensus) are not . . . identical with the rules that guide the pursuit of truth' (p. 224).

Why do we want to discover the 'truth' about society? What are the advantages of achieving 'objective understanding'? Bauman's answer is that knowledge is a substitute for control. Imagine that you or I had sufficient control capacity to turn our will into truth through action – that we could say 'this is how things shall be' and arrange for things to be exactly like that. If that were the case, we would not need to look for accurate knowledge about the world. We would be able to create truth through acts of will.

If our control were sufficient, we could 'make' truth and would not need to search for it. Since we cannot control the world we live in, the only way to reduce uncertainty is to discover the truth and try to avoid its worst consequences. How, then, are truth or objective understanding to be obtained? Bauman discusses various possibilities.

Husserl's phenomenological approach is one candidate. Husserl recommends bracketing or sealing off all the influences of specific sociohistorical contexts so that 'I' can achieve direct insight into the contents of my purified consciousness. But, asks Bauman, even if this were practical, how could such objective understanding help us to orient ourselves in a world regulated by meanings that are not purified, but are, on the contrary, thoroughly embedded in particular time-bound, place-bound and culture-bound environments?

Another approach is taken by Weber and Mannheim. They hoped that objective understanding could be based upon agreement among social scientists. However, Bauman notes, this state of agreement has not come about. Reaching agreement is made more difficult by the fact that 'lay' people have much more influence on sociologists than they do upon natural scientists secluded in their laboratories. Atomic particles do not answer back the way people do. Social scientists have not achieved 'autonomy of practices' (p. 234) to the same degree as, say, physicists or chemists. As Bauman puts it:

> the truth of sociology is the derivative of an agreement reached (if at all) in the debate between sociologists and the objects of their study regarding phenomena whose control is shared between sociologists and the objects of their study to the clear disadvantage of sociologists. *The truth of sociology has to be negotiated in the same way the ordinary agreement is*; more often than not, it is not the sociologists who set the rules of negotiation. (p. 234; emphasis in original)

Yet another strategy derives from the work of Dilthey. Initially, it involves exploring the particular experiences and meanings found in specific forms of life. The next step is to interweave these explorations of the particular with repeated attempts to intuit and describe the general principles embodied within them. The hermeneutic explorer follows a circular path, going from the specific to the general, returning to the specific, moving back to the general, and so on. One problem with this is that there is never a point when one can say that general 'truths' have been finally discovered. Another trip around the hermeneutic circle is always possible.

Bauman faces up to the threat of relativism – the possibility that all standards of truth are specific to particular forms of life: 'our' truth, 'their' truth and so on. He accepts that absolute and incontrovertible truth, apodictic truth, is not available to the social sciences. However, he points out that neither is it available to the experimental natural sciences.

Bauman cites Karl Popper's argument that scientific theories can never be finally proved. They can only be refuted – shown to be wrong. The idea of truth, of 'getting it right', guides natural scientists in formulating their theories and doing their experiments. However, they can never demonstrate finally and for all time that their theories are 'true'. They are only, so to speak, 'not yet disproved'. Truth is a guiding ideal 'in line with other utopian ideals' (p. 238), but it is an ideal that is never fulfilled.

This allows Bauman to say that the idea of truth plays the same role in the social sciences as in the natural sciences. He quotes Popper's dictum that the rules for conducting science are subject to 'the general aim of rational discussion, which is to get nearer to the truth' (Popper 1972: 17; Bauman 1978: 238). Bauman then links this assertion to Jürgen Habermas's claim that pursuing truth and objectivity are 'transcendental conditions of the specifically human mode of existence' (p. 239).

Habermas's point is that human work and communication, basic to all human life, are both guided by the idea of truth. Work expresses the technical interest in understanding and controlling nature – an interest that guides the empirical-analytical sciences. Communication expresses the practical interest in discovering a broad basis of shared understandings and intersubjectivity. Where these understandings exist, it is possible to engage in argument and, eventually, achieve agreement between different forms of life.

Bauman's conclusion is that all human beings have an interest in scientific procedures that eliminate false hypotheses. They also have an interest in practices of human communication that undermine those 'conditions of communication which lead to an invalid, untrue consensus' (p. 241). The truths that human communication are concerned with relate, above all, to norms of conduct: how one *should* behave. The content of these norms can be discovered only through rational discussion.

Rational discussion can be effective only if everyone involved is genuinely committed to the cooperative search for truth. This search should serve the interest of all participants: that is, their common interest, determined by all in an open and unconstrained discussion, conducted without deception. This ideal is 'no more "utopian" (or, alternatively, no less "realistic") than . . . the model of ideal experiment or canons of inductive reasoning'. It is 'not a generalization of practice but the definition of its idealized horizon'. It provides the benchmark against which actual practices can be criticized. It allows us to spot *'distorted communication'* and to identify *'false consensus'* (p. 243; emphasis in original).

Finally, Bauman sets out sociology's mission. It is to make sure that people understand that norms of conduct and 'action-oriented meanings' are likely to be truer, more valid, if they are discussed in open and equal conditions by all concerned. Sociologists should not just sit around commenting on the consensus that society arrives at in conditions of distorted communication. Nor should they carry on their own academic business in a closed, inward-looking way without reference to the wider debate in society.

On the contrary, sociology should develop 'an evolutionary theory showing the way which the society could follow toward conditions progressively emancipated from obstacles to rational agreements'. These 'obstacles' include social inequality and the 'dominance' of the professional-bureaucratic establishment criticized by Foucault (pp. 244–5).

Sociology should also play a 'prominent role' in 'bringing into being conditions of true understanding', mainly by criticizing the inequalities and distortions embedded in existing social practice. In other words, the sociologist should be among the people, discussing their interests with them, and finding practical ways in which those interests might be better understood and articulated.

As Bauman puts it, 'Sociology cannot help but be permanently engaged in discourse with its own object.' Sociologists should pursue a rational consensus, one which approaches the truth, by engaging in 'a communal negotiation whose scale extends beyond the boundaries of professional sociology proper' (p. 246).

Conclusion

There is a grand narrative lurking beneath the surface of these four books. It begins with the break-up of the medieval feudal order when the bourgeoisie challenged the authority of the aristocracy, and the peasantry escaped their rural bondage on manorial estates. Feudal domination gave way to the authority of scientific rationality.

In its early days, Reason was a liberating force, undermining the reign of ignorance and superstition. During the seventeenth and early eighteenth centuries, the Enlightenment served the cause of human freedom. There was a humane tolerance of difference and variety in the world.

However, by the nineteenth century this tolerance had given way to a fear of disorder and untidiness, and a strong desire to force society and nature into a rigid and comprehensive system of categories. Everything and everyone had to have its place. Positivistic natural science and social science were employed in a sustained attempt to bring this about.

Rationality stopped being an emancipating power and became an instrument in the hands of the authorities, especially the state and the professions. The result was a repressive regime of social inequality and unfreedom. Intellectual order was imposed by forcing a particular vision of truth and reality upon the world. Positivism denied the artificiality of the order it constructed and refused to consider possible alternative realities.

In Bauman's view, the challenge faced by men and women in the present epoch is how to construct a new intellectual and sociopolitical order that can replace the positivistic monolith favoured by capitalist and communist regimes alike. Bauman hopes that humankind will be able to escape from the bondage of positivism, just as earlier it escaped from the bondage of feudalism. One useful weapon against positivism is existentialism. This approach refuses to treat social institutions as external constraints whose commands have to be obeyed. It emphasizes instead the creativity of human beings.

Existentialism unshackles human beings from the uniformity imposed by the managerial state and encourages them to build their own worlds through self-steered action. An existentialist approach can even provide the basis for a new vision of social order, jointly constructed by human beings whose understandings and perceptions coincide or overlap sufficiently for them to agree what reality is. However, Bauman does not simply want to replace an order imposed from above with an order jointly constructed by all. There is no guarantee that such a consensus will be based on a correct understanding of human interests or accurate information about how to pursue them effectively.

Bauman wants to develop a methodology for identifying the 'best' way to run a society: in other words, for identifying the shared interests of human groups and clarifying the norms of behaviour that will most effectively serve those interests. Habermas provides him with such a methodology – a procedure for eliminating false understandings of human interests and seeking a consensus based on truth.

In the 1970s, as in the 1960s, Bauman's work contains hints and anticipations of arguments that became central to his vision of modernity and postmodernity in the 1980s and 1990s. The grand narrative just outlined was partially reworked in Bauman's trilogy consisting of *Legislators and Interpreters* (1987), *Modernity and the Holocaust* (1989) and *Modernity and Ambivalence* (1991).

There are two main differences between the early and the later versions of this narrative. One is that, in the later version, Bauman darkens his vision of the positivistic regime of modernity. Increasing pessimism was already setting in during the 1970s. In 1971 Bauman was presenting the East European regimes as being in some ways morally superior or in the vanguard compared to the capitalist West. He pointed out the benefits they brought to the peasantry and the value of the new political paradigm they had instituted – one based upon the state's expanding responsibility to meet the needs of the population at large.[7]

However, by 1976 he was noticing that capitalist and socialist regimes alike were driven by the 'dream of a rationally organised society', which was 'a recipe for totalitarianism' (p. 132). The seeds of the analysis in *Modernity and the Holocaust* were evidently already sown at this time.[8]

The other main difference between the grand narrative produced by Bauman in the 1970s and the one he offered in the 1980s and 1990s is that in the later version Bauman places much greater stress upon the irrepressibility of difference, otherness and ambivalence within society and culture. According to Bauman's argument as set out during the 1970s, these characteristics were the legacy of feudalism's collapse, but were extirpated with great determination by positivistic science. However, again there are hints and anticipation of the later version to be found in the interstices of Bauman's earlier argument.

During the 1970s, Bauman did not treat it as inevitable or even likely that the walls of positivism would be breached, any more than he (or anyone else) expected the Berlin Wall to be dismantled. However, he was already thinking through the implications of living in a world where each individual was faced with a complex repertoire of mutually inconsistent moral codes and where the behaviour or ways of others might appear strange and impenetrable.

During the 1960s, this problem came on to Bauman's agenda as a practical issue confronting young people in socialist Poland. His recipe for coping with it included the need to assert and defend the moral autonomy of other people as much as one's own. In *Hermeneutics and Social Science* (1978), he explored this matter further, thinking through the implications of different kinds of authority relationship between 'I' and the 'Other'.

As we have seen, Bauman described two possibilities. In the first case, 'I' impose my ideals and objectives upon the 'Other', putting the latter in a situation where she or he accepts my wishes as providing sufficient authority for obeying any rules I make. Eleven years later, in *Modernity and the Holocaust* (1989), Bauman argues that this kind of authority relationship was the basis of bureaucratic rule under conditions of modernity. In the second case, 'I' accept the ideals and objective of the 'Other' as providing guidance and authority for my own actions. Here we have a central aspect of the moral philosophy that Bauman developed fifteen years later in *Postmodern Ethics* (1993).

However, during the 1970s, unlike later, Bauman was not using the vocabulary of postmodernity. His hope was that it would be possible to reconstruct modernity from within by subverting the false consciousness and alienation sustained by positivism. In a sense, that would mean rediscovering a past condition of culture, consciousness and theoretical understanding – one characterized by Marx's confidence in the creative potential of human praxis, and Montaigne's respect for the dignity of 'otherness'. This condition should be not only recovered, but also made available to the whole of society through a process of dialogue leading to praxis.

Bauman devoted his own intellectual efforts to finding ways of overcoming mutual incomprehensibility and inequality between different social groups, between 'I' and the 'Other'. This process was intended to remain within the bounds of modernity. It was inspired by values drawn from the early Enlightenment and driven by the very 'modern' ambition of planning and creating a better society.

7

The Road to the Berlin Wall

Switching routes

By the mid-1970s, Zygmunt Bauman had made a remarkable come-back. He had regrouped his intellectual and moral forces in the face of considerable adversity. From the wreckage of his shattered faith in the Party line, he had constructed the outlines of a distinctive approach to socialism.

Bauman made a careful survey of the highway towards a socialist utopia, noting the key crossroads coming up and thinking through how they could be negotiated. For example, one problem he foresaw was that people within capitalist societies would be manipulated by political and business interests into passively accepting a very narrow range of choices in respect of how they organized their lives. The example of Polish Solidarity in the early 1980s was a welcome counter-example. It seemed to show organized working people expanding the range of choices available within civil society.

Bauman wanted people to make active choices about a wide range of political and economic issues. In *Memories of Class* (1982), he plotted a strategy for increasing democratic participation within the key institutions of civil society. Bauman hoped to find ways of extending freedom in capitalist society, making it more than a matter of being able to choose which soap powder, or which politician, you preferred among those on offer.

However, during the 1980s, Bauman came to a very crowded crossroads that he had not anticipated. He found his route towards utopia intersecting with another very busy road, which led to the Berlin Wall. The Wall came crashing down in 1989, bringing with it the entire edifice of state socialism in Eastern Europe. Bauman negotiated his way with skill across this daunting intersection, through the screams, shouts and crashing masonry.

When the dust and rubble settled, Bauman was still upright, still moving strongly, but now travelling towards a different destination. He had gone into the intersection travelling on the road to a socialist utopia. He came out of it heading along the road to post-modernity. In this chapter, I trace Bauman's intellectual trajectory during the early and mid-1980s, beginning with his response to the rise of Polish Solidarity.

Solidarity

In 1970, Polish shipyard workers in Gdansk and Szczecin demonstrated against high food prices. This brought down the government of President Gomulka. In 1976 his successor, Gierek, faced similar protests. Two years later, Lech Walesa and a small group of shipyard workers founded the Committee of Free Trade Unions for the Baltic Coast. In 1980 there were renewed strikes throughout Poland over increased food prices. This time the communist government accepted the strikers' demands, which included the right to set up free trade unions independent of the Party.

This opened the way for the founding of Solidarity. By 1981, 10 million people – that is, about two-thirds of the workforce – were members of the Solidarity trade union or its rural counterpart. Membership of the Polish Communist Party fell by a quarter. At the end of the year, General Jaruzelski declared martial law and arrested Solidarity's leadership, thus forestalling a Soviet invasion. Solidarity was driven underground until 1989 when it was made legal once again.[1]

1980 was a year of high hope for Bauman. He thought Solidarity's rise marked a positive step towards 'the maturation of socialism' (Bauman 1981: 48). It touched him personally. The Polish workers were fighting the same battle that he had waged two decades before. They were trying to re-establish the idea that people could go about their own business, think their own thoughts and pursue their own individual or collective objectives, all without the state regulating every minute detail of social activity. In other words, they were trying to reclaim the lost autonomy of civil society.

Bauman realized, like Mill, that intellectuals have a vested interested in freedom within civil society. Such freedom allows them to protect their own privileges – their 'right' to cultural autonomy. However, they cannot win these rights if they are politically isolated. Intellectuals need to be allied with a powerful class that has 'won independence from the political state' (p. 53).

In the West, during the nineteenth and twentieth centuries, the intellectuals allied with the bourgeoisie. Together they managed to build up a strong public realm outside the state apparatus. The bourgeoisie supported a free press, independent political parties and associations promoting a wide range of social causes. The bourgeoisie also tolerated free trade unions.

Bauman believed that, in Poland during the 1970s and early 1980s, the working class played a role similar to the bourgeoisie in the West. In other words, it stood up for a free public sphere outside the state's control. Solidarity wanted to push back the frontiers of the state, to stop the regime interfering in ordinary people's everyday lives. Bauman interpreted this as being consistent with Marx's own vision of a minimalist government confined to 'the administration of things'. According to this vision, society would become an association of free producers.

Bauman saw ordinary Poles acting collectively and with a sense of purpose. In 1980, Poland 'came close to the model of historical creativity, when praxis takes over from structure as the main determinant of events' (p. 48). People showed that they were able to change structures rather than being trapped by them. The Polish experience showed that praxis made learning possible. The consciousness of the working class, especially its leadership, was changed by the shared experience of political struggle. The rise of Solidarity demonstrated that 'True collective learning is an aspect of collective action' (p. 50).

One vital lesson that working-class leaders learned was not to become entrapped in the discourse of its opponents – the regime. Solidarity refused to argue on the regime's terms. It denied that its actions were 'political', refused to accept that those actions had any relevance to the regime and its policies, and insisted that its trade union activities were solely a matter for its own members. In making this claim, Solidarity was asserting something highly novel within a state socialist country. It was saying that trade union activity could and should, quite legally, express the aspirations of social groups without reference to the political regime's objectives and desires. By asserting this point successfully, Solidarity changed the rules of the game.

The Solidarity movement in Poland must surely have been at the back of Bauman's mind as, in the early 1980s, he turned his attention once again to the way Britain had developed as a capitalist society.

Memories of Class

Memories of Class (1982) is much more lively and exciting than *Between Class and Elite* (1972), Bauman's earlier venture in analysing British society. The text is a rich mixture of theoretical analysis and empirical data, synthesizing work by historians, economists and sociologists. It is a very stimulating read.

The central argument can be quickly stated. *Memories of Class* is a tale of two crises. Bauman believes that British society and, by implication, the capitalist system entered a period of systemic crisis in the late twentieth century. This recent crisis is as profound, he says, as the earlier systemic crisis that accompanied the collapse of the traditional rural social order in the early nineteenth century. Each crisis, the one in the late eighteenth and early nineteenth centuries and the one beginning in the late twentieth century, arose because of a contradiction between two things: on the one hand, the expectations and motivations of the people and, on the other hand, the form of social control.

In the earlier crisis, new forms of control succeeding in crushing workers' resistance to the imposition of much greater discipline over their daily lives. Class identities were shaped in the long fight for domination in the workplace – a fight that was eventually won, decisively, by the employers. The 'discipline power' imposed by employers shifted the ground upon which workers and bosses fought. Conflicts over control were transformed into conflicts about how the surplus should be distributed. People 'redefined the problem of personal unfreedom as the lack of access to marketable goods, and personal emancipation as the broadening of such access' (p. 197). This encouraged the 'economisation of politics' (p. 129).

By the time of the later crisis, two hundred years later, the scene of battle had shifted from production to the sphere of consumption. In this later case, the systemic crisis was once again the result of popular resistance to regulation. However, this time the resistance was being mounted by groups of consumers rather than groups of producers.

In the late-twentieth-century crisis, the factors involved were the same – popular expectations and the forms of social control – but the problem was different. Instead of popular expectations being crushed, these expectations remained powerful. They were backed by enough political muscle to challenge the forms of social control. Bauman argued that these forms of control, inherited from the previous epoch, were no longer effective. As a result, they were unable to regulate or satisfy the people's demands for goods and services from capitalism and the welfare state.

In *Memories of Class*, Bauman drew upon a well-stocked arsenal of sources, ranging from Michel Foucault to E. P. Thompson.[2] He trespassed with some relish on ground that Marx made his own: that is, the historical experience of capitalist development in Britain. In doing so, he trod heavily upon some orthodox Marxist assumptions.

Bauman emphasized that the working class was hostile not to capitalism as such, but to the intrusive discipline imposed by industrialism with its demands for regular attendance at work and strict obedience. In fact, this disciplinary regime was not brought into existence by the needs of capitalist manufacturers. It was implemented much earlier by state bureaucrats, religious ministers and local government in order to fill the void left by the collapse of the traditional rural order.

Hundreds of asylums, poorhouses, prisons and schools were established to help those with power regulate society as it became more fluid and mobile from the sixteenth century onwards. The capitalist factory was a late comer on the scene. The factory owner benefited from the climate of discipline that existed in society, but he was not responsible for bringing it about.

In any case, adds Bauman, ordinary working people were not the only ones struggling against a system that imposed a rigid framework of control upon human beings, regulating their ways of thinking and behaving. It is true that the working class were the first victims of industrial work discipline and, in this respect, were 'for almost a century alone on the battlefield' (p. 20). However, during the twentieth century most of the rest of society, including the middle classes, have become subject to similar controls.

Bauman refuses to treat the 'moving force in history' as always being 'the thrust of a new class to take over the management of the social surplus' (p. 27). That was certainly not true in the second half of the twentieth century. By that time, capitalism had acquired a 'corporatist' character, as major functional interests such as trade unions and employers' organizations became part of a permanent network of consultation and negotiation with each other and government.

Corporatism drew governments into detailed regulation of the capitalist economy. They helped maintain the production of goods and services during periods of economic turbulence and, more generally, tried to make sure that companies received an adequate supply of suitably educated and properly motivated human labour. However, all participants in the system were in a deeply ambiguous situation. No single class had a clear and unshakeable commitment to the corporatist system as a whole. It was endemically difficult for any group within the system to decide what action served its best interest. For example, everyone benefited from government-provided services but, at the same time, everyone resented paying taxes.

Ironically, all attempts by the state to strengthen capitalism in the short term undermined it in the long term. The bureaucratic principles on which state regulation were based weakened the place taken by profit-seeking behaviour. As a result, the motivations and incentives on which capitalism relies were weakened.

On the one hand, intervention by government was weakening capitalism. On the other hand, the commitment of governments to the capitalist system meant that they could not take effective action to tackle the growing poverty gap that capitalism was producing globally. Capitalists responded to 'market demand' and not to the much larger level of demand represented by the millions who, by Western standards, were badly fed, badly housed and badly supplied with material possessions. Economic growth could not solve this problem. On the contrary, accelerated growth was likely to produce further pauperization, increased awareness of inequality and environmental disaster.[3]

In Bauman's view, the late-twentieth-century crisis signalled the arrival of 'a qualitatively new stage in history' (p. 33). People had failed to recognize this because they relied too much upon the historical memory of their society, class or group to provide categories through which to interpret the present and envisage the future. Their thinking was shaped by the remembered past – by the 'grammar' (p. 2) of tradition and received wisdom.

Bauman called for 'a change in the type of social power' (p. 33). He wanted his fellow citizens to abandon 'discipline power' – the characteristic control mechanism of industrial society. Discipline power had been very successful in its day. It had displaced conflict from the question of workplace control and focused workers' attention on to wage bargaining and the pursuit of tax-funded social benefits. However, pressures had built up that destabilized the system of corporatist capitalism.

An increasing proportion of the population had a claim to a share of the surplus without being able to participate in production, mainly because they were unemployed, marginalized or dependent in some way. Such people relied not upon market power, but upon their direct or indirect political influence. As a result, distribution conflicts were increasingly politicized.

Bauman hoped it would be possible to seize the opportunity to renegotiate the problems of freedom and emancipation. He wanted politics to be more directly concerned with how social life is organized. This meant giving ordinary people a much bigger say in how the institutions that shaped their lives (the schools, hospitals, banks and so forth) were organized. Bauman wanted politics to be about 'self-management, restitution and preservation of human control over the ways in which human bodily and spiritual potential is developed and deployed' (p. 197).

These words were written in the early 1980s, at a time when the impression made by the early successes of Poland's Solidarity movement was still very vivid. In the United Kingdom, the political atmosphere was tense. The Keynesian welfare state was being dismantled by the new Conservative government that had ousted Labour in 1979. In 1981 there were riots in many of the UK's large cities.

Social and political structures in the UK were apparently becoming a little more fluid in the early 1980s. There were, perhaps, grounds for hope that, as in Poland, a moment of historical creativity had arrived: that for a while 'praxis might take over from structure as the main determinant of events' (Bauman 1981: 48). In fact, the most effective agent of praxis was, for a while at least, the new leadership of the Conservative Party under Margaret Thatcher. During the next half decade, the powers of organized labour were steadily reduced, the privatization programme pushed ahead and market forces were allowed much greater freedom.

When Bauman came to write *Freedom* (1988), published six years after *Memories of Class*, the hope and excitement of the early 1980s had been replaced by sardonic bemusement, even a touch of satire.

The message conveyed was that the prospect of a better society was receding rather than coming nearer.

Freedom

When Bauman looked at the way capitalist society was being regulated in the late 1980s, he concluded that 'the future of capitalism looks more secure than ever' and 'the whole operation of "social control" may be now counted among systemic assets' (1988: 61). A change in the type of social power had indeed occurred. As Bauman saw it, the old system of discipline power had been largely discarded. However, the new system was not the one he had hoped for. Modern capitalism was governed in the name of freedom, but it was not the type of freedom he wanted to see.

Bauman's argument in *Freedom* starts with the Roman Empire. Then, as now, freedom was a privileged state. The freed slave was released from bondage by a special act of manumission.[4] Early Christian theologians were influenced by the analogy with manumission when thinking about human free will. For example, according to Pelagius, God gave humans their freedom to use as they wished, choosing good or evil. St Augustine responded to Pelagius by insisting that we were all more inclined towards evil. It was only the gift of grace offered by God, our all-seeing and omnipresent master, that allowed us to recognize and follow the road of virtue leading towards salvation. From this point of view, our freedom was best expressed as willing obedience to God.

The career of freedom in the West was closely tied to the spread of individualism and the rise of capitalism. Individualism was a product of the breakdown of a single centre of authority within Europe, argues Bauman. In classical Greece, the basic unit of social life had been the *polis* or political state. This had a continuing life of its own down the generations. Individual citizens participated in its affairs, but the *polis* existed before they were born and continued after their deaths. However, by the time of Thomas Hobbes in the seventeenth century, the basic unit of social life had become the solitary individual trying to survive in a hostile world.

Bauman argues that individualism, in the sense that each person has responsibility for his or her own actions, became possible when authorities multiplied in Europe. He dates it from the thirteenth century in England and a little later in the rest of the continent. The point is that, if several would-be lords (dukes, counts, bishops, princes and so on) are all trying to tell people what to do, people have a great deal of practical discretion about how they behave. Their freedom is increased. However, as Bauman points out, one group's freedom may depend upon another group's lack of freedom.

Capitalism needed freedom in order to develop in the first place: freedom from predatory feudal lords, freedom for merchants to move about buying and selling, freedom of labour to move where the jobs were, freedom to set prices according to the state of the market, and so on. However, at the turn of the millennium, large business organizations do not give their employees a great deal of freedom. They are subject to constant surveillance, continual monitoring of performance and unrelenting pressure to conform.

There is a certain amount of freedom at the top of business organizations, but very little at the bottom or in the middle. Max Weber analysed this aspect of the modern condition in his writings on rationality and rationalization. He believed that planners and organizers in modern society needed to be free in order to create rational conditions of life for everybody else. But the smaller fry would inevitably be cogs in the wheel, captives in iron cages. Their lives would be rationalized, but they would not be free.

Bauman shows that Weber's vision of modern rationality was very similar to Jeremy Bentham's Panopticon[5] – his model of a disciplinary regime. In Bentham's 'inspection house',[6] inmates were to be observed twenty-four hours a day and subject to complete control by the inspectors set over them. The inspectors could manipulate the inmates' conditions of existence so that they were forced to behave in the 'right' way, following rational rules laid down by the head inspector. Like Foucault (1977), Bauman finds this a very powerful metaphor for modern society.

In most careers, for most people, 'the road to an agreeable life now leads through excelling in conformity to institutionally set purposes, rules and patterns of conduct. . . . They have to accept commands, demonstrate a willingness to obey, cut their actions to the measure designed by their superiors' (Bauman 1988: 57). Bauman notes that they are helped in this task by the skills and habits of self-discipline. Drawing on Elias, Bauman argues that these attributes are shaped, in part, by the constraints imposed upon people within social networks, including bureaucratic hierarchies.

Conformity is made more agreeable by some uncomfortable aspects of the alternative way of life offered by freedom. Free human beings may have responsibility for deciding 'who' they are and how they 'should' behave, but their freedom has a price. No unchallengeable authority exists outside themselves to reassure them that their identity is a 'good' one or that they are behaving 'correctly'.

So, has freedom run its course, acting as a kind of booster rocket for capitalism and the modern age, getting them into orbit, then dropping back to earth – a cumbersome nuisance to be got rid of? Bauman does not make that argument. Instead, he pulls a rabbit out of his hat. He declares that a new frontier of freedom has appeared in the sphere of consumption: the world of the car showroom, the carpet warehouse and the special offer. This is a sweet and painless freedom, bringing happiness without insecurity.

For the consumer, 'Freedom is about the choice between greater and lesser satisfactions, and rationality is about choosing the first rather than the second.' There is pressure to spend, but this does not feel like oppression. Instead, spending offers 'the joy of submitting to "something greater than myself"' and the 'straightforward, sensual joy of tasty eating, pleasant smelling, soothing drinking, relaxing driving or the joy of being surrounded with smart, glistening, eye-caressing objects. With such duties, who needs rights?' (pp. 76–7).

In fact, Bauman says all this with a sardonic twinkle in his eye. He has great respect for the immense power and effectiveness of consumer culture, but little admiration for its underlying values. His basic point is that, in the early years of industrial society, work gave people identity and a sense of purpose. Social groups and the industrial system were integrated by the links between different occupations. More recently, the production function has ceased to play these roles. Instead, the consumption function has taken its place. When we spend and consume, we create and express our identities, define our relationship to others and keep the capitalist system going. Consumption now does what work used to do.

The culture of consumption is reinforced by the values conveyed through the medium of television. The key idea conveyed by television, argues Bauman, is that life, in fiction and in fact, consists of a 'multitude of mini-dramas' with 'no clear-cut direction'. These dramas are set in motion by individuals: 'they happen because they have been chosen to happen' (p. 78). By implication, if the individual had chosen differently, the story would have been different. So each life, it seems, is self-assembled in a controlled way, just as the self is assembled by a set of consumer choices: *this* house, *that* dress, *this* school and so on.

The consumer society is surrounded by 'thick walls. One does not see the "other side". Neither is one curious to see it: it is the other side, after all' (p. 92). One large part of life left 'outside' is the real world of political decision making. As a result, politicians are able to pursue their own interests without close attention from the public. Like Bentham's inspectors, they can see without being seen.

In fact, the state itself plays a smaller part in integrating society as the consumer market penetrates more areas of modern life. State bureaucrats in advanced capitalist societies do not feel under pressure to impose conformity upon the population; nor do they feel responsible for keeping their citizens in work. Citizens respond by staying home on election day in greater numbers. Voting seems to matter less when government stops trying so hard to save jobs and when spending on the public sector is inadequate whoever is in power.

Who else is on the other side of the consumer society's thick walls? The poor are there. Weak, divided and disenchanted, they are forced to rely upon public welfare. They can neither 'exit' to the soft pastures of the consumer world nor 'voice' their demands effectively within the political arena.[7]

There are also other, more nasty and threatening things outside the walls. Writing in the late 1980s, before the Berlin Wall had fallen, Bauman pointed out that under the communist system there was no large consumer society seducing the mass of the population. On the contrary, the people as a whole were treated according to the same principles applied to members of the poor minority in the capitalist West. In other words, they were told what they needed, informed what was good for them, and more or less forced to accept it. They were not seduced but repressed.

Meanwhile, over the horizon were the hungry millions of Africa and Asia. In their eyes, freedom meant breaching or clambering over the thick walls keeping consumer goods like cars, refrigerators, lap-top computers and air conditioning systems in the hands of rich Westerners.

Bauman did not anticipate that either of these two challenges would undermine consumer society. He saw that consumerism was a powerful obstacle to fulfilling his hope that people would learn to exercise and enjoy greater freedom as citizens – the project he had set out in the final pages of *Memories of Class*. His only recourse was to remember the origin, as he saw it, of consumer freedom. In his view, people turned to the pleasures of shopping when they lost real power in the workplace and in government. Men and women might recover their desire for fuller citizenship if other fields of social life became 'open to the exercise of individual freedom; in particular, the areas of production, of community government, of national politics' (p. 95).

Unfortunately, the people with most to gain from such a change, the poor, are the worst equipped to organize themselves to achieve it. The most ambitious and cunning among them succeed in climbing out of poverty, leaving the less ambitious and less clever behind. Bauman does not write off the goal of 'communal self-management'. It remains 'an unexplored possibility'. However, 'the overall picture is one of consumer, self-centred freedom remaining alive and well, coping effectively with challenges, dominating the social scene and having enough self-propelling force to keep it going for a long time' (p. 98).

The year after *Freedom* was published, part of the 'thick wall' surrounding the consumer society was breached in Berlin. The first destination for most of the East Berliners who spilled across into the West was the shopping district where they could see at first hand the consumer goods that they had been denied for years. One of the first things the West German government did when faced with this flood from the East was to make special provision to provide the newcomers with some Deutschmarks. This helped them to become capitalist consumers and share the central experience of modern Western culture.

After communism

Bauman summarized his first reactions to the momentous events of 1989–90 in two articles entitled 'Communism: a postmortem' and 'Living without an alternative', both of which were reprinted in *Intimations of Postmodernity* (1992a).

Bauman's response is tinged with irony. He notes that the forces opposing the old order were united only by their hostility to the communist state. Once that collapsed, they quickly fell to fighting among themselves. The intellectuals and visionaries who inspired the crowds and took immense personal risks were pushed aside by power brokers after the revolutions.

More specifically, the Poles had played a vanguard role in mobilizing civil society to resist the deep conservatism and repressive instincts of the communist bureaucracy. The example of Polish success made it easier to achieve victories in neighbouring states. However, the very success of Solidarity in awakening civil society meant that post-revolutionary governments in Poland had to run the gauntlet of an alert citizenry.

Many of those citizens were sorry to lose the sense of security they had enjoyed under the old regime, even if they paid for it by sharing a low standard of living. As Bauman points out, some of the criticism directed against new market-driven economic policies carried echoes of Carlyle's complaints about the end of old-style paternalism in early-nineteenth-century England. The revolutions had been carried out in the name of bourgeois freedoms, but they left still undone the task of creating a class of people able to carry forward the task of building up a thriving capitalist economy and a vigorous civil society.

The most important conclusion that Bauman reaches in these two papers is that the death of communism meant an end to the dream of modernity. This was because the Soviet experiment in Russia and Eastern Europe had been the most thoroughgoing attempt in history to put into practice the 'passionate conviction that a good society can only be a carefully designed, rationally managed and thoroughly industrialized society' (Bauman 1992a: 166). The planners of Russia and Eastern Europe tried to impose a system that would organize the population into rational categories, define the needs of all citizens, supply those needs, teach the population to want what they needed and, finally, cultivate a shared commitment to a common set of values.

The system failed because it could not match the performance of capitalist economies or prevent capitalist needs and values from infiltrating socialist societies. The socialist vanguard of modernity could not face 'the challenge of the postmodern world' – a world in which consumer choice is central, conscience is a private matter and the state lets the market take up the task of disciplining the people.

Conclusion

Communism's decline and death during the mid- and late 1980s was a profound challenge to Zygmunt Bauman's intellectual and political strategy. It should be seen in the context of his efforts during the previous four decades.

During the 1950s and 1960s, Bauman investigated the network of relationships – political, economic and sociocultural – that linked the state bureaucracy, intellectuals and the main body of the population. As a leading academic at Warsaw University, Bauman examined these relationships, which were at the core of civil society and the state, both from a theoretical perspective and as an object of policy. He tried to inject his ideas and strategies for reforming Polish society, especially its education system, into the debate.

As we have seen, during the 1970s, Bauman retained his deep interest in the social agents of political change, but paid increasing attention to the mechanisms through which social and political change occurred and could, perhaps, be engineered. He looked, in particular, at the part played by culture, the contribution made by critical sociology and the orienting function of the idea of a socialist utopia.

During the early 1980s, the success of Solidarity strengthened Bauman's hopes for the 'maturation of socialism' (1981: 1). In the United Kingdom, the end of the political consensus around corporatist strategies for managing the Keynesian welfare state encouraged him to believe that a systemic crisis was under way and that a new stage in history had arrived.

Bauman believed that an increase in active democratic participation by citizens had become more feasible in both cases. However, both Poland and the United Kingdom moved further away from the kind of socialism that Bauman hoped for during the rest of the 1980s. Furthermore, the systemic crisis that came to a head during that decade fundamentally altered the situation of all three of the key agents of change with which he was particularly concerned: the state, the people and the intellectuals. The national state went into retreat, leaving the centre stage for global capitalism. The people paid less regard to their duties and rights as citizens and more to their opportunities as consumers. Finally, intellectuals lost much of their influence and prestige in national affairs.

These transformations occurred gradually over a number of decades, but they were dramatized by the withering away of state socialism during the late 1980s. The East European regimes had been highly imperfect, but their existence had made working towards a socialist utopia a reasonable strategy – one in contact with real-world politics. The end of communism and the virtually unchallenged reign of the market produced a very serious problem for Bauman's long-standing project. What should be the key levers of change now that the central state was no longer so dominant? What role could intellectuals fill now that so many decisions were left to the market? What part could Bauman himself now play?

8

The Trilogy

Three narratives

The late 1980s were a watershed for Zygmunt Bauman. He arrived at the conclusion that modernity, including the socialist project with which he had identified strongly, was bound to fail. Bauman set himself the task of understanding why it had failed and what could be salvaged from the wreckage.

Bauman continued to be preoccupied with the same issues: for example, relations between intellectuals, the state and the people, the search for truth, the nature of culture, the role of sociology, and the dynamics of societal and individual choice. However, the dynamic relationship between modernity and postmodernity replaced the contest between capitalism and socialism at the heart of Bauman's thinking.

Between 1987 and 1991, Zygmunt Bauman published three books: *Legislators and Interpreters* (1987), *Modernity and the Holocaust* (1989) and *Modernity and Ambivalence* (1991). Each book contains a historical narrative from which Bauman draws several lessons. In *Legislators and Interpreters*, the central actors are the intellectuals. They play the leading part in a story that begins during the European Reformation of the sixteenth century and ends in the late twentieth century. The two main settings where the scenes take place in *Legislators and Interpreters* are modernity and postmodernity. The two settings are, in fact, two aspects of the same setting: two perspectives on the same landscape.

In the other two books of the trilogy, the central actors are the Jews. In *Modernity and the Holocaust,* Bauman argues that Jewish suffering under the Third Reich illustrates in an intense form the essential inhumanity of the 'civilizing' mission undertaken by *modernity.* In *Modernity and Ambivalence,* Bauman argues that Europe's Jews, especially the German Jews, filled a vanguard role. They were the first to experience and analyse the ambivalence underlying the *postmodern* human condition.

Legislators and Interpreters

One of Bauman's working assumptions, which appears repeatedly in his books, is that power flows to social groups who can influence or control the sources of uncertainty. In *Legislators and Interpreters* (1987), Bauman argues that shamans, magicians, priests and intellectuals have all been able to seize this form of power. People have turned to them to propitiate evil forces, summon divine help and generally provide guidance or give directions.

As in *Hermeneutics and Social Science* (1978), Bauman makes the case that the weakening of the aristocracy's rule in early modern Europe made possible an enhanced awareness of difference, an increase in reflexivity and greater detachment in the sphere of thought. In particular, it allowed thinkers to break away from their previous preoccupation with the norms of perfection expressed in the European aristocratic way of life.

Other ways of life and other norms came on to the agenda. These included the manners of the people: brutish swine, it was thought, drenched in superstition and ignorance, badly needing regulation and improvement. Intellectuals also became more self-conscious about their own way of life and saw their task as providing the people with the guidance they required. *Legislators and Interpreters* tells the story of how the intellectuals managed to acquire this 'legislative' role, and how they then lost it.

Bauman argues that the key historical place and time was eighteenth-century France. The *philosophes* shared a common vocabulary, common assumptions and common purposes. They managed to secure a privileged place in the counsels of government. This alliance between the state and the intellectuals in France is the historical basis for the 'power/knowledge compound' (p. 26) in modern societies.

There were many reasons why this was able to happen. For example, the decline of the old nobility and its feudal values meant that new ways were needed to justify political authority and exercise social control: the *philosophes* set to work on these problems. Moreover, during the eighteenth century there was no other powerful social force ready and able to step into the old nobility's shoes and provide government: the *philosophes* stepped forward.

The absolutist state undertook an ambitious programme of imposing order and high standards on the people it governed. There were vacancies for innovative planners to administer, organize and manage society. The *philosophes* were equipped for this role. They came from many walks of life. As 'freelance intellectuals', they were not bound to the interests of any particular institution, such as the Church or the legal profession. They could identify themselves with the whole society.

The *philosophes* established a dense network of communication among themselves. They wrote to each other, visited one another, reviewed each others' books and attended meetings together. They created a *république de lettres* governed not by economic or political interest, but by highly educated opinion. 'They were a group, an autonomous group, and a group which introduced opinion, writing, speech and language in general as a social bond to do away with all social bonds' (p. 26).

The Reformation and Counter-Reformation movements during the sixteenth and seventeenth centuries had ended the Catholic Church's monopoly upon 'truth'. The ' "command economy of thought" ' administered by the Church was replaced by new 'counterfactual rules of secular truth-seeking' (p. 35). These new rules were favoured by the *philosophes'* 'horizontal' structures: in other words, by the strength of the ties between them and the fact that they depended on no single outside power for their income and security.

The *philosophes'* rules of truth seeking began with the requirement that all participants in the search should ignore the selfish concerns flowing from their particular social circumstances as individuals. All statements were to be subject to only one test of their relevance and validity: the intellectual power of the argument as judged by all participants. If consensus were reached among such a group of highly educated participants committed to testing every argument to destruction, then it could be accepted as an advance along the road towards truth.

When the absolutist monarchy set out to reshape French society, it turned to the *philosophes* for guidance. The various grand plans for reforming society that they came up with were generally based upon the hope that French society as a whole could be made to resemble the way of life enjoyed by its leading intellectuals. However, in practice they became implicated in the construction of a vast system of top-down surveillance designed to keep an eye on the crowds of 'masterless men' (p. 40), vagabonds and rootless strangers thrown up by a modernizing society.

The *philosophes* helped to design the prisons, workhouses and other institutions intended to impose disciplinary power. They became expert horticulturalists in the 'garden' (p. 51) being cultivated by the modern state. They helped to identify and remove the weeds (the corrupt, the superstitious, the criminal and so on), while rearranging the flowers (the potentially educable, useful and conforming subjects) into convenient patterns.

Increasingly, the poor were seen as bad and dangerous, while their masters thought of themselves as good and benign. The common people were 'common' – that is to say, ignorant and unworthy – in their behaviour and aspirations. The administrators were 'noble': that is to say, intelligent and high-minded. Terms which originally referred to social position (the common people, the nobility) came to be associated with moral character and personality. The common people had to be 'civilized'. In other words, their minds and bodies had to be reformed. Low culture had to be brought up to the standards of high culture.

This approach was not developed overnight. It took over a century to mature. The intellectuals' discovery that the people were 'different' – in fact, that there were many varieties of difference among human populations – had been made in the sixteenth century. At first, the discovery reinforced the modesty and humility of writers such as Montaigne and, later, Pascal. Their intellectual response was grounded in a cautious pragmatism. The best they hoped for was to produce some tentative working hypotheses about life and conduct.

However, by the eighteenth century intellectuals were engaged in a 'conscious proselytizing crusade' to install 'a knowledge-led management' of society: one 'aimed above all at the administration of individual minds and bodies' (p. 93). The peak of their ambition was reached in the early nineteenth century when Destutt de Tracy and the so-called ideologists proposed a vast scheme of education to be administered by experts such as themselves. Each group within society would be given the schooling it 'needed' to become properly trained for its proper place within the 'good' society.

In the late twentieth century, some intellectuals, such as Habermas, looked back with nostalgia to the eighteenth century when the *philosophes* sought truth through 'undistorted' communication among enlightened men and women who accepted the authority of the best argument. This was also a time before intellectual life was split up into separate compartments for scientific, aesthetic and moral concerns. Unfortunately, these dreams had to contend with two realities.

The first was that the heirs of the *philosophes* were increasingly drawn into a system of top-down regulation of the masses, whose primary object was not so much to free the minds of ordinary people as to subject both mind and body to a strict discipline. This regime served the interests of the state and its ruling establishment. The second reality was that, by the late twentieth century, the state had far less need of the services of general intellectuals: in other words, men and women who have a vision of society as a whole.

Instead, the demand was increasingly for specialized experts – high-grade technical minds that could operate and improve the systems that capitalism required to keep its wheels turning. There was no more demand for educators who would help men and women understand the way society as a whole fitted together and their own particular roles within it. This task was now being done by the capitalist market, increasingly the main 'judge, . . . opinion maker [and] . . . verifier of values' (p. 124).

The market seduced consumers into buying commodities, helping to maintain and reproduce the capitalist social order. The state's function was, increasingly, to keep an eye on the margins of the system – to patrol the dingy corners where those too poor to become significant consumers were located. They had to be subjected to rigorous repressive controls. Again, this was a job for specialists, experts in policing techniques, not for general intellectuals.

This radical change of circumstances has seriously undermined the self-confidence of intellectuals as a group. Their power has been expropriated by the advertiser, the marketing manager, the public relations expert, the television producer, the game show host and other agents of mass seduction. Management of the culture has been taken out of their hands. Increasingly, intellectuals have become aware that a new set of rules and functions is being established.

The 'old' regime of modernity, in which intellectuals had a leading place, was full of confidence that its principles were sound, well grounded and effective. In the new postmodern regime, profound uncertainty has returned. It is expressed through a mix of anxiety, scepticism and fatalistic acceptance of relativism.

In postmodern society, it is the advertisers who set standards of taste and create consensus within the population, not the general intellectuals – heirs to the *philosophes*. In fact, the market is broad and flexible enough to accommodate a wide range of different tastes and values. There is no more need to impose cultural uniformity as in the old days of the 'gardening state' in the regime of high modernity. Postmodernity provides the conditions for a host of variegated subcultures to blossom.

This fact offered an opening to the newly redundant legislating intellectuals or, rather, to their postmodern heirs. Instead of legislators they became interpreters. They took up the task of penetrating beneath the surface of the mosaic of cultural styles around them, investigating the various languages and forms of meaning embedded in different ways of life. In fact, this mission had already been formulated by writers such as Dilthey in the nineteenth century. It was part of the strategy of the hermeneutic circle: in other words, the search for truth by shuttling back and forth between specific local cultural traditions and general philosophical principles.

The postmodern role of interpreter does not involve the search for absolute truth. Instead, the interpreter has two tasks. These are, first, translating the language of each special community into a form that members of other communities can understand and, second, interpreting the values of a particular community to its own members. In the first case, the intellectuals are fostering dialogue between different groups who are potential rivals or enemies. They are making an important contribution to peace by encouraging 'the art of civilized conversation' (p. 143). They do this best by not wasting energy on searching for some ultimate truth. At least, this view says, the translator between traditions is being useful.

In the second case, sub-groups of intellectuals may establish strategic positions *within* communities – a fact that allows them, in effect, to define or codify the value systems of these communities. One example is the part played by intellectuals in nationalist or liberation movements. They provide coherent philosophies or ideologies and define what is correct orthodox thinking for each movement. Such intellectuals have a quasi-legislative role. They can define what is 'true' for the particular communities with which they are identified.

One response to postmodernity has been for intellectuals to put their faith in the construction of communities committed to value-systems of which they approve. Bauman believes that these hopes are ill-founded. Communities cannot be deliberately 'made'. They happen unintentionally. Once their members begin to be self-conscious about the sources of their strength and solidity, it is a sure sign that they are beginning to weaken and fragment. 'Made' communities are likely to be repressive, imposing their rules upon backsliders.

Apart from these two responses – translating between different subcultures or meaning-systems and becoming legislators within specific subcultural communities – what other options are there? One possible approach for intellectuals is to withdraw from the world and cultivate the practice of reason for its own sake. A less drastic strategy of withdrawal involves a collective retreat by intellectuals into esoteric science and high culture.

Alternatively, intellectuals could look around for a social force and help it to 'discover its own possibility' (p. 195), just as Marx and Engels hoped to educate the working class about its role in overthrowing capitalism. Or they could just 'do their own thing'. For example, philosophers could carry on philosophizing to the best of their ability without wasting effort justifying themselves to the world at large.

The possible responses listed above are all mentioned in Bauman's 'Conclusion, post-modern style' (p. 192). However, he offers two alternative conclusions. In the pages before his 'post-modern conclusion', Bauman inserts a 'Conclusion, modern style' (p. 188). Here he paints a picture of late modernity as a scene of fragmented authority. Each fragment (nation, company, community, etc.) has rational technology at its disposal and they are all linked to each other through the market. Taken as a whole, the fragments produce a lot of irrational waste. The state is no longer coordinating their efforts. Its only task is to make sure that the market is able to function. The state is 'first and foremost, an agent of re-commodification' (p. 188).

Bauman's 'modern' conclusion notes that the shrinking of the state has shrivelled up the channels through which men and women might discuss and criticize the system's wastefulness. Instead, they seek satisfaction as individual consumers. The market makes sure they are never truly satisfied. It 'feeds on the unhappiness it generates' (p. 189).

How can modernity be brought to a more fruitful state – one serving human needs to a greater extent? The values of 'autonomy, self-perfection and authenticity' need to be reclaimed from the advertising agencies and restored to 'the realm of public discourse'. Moreover, intellectuals have to show that, in order to achieve these values, society must be made rational once more. The market cannot do this job. Commodification does not serve 'person-oriented ends'.

Intellectuals must explain what can still be achieved and promote 'genuine democracy by involving ever wider sections of society in the redemptive debate' (p. 191). Their task is 'discursive redemption' of the project of modernity. People must be allowed to see that the present state of society is not necessary or inevitable. The 'functional requirements of instrumental reason of industry and commodity production' have subordinated 'individual autonomy and democratic tolerance'. Intellectuals are carriers of these values. Their job is to bring them to fruition – to 'bring the project of modernity to its fulfilment' (p. 192).

I have reversed the order in which Bauman sets out his modern and postmodern conclusions. He puts the postmodern one last. However, does this matter? Bauman does not choose between the two sets of conclusions. Is he, instead, offering his readers that choice?

Cruelty, dehumanization and estrangement

In 1986, presumably while Zygmunt Bauman was writing *Legislators and Interpreters*, his wife Janina published a remarkable book. It is the story of her early life in Poland during the 1930s and 1940s.

In *Winter in the Morning* (J. Bauman 1986), Janina describes the horrors that she and many other Jews endured in the Warsaw ghetto during the early years of World War II. Those who escaped starvation lived with the ever-present threat of deportation to the Nazi extermination camps. Janina managed to escape from the ghetto and, along with her mother and sister, lived life on the run and in hiding till the end of the war. Her father did not survive the war. He was killed by the Russians. This occurred in the Katyn Massacre of 1940 when about 14,500 prisoners of war, mainly Polish officers, were executed.

The underlying theme of Janina's book is how human beings respond to situations of ambiguity, loneliness and threat. She recalls her own confusion about being Jewish. As a very young girl,

> The queerness, the strangeness of those people who were Jews like us had puzzled me as long as I could remember. I used to see many of them in the park in Warsaw, but I saw them first of all in my father's surgery.
>
> Some of them looked very poor, but some did not. Still, they were all strangers and I felt frightened whenever I had to pass the corridor where they would sit and talk very loudly while waiting for my father to see them . . . I feared them, perhaps I slightly despised them as sometimes children do when they meet people who speak in a broken language and look different. But most of all I wondered and wondered how they and we were Jews while other people, as sweet and familiar as Auntie Marie [a close Christian friend of the family – DS] were not. Obviously it had nothing to do with being poor or rich.
>
> I learned somehow that Jews could be recognised simply by their looks – dark, curly hair, black eyes, high-bridged noses. But this did not work either. Uncle Jozef was blonde, my own eyes were pale green and there were many straight noses in the family. What then? (pp. 3–4)

Being not only Jewish but also from a well-off family, Janina had felt isolated and estranged at school: a 'double stranger' (p. 11), as she put it. Later, during moments of intense danger, she was forced to rely on the help of people she did not know, who hid her mother, sister and herself from the Nazis. These experiences gave her an important insight: 'Some time and several shelters passed before I realised that for the people who sheltered us our presence also meant more than great danger, nuisance or extra income. Somehow it affected them, too. Sometimes it divided the family, at other times it brought the family together in a shared endeavour to help and survive' (p. 141).

In other words, the presence of strangers making very great demands presented a great moral and psychological challenge to the host. Janina also learned another 'truth we usually leave unsaid: that the cruellest thing about cruelty is that it dehumanises its victims before it destroys them. And that the hardest of struggles is to remain human in inhuman conditions' (p. ix).

In her book she thanks 'Zygmunt, my husband, who had to put up with my "absence" when, for almost two years, I dwelled in the world of my youth that was not his world' (p. vi). These words affected her husband profoundly, as he openly admits in his preface to *Modernity and the Holocaust* (Bauman 1989). Zygmunt Bauman realized that he had never tried to explore the Nazis' 'world of horror and inhumanity' (p. vii). He decided to make the effort to 'comprehend' the Holocaust. This would not be easy, he thought, because 'This event had been written down in its own code which had to be broken first to make understanding possible' (p. viii).

In *Modernity and the Holocaust*, Bauman described the systematic dehumanization conducted by modern bureaucracies. He looked at the cruel way people who did not fit into tidy categories were treated. He thought about how societies created strangers and how strangers were dealt with.

These themes were by no means completely new to Bauman. Early signs of them can be found in his writings as far back as the mid-1960s: for example, in articles such as 'Three remarks on contemporary educational problems' (1966c) and in his book *Culture as Praxis* (1973a). However, a combination of factors may have helped to bring these themes to the front of his mind.

Three factors may have been particularly significant. Janina Bauman's book is obviously relevant. There is also the fact that state socialism in Eastern Europe was in a highly advanced state of decay – an increasingly hopeless case. Furthermore, Bauman was coming to pensionable age and his career as a full-time university teacher was drawing to a close. It is not unreasonable to suspect that Bauman heard the sound of scaffolding collapsing all around. He needed a new base, a new identity and a new horizon.

Modernity and the Holocaust

In *Modernity and the Holocaust* (1989), Bauman attacked an approach to life that had once absorbed him totally. This book marked the culmination of a process of disengagement from modernity that had been gradually occurring for more than three decades. Bauman began his adult life as one of modernity's fervent warriors. Serving as a junior officer, he played a part in the communist takeover of Eastern Europe. After the war, as a major in the Polish army, he was a relatively high-ranking manager of modernity – an intellectual bureaucrat.

Bauman stopped being a modernizing bureaucrat in the early 1950s when he was dismissed from the army on the grounds that his father had visited the Israeli Embassy to enquire about emigration to Israel. Although Bauman lost his position as a communist 'insider' as a result of anti-Semitism, it took nearly half a lifetime before he explicitly embraced the role of estranged victim into which he had been cast, as a Jew, in the early 1950s. Perhaps Bauman was unwilling to explore this role until, finally, he became totally disenchanted about the prospects for achieving a 'good' modernity – the kind he once hoped socialist states could bring about.

In *Modernity and the Holocaust*, Bauman mounts a full-scale attack on modernity. He takes the position that modern rationality, especially in the form of rationalization, has proved to be bad for human beings. In previous works such as *Socialism: the active utopia* (1976a), Bauman had envisaged that reason in alliance with democratic openness and equality could be an emancipating force. However, he concluded that, in practice, rationality bonded much more readily with centralized political power – a fusion that generated repression and heteronomy.

In *Modernity and the Holocaust*, Bauman rediscovers his Jewishness. He had long insisted on the relative unimportance of ethnic differences in the socialist utopia for which he had been working. Bauman had not denied his Jewishness. He had made no effort to disguise it. However, he had neither cultivated it nor paid it particular attention. He had not, for example, been especially attracted by the idea of living in Israel.[1]

When Bauman rediscovered his Jewishness, he also found out how little he knew about the Jewish experience. Ironically, Bauman was an outsider to his own outsiderness. He wanted to get inside his outsiderness – to 'break the code'. This was his mission not only in *Modernity and the Holocaust*, but also in *Modernity and Ambivalence* (Bauman 1991).

In *Modernity and the Holocaust* (and, again, in *Modernity and Ambivalence*), Bauman tries to forge a strong link between the Jewish experience of modernity and the experience undergone by the rest of humankind. Bauman sees Europe's Jews, especially the German Jews, as filling a vanguard role. In his view, they experienced the modern (and the postmodern) human condition before others did. They also underwent its miseries in a more intense form.

These strands in Bauman's analysis are drawn together in his answers to the following questions. Why was the Holocaust possible? Why were the Jews its main victims? Why was the Holocaust not prevented?

In Bauman's view, the systematic murder of Jews and others was possible, and remains possible, because the moral capacity of human beings is systematically suppressed by modern society.

According to Bauman, our inclination to act as moral beings – our impulse to do right things and avoid wrong things – is 'pre-societal' (1989: 179). We are born with a natural tendency to care for other human beings whom we see are weak and in need. We want to protect those we observe to be under threat.

However, when we come under the control of bureaucrats, professionals and other 'experts' acting on scientific or political authority, we are trained to ignore these moral promptings. We are socialized into accepting that we should obey commands 'from above', that our responsibility is fulfilled simply by obeying dutifully, that we need not consider the moral implications of our actions beyond that.

As a consequence, we will carry out evil actions without feeling a sense of personal moral responsibility as long as we are ordered to do so by a bureaucratic or scientific authority that we consider to be legitimate. Bauman reinforces this point by quoting the well-known experiments of Stanley Milgram. Subjects were invited to participate in a scientific experiment. They were told to administer electric shocks of increasing severity to an unseen person. Under these conditions, many people were prepared to obey orders that led them to inflict considerable pain on the unseen Other.

Bauman argues that these experiments support the view that we are likely to follow instructions that harm someone else when the Other is far away or, at least, out of our sight. We comply more readily if the instructions are set in a rational framework: that is, if we are given a chain of reasoning that explains why the actions are to be taken. It also helps if we are one of a group acting in this way, if responsibility for the actions is diffuse and shared within that group, and if the harm we do to others is small at first and only gradually increases.[2]

The willingness to obey revealed in the Milgram experiments is, in Bauman's view, one result of the 'civilizing process'.[3] This process also provides the technology and organizational skills required to carry out evil on a large scale. As he puts it, 'Modern civilization was not the Holocaust's *sufficient* condition; it was, however, most certainly its *necessary* condition. Without it, the Holocaust would be unthinkable. It was the rational world of modern civilization that made the Holocaust thinkable. The Nazi mass murder of the European Jewry was not only the technological achievement, but also the organizational achievement of a bureaucratic society' (p. 13; emphases in original).

Genocide was the product of the union between two things: on the one hand, an efficient and dedicated bureaucracy determined to fulfil the tasks it was given and, on the other hand, a regime determined to put into practice its own design for a 'better' social order. Bauman's point is that efficient bureaucracies and single-minded regimes are not rare phenomena. As long as they have no effective opposition, events like the Holocaust are possible, not just in Germany but in any modern society.

Bauman does not accept the idea that the Holocaust resulted from an intense outburst of German anti-Semitism. French anti-Semitism was worse. In fact, the Nazi regime worked hard to avoid encouraging either sympathy or hatred for the Jews. They had learned this lesson after *Kristallnacht*[4] when the Nazis unleashed organized mob violence against the Jews. The public reacted with sympathy for the victims.

Turning to the issue of why the Jews became victims of the Holocaust, Bauman begins with the argument, which he accepts, that anti-Semitism has premodern roots. The idea that Jews were separate, standoffish and best avoided grew up in the cities following the Jewish diaspora – the scattering of Jews from the Holy Land. In Germany, Poland, Hungary and elsewhere, Jewish ghettos grew up. They contained a population without a homeland – a foreign minority who were 'inside' but kept themselves separate. Jews did not marry out of the ghetto, or invite non-Jews to their dinner tables.

In medieval Europe, Jews fitted quite easily into the social order. Estates and castes were all separated from each other, and each had distinctive privileges or tasks. When contacts between Jews and other groups were necessary – for example, in matters of trade and finance – business was formalized and surrounded by codified ritual. The Jews had to accept an inferior status. They also had to obey whatever laws the host population made about their privileges and obligations. However, the presence and separate existence of Jews were both institutionalized. They were widely accepted as a fact of life.

There was another dimension to the problem, according to Bauman. The Christian Church was struggling to define itself throughout the Middle Ages. The idea of 'the Jew' challenged all its attempts to impose sharp boundaries and tidy distinctions. Where did the Jews fit in? They were neither heretics nor heathens. They had brought Christianity into existence, yet rejected it. They challenged Christian certainty. The Jews were Christianity's 'alter ego' (p. 38), both upsetting and fascinating. In Bauman's words, 'The conceptual Jew was *visqueux* (in Sartrean terms), slimy (in Mary Douglas's terms) – an image construed as compromising and defying the natural order of things' (p. 39).

The Holocaust is explained, Bauman believes, by the Jews' estranged and exposed position following the transition from medievalism to modernity in European societies. During the early phases of modernization, when monarchs and aristocrats were learning how to organize and exploit their subjects more effectively, Jews were used as tax collectors, rent collectors, estate managers and so on. This made them hated from all sides.

Later, Jews became highly vulnerable as modern states turned their attention to three tasks: firstly, organizing the population into tidy categories; secondly, transmitting a coherent ideology throughout the society; and thirdly, drawing the different social groups together into an efficiently functioning whole.

Once again, the issue was: where did the Jews fit in? They were not a class or a separate nation. The breakdown of the premodern order brought Jews out of the ghetto and into the wider society. Many of them did very well. They began to dress like everybody else. Jews became less easy to point out in the street. However, it was easier to say that they were a hidden threat. According to Bauman, Jews became the focus for deep hostilities. These hostilities were brought on by the breakdown of the old order and the triumph of modernity.

Jews were identified with many hated things: the corrosive power of money, the curse of industrialization, the destabilizing critique of the intelligentsia and the rise of the modern state, tearing up old certainties. Jews did not have a clear location, a fixed place, within modernity. Jewish intellectuals tended to speak of universalistic values rather than national virtues.

Jews were outsiders. They were mobile between nations and states, ultimately committed to none. In modern societies, the Jews became a 'problem' that had to be actively handled by the tidy-minded planners controlling government and by the intellectuals who helped shape their thinking.

In the modern age, Judaism, the religious creed, became less significant. More important was Jewishness – a set of supposed racial characteristics. Jewishness came to be regarded as something biologically given – an essence subject to unchanging natural laws. Racist theorists in the National Socialist movement appealed to popular hopes and fears. They claimed that eliminating Jewish influence would at the same time undermine the hated forces of modernity.

Bauman points to a deep irony. On the one hand, the Jews were hated because they were strongly associated with the onset of modernity – a process that many Jew-baiters wanted to resist. On the other, the programme of eliminating the Jews became feasible precisely because of modern technology and modern forms of systematic thinking. In Bauman's view, modernity is hostile to ambiguous categories. It opposes anything that resists being shaped in conformity with an overall plan. It also provided the practical tools, the science and engineering skills, for moulding populations in ways that planners wished.

In other words, anti-modernist racism combined with an expanded, modern sense of 'what is possible'. The Jews were defined as an irremediable problem. So, as with all things that are beyond repair, the Jews had to be expelled or eliminated. They had no place in Hitler's German Reich.[5]

Eliminating the Jews was regarded as an act of sanitation. It was a work of cleansing to be guided by the standards of advanced science. It was a piece of rational management for the purpose of producing a better society. The German public did not like the mob violence of *Kristallnacht*, but they were ready to tolerate administrative measures that removed Jews from their midst. This fact, among others, made the Holocaust possible.

Bauman makes distinctions between three things: firstly, 'heterophobia', which is resentment of people or things that are different; secondly, racism, which contains a desire to remove or eliminate the object of resentment; and thirdly, genocide, which is the product of 'a specific and not at all universal relationship between state and society' (p. 82). The passage from heterophobia to racism is fairly common. The further step to genocide happens much less frequently.

Why was that step from racism to genocide taken in the German case? Bauman takes the view that one cause was the mind-set produced among bureaucrats by modernity. They are trained to solve technical problems and fulfil the tasks they are given. Hitler made it clear that 'finding a solution' to 'the Jewish problem' had a high priority. He left the details of how it was to be done to the bureaucrats. As a consequence, 'bureaucracy made the Holocaust. And it made it in its own image' (p. 105).

The first strategy for making Germany *judenrein* or 'clean of Jews' was to force Jews to emigrate from German soil. However, as the territorial extent of the German empire increased, more European Jews were brought under Nazi control. At the same time, it became increasingly difficult to find convenient non-German territories where Jews could be sent. Physical extermination was the only practical alternative. The logic was clear. Killing the Jews became the most effective means to achieve the end given to the bureaucracy by its master.

Why was the Holocaust not prevented? Genocide would not have occurred so readily if there had been forces prepared to oppose mass extermination of the Jews. However, the population at large was unable to resist the organized violence in the regime's hands. Powerful professional groups were unwilling to intervene. For example, scientists in Germany, as elsewhere, were trained to see their job as searching for knowledge, not getting involved in arguments about the political uses of that knowledge. They were more concerned about keeping their laboratories open and well supplied than challenging the regime or questioning its values. Like the bureaucrats, the scientists wanted to demonstrate how efficient and effective their techniques were. Some gave active backing to the regime, lending it the prestige of their scientific credentials. Others tried to give the Nazis' racial policy a scientific basis.

Unfortunately, political democracy was not well established in Germany between the wars. The collapse of the German empire in 1918 pushed aside the old aristo-military establishment, leaving a void at the centre. Furthermore, argues Bauman, local communities no longer gave the social support and moral guidance that they had provided for their inhabitants before the upheaval of modernity.

As the Nazis manoeuvred their way into power, they deliberately undermined, then disbanded, the free trade unions. This weakened the working class. The centralized state enforced an almost complete monopoly of decision making in all matters of political importance.

A final factor was the sense of emergency created by the war, which allowed Hitler to press ahead more rapidly with implementing his grand design for a more perfect society. Genocide was the result: *'The design gives it the legitimation; state bureaucracy gives it the vehicle; and the paralysis of society gives it the "road clear" sign'* (p. 114; emphasis in original).

One other group gave little resistance: the Jews themselves. In fact, leaders of Jewish communities cooperated with the Nazi authorities. This allowed German bureaucrats to carry out their complex operation more easily. It suited the Nazis to boost the authority of Jewish leaders. These leaders were able to take over many of the administrative tasks entailed in keeping the Jewish population calm and orderly. This kept them quiet until the time came for them to be killed.

How did the Nazis manage to incorporate the Jews themselves into the very bureaucratic mechanisms that were designed to destroy them? Bauman argues that a number of conditions were necessary for this to happen. Firstly, the relevant bureaucracy had to be solely concerned with members of a specific category. Secondly, members of that category had to be subject to the control of that single bureaucracy alone. This ensured that there was no appeal elsewhere. The clients or victims were isolated.

One way in which the Nazi regime reinforced the isolation of the Jews was by creating a new legal framework, which gave Jewishness a precise definition. This allowed non-Jews to feel that they were in the clear – that the fate of the Jews had no connection with their own. Within the 'sealed off' world (p. 123) of the Warsaw ghetto and similar places, the governing bureaucracy was able to make, vary or waive the rules according to the purposes of those in command. They determined the day-to-day real-life choices available to those over whom they had power.

Those who controlled the bureaucracy were able to manipulate this situation so that it was generally in the victim's interest to cooperate with the oppressor. For example, they could split up the victim population into several categories, by age, health, occupation, education, place of residence and so on. This meant that, when some were taken away for slaughter, those who were not in that sub-category could breathe a sigh of relief and hope for the best. One consequence of this approach was that there was never a clear point at which mass resistance seemed the most rational strategy. As a result, the pursuit of individual survival led to a collective failure to survive.

This piecemeal approach ensured the smooth cooperation of all concerned – victims as well as persecutors. On the one hand, many Jews must have found it difficult to believe that Germany's leaders would be irrational enough to devote massive resources to eliminating millions of potentially useful human beings during a major war effort. On the other hand, the bureaucrats themselves were each focused on carrying out a small aspect of the total operation as efficiently as possible. They could do their jobs without considering the overall purpose to which each was contributing. The rational frame of mind tranquillized both victim and oppressor.

Modernity and Ambivalence

Two years after *Modernity and the Holocaust*, Bauman published *Modernity and Ambivalence* (1991). This book is also concerned with the historical fortunes of German Jews, especially in the nineteenth and early twentieth centuries. However, on this occasion Bauman is concerned less with the Jews' role as the *victims* of modernity than with the part they played in discovering how we can both *survive* and *understand* modernity.[6]

Understanding modernity, as far as Bauman is concerned, means standing outside it to some extent. In other words, it involves an appreciation of the *post*modern perspective. Such a perspective means, among other things, accepting as quite normal that the messages we receive from the world around us will be disjointed, fragmented, ambiguous and confusing. It means expecting nothing else but this. A postmodern consciousness of modernity realizes that the modern aspiration to impose a systematic grid of watertight categories upon the complexities of human existence is doomed to failure. According to Bauman, the Jews, especially those in Germany, developed this consciousness at an early date.

Bauman's study of the German Jews reminds me of some aspects of *Between Class and Elite* (Bauman 1972). In that earlier book, Bauman showed that he was impressed by the combination of bravery and intelligence displayed by the 'heroic' (p. 113) first generation of labour leaders in Britain. These men had a vision of a socialist utopia before their eyes and tried to share it with their followers. Later, Bauman observed a similar combination of courage and insight among the early leaders of Polish Solidarity.

Bauman is very interested in pioneers. He likes to study men and women whose experience is, or might turn out to be, prototypical. He wants to know about people who discern new challenges and potentialities opening up within society long before others have noticed. *Modernity and Ambivalence* draws attention to one such group of pioneers. Bauman argues that ambivalence, an experience that has become dominant in late modernity, was first discovered by Jews attempting to assimilate into modern national societies during the nineteenth century.

In this respect, 'the story of the German Jews occupies the central, and in many senses a prototypical, place' (Bauman 1991: 108). In fact, 'almost all Jewish, or Jewish-born founders and heroes of popular culture, from Marx to Freud, Kafka or Wittgenstein, wrote their seminal contributions to modern consciousness in German'. In the German-speaking lands, writers such as these observed and thought about the process of 'becoming modern'. Through their work the modernizing experience was monitored and theorized.

What was this experience? What did these writers discover about the nature of modernity? The experience was one of disappointment, disillusionment and confusion. Many German Jews were deeply committed to the liberal values of the 1848 revolutions. They wanted a Germany that was democratic and free. Some of them tried to turn this liberal ideal of the German nation into reality through their writing and campaigning. Ironically, these efforts were condemned by many non-Jews as an alien take-over of cultural and political life.

In other words, although educated Jews joined wholeheartedly in the process of nation making, although they wanted very much to be 'Germans', they found that their non-Semitic neighbours still regarded them as, before all else, 'Jews'. This meant that they were not regarded as being qualified to belong fully to the nation. They were in a sort of half-way house.

German Jews who tried to assimilate within German society had to accept the anti-Semitic feelings embedded in German life. They were forced to acquiesce in the stigmatization of their parent culture – to listen in silence as their old way of life was stereotyped and abused. In spite of this, Jews were not rewarded for their tolerance. They were not allowed to become Germans in the same way as non-Jews: 'Much to their despair, the assimilants found that they had in effect *assimilated themselves solely to the process of assimilation*' (p. 143; emphasis in original). They were condemned to remain in a deeply ambiguous situation, caught between being German and being Jewish, between acceptance and rejection, between optimism and despair.

Bauman's central point is that the confusion and contradiction that German Jews experienced in the nineteenth century later became the dominant experience of life throughout modern society. We all now experience the world as a confusing and contradictory phenomenon. This has happened in spite of – or, better still, because of – all the efforts made by the modern state. This 'gardening state', this would-be all-powerful, all-knowing regulator, has tried without success to impose perfect order upon society. Stalin tried. Hitler tried. The architects of the welfare state tried. However, they all failed.

When legislators tried to put society into the straitjacket of rationality, they kept finding pieces – individuals, groups, institutions, subcultures – that would not fit or refused to conform. When they invented more complicated 'systems' to cope with these anomalies, all they got in return were more anomalies and even more complexity and confusion. Ambivalence would not go away. It just got worse. The point about the German Jews is that their failed attempt at full assimilation into the German nation gave them an early reading of our common fate. Freud, Kafka and Simmel were able to use this experience to map out how life was to become for us all.

When the gardening state has tried, and failed, to impose order, what is left? The answer is: a society of strangers artificially homogenized within the 'imagined community' (p. 65) of the nation; rootless, lonely people confronted by an impersonal, highly bureaucratized institutional order. However, once it becomes clear that large-scale social engineering is failing by a very large margin to subject the natural and social worlds to perfect human control, once people stop trying to make that impossible dream come true, then a new way of life may be built that accepts ambivalence.

How shall we live in this fragmented, ambivalent world? Each one of us has to find their own salvation. Each person is left with the task of putting a more or less coherent world together. The self is responsible for finding some way of integrating individual experience and identity. However, the self is not quite alone. If we turn on the television, listen to the radio or go shopping, we find that there are plenty of mediators about to help us fashion ourselves and come to terms with the world around us: counsellors, consultants, experts, salespeople and so on.

These willing helpers selling their wares offer a useful service. Their job is to find out what our personal needs or desires are and then show us options for satisfying them that they can make available through their specialized knowledge or expertise. Putting our trust in them, we can establish our individuality against the rest of the social world while also drawing approval from it. The emotional costs of obtaining this individual confirmation may be reduced by the fact that we are paying for it.

A variety of socially approved life-styles are available for purchase, advertised through the mass media and in shop windows: 'One can learn how to express oneself as modern, liberated, carefree woman; or as a thoughtful, reasonable, caring housewife; or as an up-and-coming, ruthless and self-confident tycoon; or as an easy-going likeable fellow: or as an outdoor, physically fit, macho man; or as a romantic, dreamy and love-hungry creature; or as any mixture of all or some of these' (p. 206).

Bauman is ambivalent about all this. Here his argument recalls his views at the end of *Freedom* (Bauman 1988). The world of wonder pills and quick fixes that he has described feels like freedom, but in reality modern human beings are being forced to live in a kind of giant playpen. We enjoy all these wonderful benefits at the cost of forgetting how to make do and mend on our own account. In other words, we are being Taylorized and Fordized.

The ancient 'cat-and-mouse' (Bauman 1991: 210) skills of chase, hide, attack and flee are taken from us. Our claws are cut back and our teeth are drawn. Our progressive de-skilling makes the list of problems needing expert solutions longer every day. At the same time, the development of society's technological capacity generates an inexhaustible supply of 'solutions' seeking 'problems' ('I've found a new way to fix things. Now, let's find something that's broken').

We are locked into an expanding network of dependency. When one set of experts fails to satisfy us, we go out and look for other experts to put the matter right. The market is the place where problems and solutions meet. This arena is fuelled by the restless drive of individuals constructing self-identity from the goods and services they find there. These arrangements are irrational and wasteful. However, an atmosphere of order and rationality is produced by creating insulated shopping environments offering straightforward choices, all of them apparently 'safe'.

But who will actually guarantee the safety and effectiveness of goods and services? Who will ultimately say that you and I are 'good', 'well', 'right' or even just 'OK'? Bauman's answer is 'nobody'. There is no source of ultimate responsibility outside the de-skilled self – no external authority that can eliminate ambivalence, uncertainty and fear. In the meantime, how is it possible to live a reasonable life under conditions of profound uncertainty?

One false trail is to try and find security and comfort by joining up with others, searching for community. However, 'Such communities will never be . . . cosy and natural (cosy because natural) homes of unanimity.' This is because such 'communities evaporate the moment they know of themselves as communities' (p. 250). It is far better to accept ambivalence and contingency as facts of life. In fact, we should cultivate toleration of diversity, making it the basis for human solidarity against oppression and neglect.

Conclusion

In the trilogy, Bauman reworked the grand narrative that runs through his earlier work from the 1960s and 1970s. The structure of the new-style grand narrative, the one produced in the late 1980s and early 1990s, is similar to its predecessor: a story about the past is fused with a description of the present and a vision of the future. However, the past, present and future are analysed in different ways in the two cases.

Three works from Bauman's earlier period that parallel the later trilogy are *Between Class and Elite* (1972), *Socialism: the active utopia* (1976a) and *Hermeneutics and Social Science* (1978). In the first book, Bauman lauded the pioneers of the British labour movement who had fought for equality and justice. In the second work, he produced a brief history of socialist modernity and pointed towards an ideal modern future. In the third, he provided intellectuals with a history of successive attempts to define their task of understanding society, and showed how that task could be pursued with increasing success in order to help bring society nearer to the socialist utopia.

In *Modernity and Ambivalence*, Bauman discovered a new set of spiritual ancestors. The pioneers to which he now looked were not working-class socialists struggling against exploitation, but Jewish intellectuals struggling to come to terms with the ambiguity of culture. In *Modernity and the Holocaust*, he revised his history of modernity and depicted a ghastly modern future. In *Legislators and Interpreters*, Bauman recast the history of intellectuals, describing a present and future in which this group suffered a loss of their authority and their capacity to shape society.

The trilogy has the structure of a three-act drama. Its two tragic heroes are the Intellectual and the Jew. The first act, *Legislators and Interpreters*, is The Intellectual's Tale. It describes the rise, fall and metamorphosis of a status group. The second act, *Modernity and the*

Holocaust, is The Jew's Tale. It is the dark centre of the work. It takes us into the depths of human suffering. The third act, *Modernity and Ambivalence*, is the Jewish Intellectual's Tale. The main protagonists meet and merge to found a line of intellectual Jewish prophets: Freud, Simmel and Kafka. They make their way to a new unpromised land. This is the State of Ambivalence, a home for all postmodern exiles.

Bauman's trilogy is the axis on which his whole career has turned. His arguments caught the imagination of many readers and established Bauman's claim to be heard as an analyst of modernity and a prophet of postmodernity. The most powerful book, the one that made the biggest impact, was *Modernity and the Holocaust*. This is a work shuddering with flashes and explosions like a spire struck by lightning. It is a deeply angry book that demands your attention. Reading it is like being jabbed in the chest repeatedly. Rows of italics splash across every second or third page.

Modernity and the Holocaust is one of only two books by Bauman that carry a personal dedication. The other, published just over a decade earlier, is *Socialism: the active utopia* (1976a). Both books are personal testaments. The earlier book on socialism expressed a strong and deeply felt commitment that had survived immense disappointments. It has a 'here I stand – I can do no other' feel about it; a kind of nakedness.

By the late 1980s, that nakedness was being tested by a very cold climate. Socialism had very little hope to feed on. My reading of his work suggests that Bauman responded to this in two ways. Firstly, he cast aside the socialist shell surrounding his values, but he kept a very tight grasp on the precious kernel within that shell: his belief in freedom, his hatred of inequality, especially poverty, and his sense of justice. Secondly, he looked around for fresh garments; a persona that he could pour himself into; a platform on which to stand. The role of the outsider provided these things. *Modernity and the Holocaust* is the book in which Bauman made this necessary transition.

9

Bauman's Vision of Modernity and Postmodernity

Elaborating the vision

Bauman's project for the 1990s has been to elaborate his vision of modernity and postmodernity – his interpretation of the human condition at the turn of the millennium.[1] He has been exploring a newly discovered world or, at least, exploring the world from a newly discovered perspective. His books are map-making exercises of the kind an astronaut circling the globe might carry out with the aid of photographic equipment. As the module moves, as more of the earth's land surface comes into view, the camera clicks. The overlaps on the resulting photographs help in the task of piecing them together to make a whole picture.

In the rest of this chapter, I shall condense Bauman's analysis of modernity and postmodernity into a single account. I will look first at the main arguments deployed by Bauman with respect to modernity. In the following section, I turn to his arguments on postmodernity.

Tending the garden

Bauman argues that human beings seek energy and information from their natural and social environment. People also classify the world. In other words, they impose order upon it by sorting its elements into categories, some of which are hierarchical. One example of this is the distinction between the nobility and the common people.

In medieval or premodern societies, human beings had a strong sense of inhabiting a 'natural' order, ordained by God. However, in modern societies, the task of defining and imposing a coherent system of social categories is undertaken by bureaucrats, planners and experts of various kinds (scientists, demographers, health advisers and so on). In some societies, especially communist states, bureaucrats also take overall responsibility for managing energy and the material resources associated with it. In other words, production and distribution of goods and services is state-controlled. This is not the case in capitalist societies. In those societies, the creation and processing of energy are to a considerable extent outside of state control. These processes take the form of capital accumulation. Production and distribution are driven by the systematic pursuit of profit. Managers responsible to shareholders undertake these tasks in a competitive environment regulated by the market.

The 'classifying' bureaucrat and the 'accumulating' capitalist operate at several societal levels, from the very local to the global. However, a key feature of modernity is that in this epoch the national state becomes the most important arena in which bureaucrats and capitalists operate, although not the only one. The central state apparatus is the principal source of bureaucratic authority. The national market is the main object of the capitalists' attention. Bureaucrats and planners provide a framework of rules and regulations for national citizens, telling them their rights and duties. Businesspeople cultivate the national labour market and advertise their goods in ways that appeal to national consumers.

Modernity has lasted half a millennium. The national state has been one of its central aspects for the past two centuries. Bauman's analysis focuses upon three things: firstly, how modernity 'works' (in other words, the mechanisms that have kept it in existence); secondly, the human cost of modernity; and thirdly, the social processes that are undermining the mechanisms which have underpinned modernity in the past. The erosion of these mechanisms is creating a void that is filled, in part at least, by other mechanisms. These new mechanisms are taking over the task of regulating capitalism, creating a new balance of benefits and costs for human beings.

Postmodernity is the human condition of trying to construct a viable and meaningful existence when modernity has been undermined by its own contradictions. This involves coping both with the void left by the disruption of the old mechanisms of social reproduction and the challenges posed by the new mechanisms, which only partly fill this void. However, that is to anticipate the argument.

According to Bauman, modernity requires a large administrative machine to maintain orderliness within society. The administrators, the 'elite', are like gardeners. They try to make sure that every plant is in the correct part of the garden, that it is growing correctly and that weeds, plants for which there are no places, are removed from the garden.

Bauman often uses this gardening metaphor. For example, it helps him to explain the role of the education system in preparing young people for 'planting out' as dutiful workers, keen consumers and patriotic citizens. It also accounts for the 'greenhouse' role played by the health and welfare systems in keeping workers fit and giving them an elementary sense of security and confidence. Finally, it indicates the 'pest control' function of prisons and reformatories, where unwanted elements are kept out of the main garden, so to speak. Some may be disposed of by being executed or given very long sentences. Others may be returned to the garden in the hope that they have developed more acceptable characteristics.

Discipline and sacrifice

Before modernity, the main techniques used to keep society in order were as follows: direct physical force in the form of violent repression; impressive public displays reinforcing the prestige, authority and awesome character of rulers; and control exercised through close personal contact within households and work groups. By contrast, the key control mechanism in modernity is surveillance – the impersonal and anonymous monitoring of human behaviour. Since the early nineteenth century, this form of control has displaced its main rivals.

Like Foucault, Bauman finds the main principles of the modern system of surveillance crystallized in Jeremy Bentham's design for a Panopticon. The inmates of this establishment are informed what rules they must follow by the person in charge. Their behaviour is then kept under constant observation by supervisors, who cannot be scrutinized by inmates in the same way.

If the inmates step out of line, if they infringe the rules they have been given to follow, then they are corrected. The object of the corrective behaviour is to discipline the mind and body of the inmates so that they conform to the rules. The ultimate aim of observation and correction is to produce disciplined inmates who do not require correction – men and women who will behave as if they are always under surveillance even when they are not.

Bauman argues that it is not just the 'masses' who are subject to surveillance in this way, although they were the first to have it imposed upon them. By the late twentieth century, all members of modern society had learned to live under a regime of constant surveillance, or at least to behave in a highly conformist manner as if they were indeed being monitored all the time.

This pattern of behaviour was reinforced in the nineteenth century by instilling a 'work ethic' into employees. Before industrialization, the workers' dedication to their labour was an expression of the 'wholehearted, dedicated workmanship and the "state of the art" task performance which once upon a time came to the craftsman naturally when he himself was in charge of his work' (Bauman 1998b: 7). This kind of work ethic had no relevance to workers doing monotonous, meaningless tasks under the command of factory owners.

The new work ethic drilled into factory employees demanded that they should labour to their utmost and give 'unthinking obedience' to their masters, in spite of the fact that their occupations gave them very little personal satisfaction. Hard and disciplined work in return for a wage; no right to an income unless you worked: these were the main principles of the new work ethic. They enabled those with economic and political power to force people into the factories while punishing those who could not adapt due to illness, incompetence or stubbornness. The workhouse was a place where you had to labour in return for your pittance.

The welfare state developed later. It came into being as a result of many pressures; it was 'indeed "overdetermined"' (p. 46). For example, in part it was intended to provide a safety net that gave a softer landing than the workhouse had done to people denied employment by the tribulations of the economy. This helped to reconcile working people to their situation in the capitalist labour market. In that sense, it reinforced the work ethic. At the same time, however, the welfare state 'sapped the work ethic's most sacrosanct and least questioned premise. It rendered the right to dignified life a matter of political citizenship, rather than economic performance'

(p. 46). This was one of a number of contradictions within modernity to be mentioned shortly.

The welfare state is also significant in another way. It has made an important contribution to one of modernity's main ambitions. This is the wish to conquer nature, including our own bodies. National health services are engaged in a constant battle against death. In this way, they join in the struggle to overcome, bury or marginalize the unavoidable fact of mortality – a hidden struggle that lies at the centre of every culture, in Bauman's view. Modernity's key strategy for coping with mortality is to defer particular deaths by treating specific diseases.

Bauman argues that 'Hygiene is . . . the product of the deconstruction of mortality into an infinite series of individual causes of death' (1992b: 155). This way of thinking is carried over into racist discourse that sees the elimination of 'diseased' or 'unhealthy' races as a means of preserving the life of the society as a whole.

Modern 'elites bent on the preservation of the social order which made their privilege secure' disguised the harshness of the discipline imposed by themselves on the masses by saying that it was a collective self-sacrifice endured by all in the name of a higher cause. This higher cause was collective survival of the group. Nationalism has been the most common form taken by this strategy for concealing repression. Individual suffering is glorified as a patriotic act. This strategy is powerful and effective partly because it promises to let individuals have a share in a form of 'group immortality' (p. 105). It enables men and women to be part of a project that promises a perfect life in the future. This project is the nation.

Following Derrida, Bauman notices an 'astonishing paradox' (p. 112). This is that nationalist ideology typically claims that the *particular* nation to which the nationalist belongs embodies *universal* values. French revolutionaries made this claim after 1789. So did Hitler in the 1930s. It follows from such a claim that the only way to realize those universal values, to make them active in the world, is to conquer and, perhaps, destroy other groups, other nations, which stand in the way of your nation's supremacy.

Why are modern men and women so vulnerable to nationalism and similar ideologies? Bauman's answer is that the processes that brought modern society into being 'destroyed the spontaneous *sociability*' of primordial communal bonds. Modernity has to fill the gap this has created. It has tried to do this by '*socialization* . . . Men and women had to be *made* into members of the community' (p. 114; emphasis in original), especially through popular education – a key agent of civic consciousness and nation building.

Modernity is about 'making' men and women into meaningful beings with identities that provide them with a sense of purpose and direction. Modern elites have tried to 'make' the masses into modern nations and also give them other collective identities related to class, religion, ethnicity and citizenship. However, Bauman points out that modernity is also about 'seeking' – the kind of seeking done by the pilgrim.

Drawing on Max Weber and Richard Sennett, Bauman evokes the world of *'inner-worldly pilgrims'* (1995: 85; emphasis in original): that is, the Protestants who early in the modern epoch chose a life strategy that later became dominant in modernity. When the Protestant looked at the world, he or she saw 'Impersonality, coldness and emptiness' (Sennett 1992: 46). Within this context, the puritan pilgrim creates meaning through acts of choice: choice of purpose, choice of destination and choice of lifestyle.

However, in modern society, 'pilgrimage is no more a *choice* . . . [but] is what one does of *necessity'*. Modern pilgrims have the project of achieving meaning and identity through their lives. Life in modernity takes the form of a journey through time towards this meaningful identity. Gratification cannot be achieved until the destination (perhaps a 'successful' career, a 'good' reputation or a 'happy' family) is reached, so the ideal is for people to choose their destinations early on and travel in a straight line towards them. Then each life will be 'a "sense-making" story' – part of a world that is 'orderly, determined, predictable . . . [and] insured' (Bauman 1995: 85–7; emphasis in original).

To summarize, the structures of modernity express the interests of a legislating elite of bureaucrats and intellectuals, which has employed its 'gardening' skills to 'cultivate' a population that behaves as if it is under constant surveillance. The elite imposes norms upon itself that are as strict as those obeyed by the masses. Modern men and women conform to the rules governing the groups and organizations to which they belong. Work and effort are highly valued in themselves.

Modernity also expresses the human desire to impose order and meaning upon nature and society, to conquer all potential sources of uncertainty and to achieve security even at the cost of freedom. As has been discussed, a number of mechanisms have developed to pursue these objectives. Lying behind and giving 'power assistance' to them all has been the modern state apparatus. The state has been able to concentrate power resources, separate itself out from the rest of society and act upon society. Bauman describes the modern state as being perched on a '"tripod" of military, economic and cultural sovereignties'.

This modern state apparatus has had 'the ability to defend effectively the territory against challenges of other models of order, both from inside and outside the realm; . . . the ability to balance the books of the *Nationalökonomie*; and the ability to muster enough cultural resources to sustain the state's identity and distinctiveness through [the] distinctive identity of its subjects' (Bauman 1998b: 62). One source of modernity's appearance of stability has been the fact that global affairs were for many decades dominated by a few large national states. For much of the late twentieth century, during what Bauman calls 'the Great Schism era', international stability seemed to be guaranteed by the apparently permanent stand-off between the East and the West.

The costs of modernity

The main cost of modernity, in Bauman's view, has been the high price paid by human beings in return for the sense of security produced by its drive for order. The highest price has been paid by members of social categories that the elite has defined as 'unwanted', 'diseased' or 'dangerous'. At worst, as in the case of the European Jews, they have been exterminated. In many cases, they have been dehumanized and treated as having fewer rights than 'normal' human beings.

As for members of the 'normal' majority, their comfort has been bought at the cost of their freedom. They live in a condition of heteronomy. In other words, their lives are spent following rules made by others. There are two reasons for this. Firstly, it reflects the elite's historic fear of the people's capacity to become irresponsible, disorderly and degenerate. This fear found its remedy in the mechanism of the Panopticon – the imposition of constant surveillance to regulate behaviour. The Panopticon represents a strategy for imposing morally acceptable behaviour: that is, behaviour that replicates the mind-set of the Puritan pilgrim – orderly, rational and purposive.

Secondly, there is another fear shared by those in power – a fear that is diametrically opposed to the first. This is the fear *not* that ordinary employees will be immoral, disorderly and degenerate, but rather that they will display *too much* moral concern. In other words, the fear is that individuals will feel *too much* personal responsibility for the good or harm they cause when acting under the orders of organizations to which they belong. These feelings, if unchecked, would weaken the capacity of organizations to act in a consistent manner to achieve their objectives.

Modern organizations respond to this danger of 'inconvenient' moral concern by trying to make sure that employees do not encounter the victims of their behaviour at close hand. All employees specialize in some limited aspect so that no one deals with 'the whole person' of the sufferer. The sufferer's face is not seen. The action of the employees is rendered 'morally *adiaphoric*; . . . neither good nor evil, measurable against technical (purpose-oriented or procedural), but not against moral criteria'. Bauman illustrated this in the case of the Holocaust (Bauman 1989). He believes that the Nazis put into practice a *modus operandi* typical of modern social organizations. This *modus operandi* depends upon

> a number of complementary arrangements: (1) assuring that there is a distance, not proximity between the two poles of action – the 'doing' and the 'suffering' one; by the same token, those on the receiving end of action are held beyond the reach of the actors' moral impulse; (2) exempting some 'others' from the class of potential objects of moral responsibility, of potential 'faces'; (3) dissembling traits, and holding such traits separate – so that the occasion for reassembling the 'face' out of disparate 'items' does not arise, and the task set for each action can be exempt from moral evaluation. (Bauman 1993: 125; emphasis in original)

Bauman argues that, through techniques of this kind, heteronomy, adiaphorization and dehumanization thrive and support each other at the centre of modernity. These mechanisms lead us to do harm to others on a regular basis without experiencing any sense of moral responsibility. We feel no need for an excuse. We are only following orders.

Contradictions of modernity

The power of modernity's formidable battery of mechanisms for maintaining order and commitment has recently been undermined. During the past few decades, a number of modernity's internal contradictions have reached a degree of severity that has led to transformations in the structure of modern society and the modern global order.

The effort by modernity's legislators to impose perfect order on society by tidying it into neat garden plots has failed. There has always been a large and lively residue that does not want to go where it is put or does not have an obvious place. It is difficult to disguise the arbitrary character of modernity's classifications. Changing the classification system to remove the residue has three effects. It undermines the legitimacy of all systems of classification by showing that they are changeable – that they simply represent the will of those with power. It normally creates another residue or 'left-over' element. Finally, it typically leads to increased complexity and more confusion.

The end result is that ambivalence becomes the dominant response of all concerned. This response was expressed, for example, in Simmel's vision of 'a yawning, unstoppably widening, oppressive and depressing gap between collectively sedimented civilization and the absorptive capacity of the human spirit' (Bauman 1991: 168). To put it more simply, the world has become too complicated to grasp. A similar reaction to the world is conveyed by the Freudian dictum that 'Things are not what we are told they are or forced to believe they should be' (p. 175). Ambivalence has undermined belief in the rules and meanings enforced through modern institutions.

Two examples of this ambivalence can be given. In the late twentieth century, Western countries are facing a much more assertive 'Third World' as the poorer countries of Africa, Asia and Latin America adapt to the end of the colonial era. The West has a deep fear of becoming embroiled in global conflicts over the redistribution of wealth, yet regularly supplies these countries with arms. Bauman notes the 'bewildering inconsistency of reactions on all levels' – a response that indicates 'acute uncertainty and ambiguity' (1982: 172).

Another sphere where ambivalence reigned was the politics of corporate capitalism in the 1960s and 1970s, as described by Bauman in *Memories of Class* (1982). During these decades, governments increasingly intervened in economic management to help maintain the production of goods and services, and to make sure that companies received an adequate supply of suitably educated and properly motivated human labour.

All participants in the system were in a deeply ambiguous situation. On the one hand, everyone benefited from government-provided services. On the other hand, everyone resented paying taxes. No class was loyal to the system when its own interests were at risk. It was intrinsically difficult for any group to know what action served those interests best.

Apart from the pervasive climate of ambivalence surrounding corporate capitalism, there were other, more specific contradictions flowing from the way it was managed. There was, for example, a contradiction between, on the one hand, the class concepts built into the thinking of managerial and workers' representatives and, on the other hand, the need to restore popular commitment to the system. Bauman, for example, believed in the early 1980s that much more influence should be given to citizens and workers at every level of the system. This would allow active participation by all involved in an atmosphere of cooperation.

However, the leading participants were strongly influenced by historical memories of the nineteenth-century battle for control over the workplace. They retained their perception of opposing class interests ranged along a battlefront. It was in this spirit that they took part in distributional conflicts about 'who gets what'. As governments became increasingly involved in economic management, politics became dominated by a lethal mixture of bitter feelings and analytical concepts rooted in a previous era. The ruling ideas were in contradiction with the actual needs of the politico-economic situation in late-twentieth-century corporate capitalism.

The 'economisation of politics' (p. 129) within corporatist capitalism was accompanied by the politicization of the economy. This process weakened capitalism. Bureaucratic intervention weakened or undermined the part played by market incentives and profit-seeking behaviour. In other words, these efforts by the state to protect the interests of capitalism were actually undermining the market. This conflict between bureaucratic and market mechanisms has a broad family resemblance to the conflict between bureaucracy and market that Bauman found in East European socialism in his analyses of the early 1970s (Bauman 1971b; 1971c).

Meanwhile, the welfare state, central to the management of modern societies, was being radically 'downsized'. It ceased to be geared to providing universal benefits for the society as a whole. It was increasingly restricted to making provision for 'the means-tested poor' (Bauman 1998e: 49). Instead of being a focus for integrating the whole community, the welfare state became a focus of social division and social exclusion.

This, too, was the product of a contradiction. It was the very success of the welfare state that led to its decline. Paradoxically, the support provided by the welfare state helped to bring into existence a generation of people who did well for themselves and developed a strong feeling of achievement. The social harmony fostered by public provision made an important contribution to their prosperity and optimism. However, these beneficiaries of the welfare state drew the conclusion that they and their families were strong enough to thrive without further assistance from it. They therefore resisted paying taxes to support it.

As Bauman puts it, 'Galbraith's "contented majority" is in no small measure a *product* of the welfare state, and the sediment of its success.' The welfare state produced 'a large enough generation of well-educated, healthy, self-assured, self-reliant, self-confident young people, jealous of their freshly acquired independence, to cut the ground from beneath the popular support for the idea that it is the duty of those who have succeeded to assist those who continue to fail' (p. 61; Galbraith 1992; emphasis in original). The idea that welfare was everybody's right as citizens collapsed before the onslaught of the self-righteous thought that economic security should only be enjoyed by those who 'deserved' it on account of their hard work.

Unfortunately, Western capitalism increasingly found labour in the rich countries too expensive to hire. The contradiction lies here in the fact that, in order to maintain social harmony and keep production levels high, business interests had stimulated consumer desires. This encouraged people to concentrate on their own private satisfactions and weakened the spirit of active citizenship. These outcomes suited capital by giving it more freedom of manoeuvre. However, a less welcome result was that workers pressed for wage increases to meet the costs of the consumer delights they wished to enjoy. Bauman sums up these conflicting outcomes as follows:

> This seems to be the logic of capitalist production: having manoeuvred itself into the use of consumer desires as the major mobilising and integrating force and the royal road to conflict-resolution and order-maintenance, the capitalist approach tends in the long run to 'price labour out of work'. Each successive plot ploughed up by the capitalist mode of production suffers sooner or later from soil exhaustion and falls victim to the law of diminishing returns. (1998e: 53–4)

This 'logic' leads capitalists to press for the dismantling of all barriers to the free movement of capital, while at the same time doing their best to keep the 'reserve army' of cheap labour bottled up in the poorer countries of the 'Third World'. The strategy of freeing up capital while keeping labour tied down suits transnational corporations that can transfer their investments very easily around the globe. They prefer to seek out labour markets where people will queue up to work at low rates rather than contribute taxes to maintaining the welfare state in the rich countries.

The globalization of capital undermines welfare provision in the West. A major benefit that companies used to receive from the welfare state was a fit and educated labour force, trained for the part it had to play in production and consumption. But capital has less and less need for this labour force. It prefers to find its workers in Central and Eastern Europe, Africa, Asia and Latin America. That way it keeps its profit levels high and its costs low.

Finally, Bauman argues that there is a fundamental contradiction between the structure of unequal exchange built into modernity and the political demand for equality that is being voiced in the 'Third World'. Although this contradiction deprives modernity of some legitimacy, Bauman does not believe that this means modernity will soon disappear. It will continue to do damage. As he puts it, 'Modernity cannot survive the advent of equality. Endemically and organically, modernity is a parasitic form of social arrangement which may stop its parasitic action only when the host organism is sucked dry of its life juices' (Bauman 1993: 215).

The net effect of these contradictions has been profound. They have undermined corporate capitalism in favour of a more freewheeling form of global capitalism, less committed to the interests of specific national societies. They have weakened central government bureaucracies within national states. They have damaged public welfare systems. They have radically diminished popular confidence in the capacity of all modern institutions to achieve their objectives. They have cleared the way for postmodernity.

The postmodern perspective

The postmodern perspective is as old as modernity – or almost. Its taproot is ambivalence – a state of mind that accompanies, with only a small delay, attempts to structure the world by classification. The classifying broom does not sweep clean; it just moves the dust around. However, as long as the broom is a big one, it commands fear and respect. For centuries the biggest broom around was the bureaucratic apparatus of the national state.[2]

During the corporatist 1960s and 1970s, the overmighty state tried to sweep round almost all society's nooks and crannies, and tried to keep everyone happy or at least quiet. The dust thrown up by this busy broom caused widespread disgust. The sufferers retaliated by breaking the broom's shaft. The chief perpetrators of this act of destruction were, firstly, the 'contented' majority who refused to pay high taxes and, secondly, boardroom executives fed up with rules and regulations imposed by civil servants. Global capitalists no longer needed the state to 'recommodify' (educate, discipline and soothe) labour for them.

The state was forced into semi-retirement. The big broom was shattered. However, as in the tale of the Sorcerer's Apprentice, the shattered broom's remnants stirred into life, became a host of little brooms and brushed away more feverishly than ever. The point is that the task of creating meaning by imposing order, the job of marking out boundaries, defining categories and assigning values, the exercise of identifying enemies and recognizing friends, all these activities did not become less pressing when the central state retreated from the scene. Instead, they were privatized like so much else in the West during the late twentieth century.

Groups of individuals in scattered pockets everywhere are making deliberate efforts to build worlds for themselves, constructing rules of behaviour, erecting value-systems and creating communities. Bauman is deeply sceptical about these 'communitarian' tendencies within contemporary society, as will be seen later. However, the main point here is that the overall effect of these multitudinous experiments is to raise the level of ambivalence within society still further. The world seems full of missionaries, each seeking converts for her or his own brand of 'religion'. The confused wanderer through the postmodern landscape is beckoned in several different directions all at once.

This postmodern habitat, thronging with people, things and ideas, all live and kicking, busy 'doing their own thing', is an enchanted place or, as Bauman prefers to say, it has become re-enchanted. In the past, the ruling elites of modernity, the bureaucrats and experts, tried to force rationality upon the 'unprocessed, pristine world', tried to disenchant it, to deprive it of spirit and animation, to make it 'an *object of willed action* . . . given form by human designs' (p. 142; emphasis in original). They tried to do this to the natural world. They also tried the same strategy on human beings. Modernity meant killing the life within nature and people, cutting and shaping them to modern purposes, then trying to make them work within an artificial plan for a new modern world order.

Bauman argues that this strategy produced very big losses and very uncertain gains. The instrinsic character of nature and human beings was stifled. New meanings and purposes were imposed from outside. Instead of 'earth, forest and water', rationalizing moderns saw 'ores, timber and waste disposal' or some other combination of resource uses. 'And as nature became progressively "de-animated", humans grew increasingly "naturalized" so that their subjectivity, the primeval "givenness" of their existence could be denied and they themselves could be made hospitable for instrumental meanings; they came to be like timber and waterways rather than like forests and lakes.'

This centuries-long experiment has failed. We have lost faith in the 'command-issuing, order-making powers' (p. 142) of the rational legislator. An important result of this, in Bauman's view, is that we have begun to doubt very seriously our capacity to carry through large-scale plans that treat the world as a repertoire of human and natural resources, passively waiting to be 'put together' and 'pointed in the right direction'. The collapse of some major efforts in that direction, most spectacularly the break-up of the Soviet Union, has lifted some of the top-down pressure upon human beings, making it less necessary to behave like hetero-nomous robots obeying orders from above.

The lifting of this pressure has had two consequences. One is that we have become more sensitive to the inner promptings of our moral nature. These promptings were systematically stifled by modernity – a regime that left such matters to 'big brother' in the form of the 'boss' or the state, aided by legislating intellectuals. The death of big brother brings about 'a *re-enchantment* of the world' (pp. x–xi; emphasis in original). We feel our moral nature springing back to life with the same wonder that we might watch the leaves return to a tree after wintertime or press an ear against the bark to hear the sap rising.

The other consequence is fear. Our inner moral promptings raise profound questions about how we should behave, what we should want, and who we should try to be. However, these promptings do not provide *answers* to such questions. They make us itch with uncontrollable irritation, but they do not supply any ointment to cure the itch. They make us feel inadequate and vulnerable. We miss the comforting touch of big brother's hand on our shoulder.

The postmodern habitat

According to Bauman, the postmodern habitat is a complex system whose dynamics cannot be reduced to statistical formulae. It is populated by many agencies (or agents), big and small. This covers a wide range: for example, campaigning organizations, companies producing specific products, sects promoting specific paths to the 'truth' and particular individuals trying to make sense of the world and themselves. None of them can determine the behaviour of other agencies, but they are all partly dependent on each other. Their actions 'remain staunchly under-determined, that is autonomous' (p. 192).

Each agency sees the wider habitat as a chaotic and indeterminate space filled with competitors promoting rival claims: different meanings, different solutions. The habitat is an unpredictable arena of pragmatic manoeuvring between competing agencies. Each competitor regards the rest of the habitat as a set of opportunities or problems that help or hinder it in pursuing its particular objectives. In other words, they tend to have blinkered, tunnel vision. For example, they systematically produce, indeed overproduce, those 'solutions' for which they have skills and resources, and then look round for problems that require these solutions.

The denizens of the postmodern habitat have a rootless and inconclusive existence. They construct their identities through trial and error. This 'process of *self-constitution*' has 'no visible end; not even a stable direction' (p. 194; emphasis in original). Its only visible point of continuity is the human body itself. This is the focus of sensation and display, both of which are pursued through 'body-cultivation'. What men and women ingest (food, drink, drugs) and what touches our skin (cosmetics, clothes) become deeply interesting topics. Individuals impose cruel regimes upon themselves to get fit and slim. These self-imposed regimes replace the 'panoptical drill of the modern factory, school or . . . barracks'.

The indeterminacy of the postmodern habitat makes it impossible to plan 'a sovereign life-project': in other words, a trajectory through life designed in advance as a meaningful journey through a fixed landscape. Instead, people orient themselves with reference to the other agencies swirling around within the habitat. They define themselves by their 'self-proclaimed allegiance' to whatever agencies they choose.

Inhabitants of the postmodern habitat show their allegiances by adopting '*symbolic tokens* of belonging' (p. 195; emphasis in original). These might include the clothing they wear, the furniture they purchase, the residential districts they live in, the types of housing they occupy, the kind of food and drink they consume, how they spend their leisure, the books they read, the works of art they admire, the opinions they repeat, and so on. The choice is their own and they can change their minds without permission.

However, freedom brings uncertainty. People need reassuring that they have chosen wisely and that they have assembled their identities competently. They need a pat on the back. They get this if their choice of symbolic tokens (these clothes, those opinions and so on) conforms to popular taste or if it concurs with the views of experts whom they trust. Experts control access to two strategic resources: knowledge and the capacity to reassure.

The freedom to choose which symbolic tokens to adopt is not equally distributed. Folk who are richer and more knowledgeable have a wider choice. The postmodern habitat is stratified. At the top are the favoured minority with access to all the credit and expertise that they need to make the world their oyster. They have a global stamping ground and can often be found in airport lounges. Then there is a broad middle stratum consisting of those who have enough money and knowledge to participate in the sensation-gathering, symbol-toting culture just described.

At the bottom are the poor. They lack the money needed for a free existence within the postmodern habitat. They are strongly influenced by the values of this habitat, since these are loudly broadcast to all. However, they are marginal beings within socio-political arenas dominated by those with credit cards and bank accounts. In fact, the majority of the poor are excluded altogether from those arenas and remain penned up in the 'Third World'. Some of these men and women may also be found in airport lounges, waiting to be deported – sent back 'where they belong'.

For most people in the richer countries of the world, the relationship between freedom and security in the postmodern habitat is the reverse of what it is in the modern habitat. In the modern habitat, panoptical surveillance is widespread and inhabitants operate according to a set of rules established by external authority. In such a habitat, people are generally keen to have more freedom – mainly freedom *from* the state and freedom *within* the market. Within the postmodern habitat, more people feel freer, but another need nags at them. This is the desire for security, especially the security supplied by popular opinion or by experts whom they feel they can trust. The freedom deficit is replaced by a security deficit.

The broader context

The postmodern habitat needs to be placed in its broader context. As Bauman puts it, 'If [the] . . . suggestion of a close relationship between the advent of postmodernity and advanced consumerism deserves credibility, it is necessary to ask to what extent post-modernity ought to be seen as a local event, a parochial phenomenon fully dependent on a temporary, and possibly transient, privilege of one group of states in the worldwide distribution of resources' (1992a: 59).

This passage should be considered alongside another. In *Globalization: the human consequences* (1998b), Bauman criticizes the self-absorption of rich, well-educated tourists who savour the world as a delightfully exotic show, not to be taken too seriously. For these jet-setters, postmodern life is a constantly shifting collage of exciting experiences. The world is a global salad bowl from which they can pick and choose – a cultural light lunch that never ends. However,

> The hybridization and defeat of essentialisms proclaimed by the postmodernist eulogy of the 'globalizing' world are far from conveying the complexity and sharp contradictions tearing the world apart. Postmodernism, one of the many possible accounts of postmodern reality, merely articulates a caste-bound experience of the globals – the vociferous, highly audible and influential, yet relatively narrow category of exterritorials and globetrotters. It leaves unaccounted for and unarticulated other experiences, which are also an integral part of the postmodern scene. (p. 101)

These globetrotters are the postmodern elite. The habitat they occupy is global. It stretches to include all the airports they fly from, all the hotels and restaurants they frequent, each boardroom and lecture hall they speak in, and every golf course, beach and tennis court they play upon. This highly mobile elite provides the models and heroes whose life-styles are pictured in the advertising that draws less-rich-but-still-affluent consumers into the retail parks and leisure facilities within easy reach of their homes.

Borrowing from Thomas Mathiesen (1997), Bauman sees a new power mechanism at work here: the Synopticon. Unlike the Panopticon, where the few watched the many, in the Synopticon, the many watch the few: on television, at the cinema, and in their magazines and newspapers. The lives of celebrities provide a pattern of existence for millions of admirers. Reports of their activities are like 'broadcasts of heaven'. The audience, hypnotized by fame, accepts the values and world-view expressed in the global doings of the mighty few. It is an effective system of social control by 'a royalty that guides instead of ruling' (Bauman 1998b: 52, 54).

The affluent stratum of society occupies a part of the post-modern habitat that is carefully insulated from the suffering and frustration endured by the poor, trapped in their urban ghettos or marooned in their rural shacks. The postmodern habitat bestows freedom, albeit anxiety-ridden and ambivalence generating, upon many people. However, as Bauman points out, the social processes that deliver new opportunities to some people place others in chains: 'postmodern freedom' coexists with what 'may feel rather uncannily like the postmodern version of slavery' (p. 92).

Seen from the perspective of the West, recent trends in the development of capitalism and political structures have given more *freedom to the rich majority* in the suburbs, while bringing increased *repression of the poor minority* in the inner city. However, seen from the perspective of the rest of the world, the balance between the majority and the minority is a different one. From that global perspective, recent trends have given more *freedom to the rich minority* in the West, while bringing increased *repression of the poor majority* in the less developed societies.

Three aspects of postmodernity

I want to show the importance of these remarks for Bauman's understanding of postmodernity. Before I can do that, I have to separate out the different ways in which Bauman uses that term. *In practice, Bauman is making distinctions among three aspects of postmodernity: the postmodern perspective, the postmodern habitat and the process of postmodernity.* These distinctions remain implicit in his work and it will be helpful to draw them out. We have already discussed the first two, but a brief summary will be helpful.

The first of the three aspects of postmodernity is the *postmodern perspective.* As has already been noticed, this perspective is permeated with a sense of the ambivalence of existence, the contingency of events and the insecurity of being. These responses are nurtured by continuing evidence of modernity's failure to achieve its objective of creating perfect order.

The sense of ambivalence is linked with a deep scepticism about modernity: an unwillingness to believe its promises and a reluctance to be taken in by its 'big stories' or meta-narratives (about socialism, democracy and so on). Since the evidence of modernity's failures began to appear very early on in the modern epoch, the postmodern perspective has a history almost as long as modernity itself. However, this perspective did not become dominant within large sections of society until the evidence of modernity's failures had become overwhelming.

The second aspect of postmodernity is the *postmodern habitat.* This is a cultural and sociopolitical arena in which the postmodern perspective, the postmodern way of looking at things, is not just a nagging doubt about modernity's world-view, but actually displaces that world-view and takes its place. It stops being a 'backseat driver' criticizing the route being taken and, instead, moves forward into the driving seat.

In a postmodern habitat, the sense of ambivalence becomes dominant. The postmodern perspective is transformed from being a *reactive stance,* flinching from the unbelievable claims or intolerable demands of modern bureaucracies, to being a *proactive force* that shapes how individuals construct their lives, identities and relationships. This change occurs because inhabitants of the postmodern habitat have achieved increased freedom from the state and within the market.

The postmodern habitat just described is fuelled by thick flows of cash and credit. Its shopping malls present themselves as a kind of consumer paradise. As has been seen, the postmodern habitat is governed by consumer desires and choices regulated by the market, public opinion and experts.

The third aspect is the *process of postmodernity.* In *Postmodern Ethics,* Bauman refers to 'the modern age reaching its self-critical, often self-denigrating and in many ways self-dismantling stage (*the process* which the concept of "postmodernity" is meant to grasp and convey)' (1993: 2; emphasis added). This postmodernization process is discussed in the next section.

Postmodernization

The postmodernization process is many-layered. Its main outlines are as follows. Structural transformations are altering the way capitalism articulates with national states. These fundamental changes within capitalism and national states are creating conditions that allow the postmodern habitat to develop in many locations. The development of the postmodern habitat is, in turn, allowing the postmodern perspective to become a strongly proactive force in the world. At the same time, a global order or 'disorder' (Bauman 1998b: 59) is coming into being, which increasingly polarizes the postmodern habitat between the rich and the poor. While the rich splash around in buoyant streams of cash and credit, the poor are excluded and humiliated. The poor are weaned on the postmodern perspective, but denied the means to thrive in the postmodern habitat.

This polarization between rich and poor is regulated on the basis of a new division of labour between capital and the state. The origins of this new division of labour lie in the globalization of capital. This has helped to bring about the shattering of all 'three legs of the sovereignty tripod' (p. 65) on which the national state used to rest. The three legs were military, cultural and economic sovereignty.

Governments have not lost their power and influence completely. They have been successful in retaining some degree of military sovereignty – in effect, control over the legitimate use of the means of force. In particular, this means that they can take responsibility for policing their own poor and making sure that the poor from other countries do not cross their borders and become a burden on the taxpayer. Meanwhile, capitalism has taken over the task of managing the cultural and economic dimensions of society. Its primary medium of regulation is the market.

Bauman has examined the transformations and challenges that postmodernization has brought at a number of levels: for example, at the global level, within the postmodern habitat, and at the level of the individual. Let us look at these different levels in turn.

Globalization

Investment capital has become much more mobile, moving round the globe with great ease. Communication of information between physical locations has become much easier, faster and cheaper, so that physical proximity has no special importance for the task of running organizations. Decision-making forums are no longer sited in public spaces closely linked to local communities. Instead, they occur somewhere in global cyberspace. Meanwhile, local public spaces follow the pattern of the shopping mall – somewhere you mingle with a crowd of strangers, all minding their own business. One locality is getting to look very much like another.

Local territories have lost their meanings. The rich and educated can join the transnational business executives, the cosmopolitan jet-setters and all the other 'globals' (p. 51). Meanwhile, the poor and disadvantaged have no choice but to stay imprisoned in their localities. These places are defined, increasingly, by what they lack: character, influence, community, public life and opportunity. The punishment for poverty is to remain one of the 'locals' – to suffer 'ascription to meaninglessness' (p. 18).

National states no longer hold the ring at the global level. In fact, Bauman argues, nobody is in control. For a few decades, the 'Great Schism' (p. 57) between capitalism and communism gave a deceptive appearance of orderliness to international affairs. However, the end of Soviet and East European communism has revealed the 'erratic and wayward nature of the global state of affairs' (p. 58). Throughout every continent, global companies compete with each other in bitter dog-fights. Governments cannot hold them in check and have let them off the chain.

The pace of change increases every year. The global economy is like an accelerating truck with no one at the wheel. Bauman agrees with Claus Offe's judgement that 'The dominant pattern might be described as "releasing the brakes": deregulation, liberalization, flexibility, increased fluidity, and facilitating . . . transactions on . . . financial real estate and labour markets, easing the tax burden, etc.' (Offe 1996: 37; Bauman 1998b: 68–9).

Seduction and repression

In Bauman's view, within the postmodern habitat there has been a radical shift away from production to consumption as the central integrating activity. Modernity allocated to work the main responsibility for giving people their identity, their social bonds and their social function: you *are* what you do for a living. By contrast, in a postmodern habitat you *are* what you buy. Advertisers train you to think this way from the moment you can blink at a television screen. Consumers are seduced into their purchasing role. In fact,

> it is the aesthetics of consumption that now rules where the work ethic once ruled. For the successful alumni of consumer training the world is an immense matrix of possibilities, of intense and ever more intense sensations, of deep and deeper still experiences ... The world and all its fragments are judged by their capacity to occasion sensations and ... to arouse desire, ... more satisfying than the satisfaction itself. It is by the varying volumes of that capacity that objects, events and people are plotted on the map. (Bauman 1998b: 32)[3]

In this environment, the poor are out of place. At best, they are useless. They are 'flawed consumers' (p. 38). At worst, they are threatening. Bored, dissatisfied, lacking self-esteem, the 'new poor' seem likely to commit violence and theft. However, the real problem with the new poor is not that they are dangerous, but that they are inconvenient. They do not conform to the way of life that is valued in the postmodern habitat.

The rich react by labelling the new poor as the 'underclass'. This institutionalizes their place on the fringes of the postmodern habitat. The hidden assumption is that the new poor do not deserve a decent place within this habitat. The rich blame and condemn the poor for their poverty. The work ethic, left over from modernity, is a very convenient mechanism for doing this. The poor, it is said, are poor because they are morally inadequate. They do not work, they do not try. They have misused their freedom and so deserve whatever comes to them.

The rich salve their residual guilt with occasional 'carnivals of charity' (p. 78), subscribing to relief funds. However, this is more than counterbalanced by the strategy of criminalizing the new poor. This response feeds on the attitude that any kind of behaviour that is inconvenient for the routines of the consumer society, that is unwanted because it does not fit in, should be regarded as a 'crime'. Throughout the 'developed' world, there is a rapid growth in the prison population.

Bauman raises the prospect that the widespread criminalization and imprisonment of the new poor could be a step on the road towards eliminating the weak and defenceless, getting rid of those who are unable to survive in the postmodern habitat unless they receive help and support. It is already more convenient to remove them from sight than to help them. Could the next step be to remove them altogether? Bauman concludes: 'We are not quite there – not yet. But the writing is on the wall' (p. 94).

If the poor suffer this fate, it would mainly be because they are, so to speak, unpleasing to the rich. They spoil the view. They do not fit into the picture. This is a vulnerable situation to be in when 'the world map in most frequent use is aesthetic, rather than cognitive or moral' (p. 32). However, how did this postmodern 'world map' come into existence?

Cognitive, aesthetic and moral space

Postmodern men and women have to adapt to a very high level of uncertainty and risk. They do not receive clear and consistent signals from 'above' or 'outside' about the nature of reality or what moral rules they should follow. As a result, there is a high level of fear that they will make massive errors of judgement and consequently get hurt.

How do postmoderns respond to this situation? They continually check their feelings about themselves, the world and each other. They compare notes constantly. They try to reclaim control over the world, or at least the small bit of it that they occupy: making their own reality, making moral rules for themselves. Where possible, moral and cognitive issues are turned into questions of taste – a sphere where opinion rules, and where opinions may legitimately differ and shift. These are strategies for reducing uncertainty or 'domesticating' it.

The everyday world of the postmodern habitat is episodic, haphazard, inconsistent and contingent. What seems 'true' today may seem 'false' tomorrow. This is a repeated experience. In order to survive upon these shifting sands, postmodern people get used to the idea that what seems real and reliable disappears, yet their lives continue. The ultimate disappearance of reality that goes by the name of death is rehearsed in a small way every day, but they survive. They experience a kind of immortality. Or, as Bauman puts it, immortality is deconstructed by this daily experience that 'dissolves the future in the present' (1992b: 187). This is postmodernity's counterpart to the modern strategy of dealing with death by deconstructing mortality: in other words, by delaying individual deaths.

Truth and reality acquire a certain plasticity in the postmodern habitat. Meanings are not handed down from above in complete and packaged form, as in the old model of modernity. In trying to cope with the ontological insecurity brought by postmodern freedom, artists and novelists take the lead in reclaiming the very process of meaning-creation. Through their work they show that meanings are always incomplete and ambiguous. Meanings change in the very process of interpretation. Readers help to determine what a novel 'means', and the audience can shape the meaning of a play. Critical opinion works and reworks the meaning of a work of art. In fact, postmodern culture is a 'consumer cooperative' (p. 140).

This seems very cosy, companionable and controlled. From this account, postmodern life seems to be like a pleasant seminar in a highly sophisticated senior common room – a seminar conducted by humane aesthetes who together construct a meaningful world for themselves, and who control their doubts by sharing them. Such people could be let loose with confidence in any shopping mall.

However, Bauman does not think life is like that. He is aware of the tremendous fear of loneliness and isolation that underlies our behaviour. He knows that the seminar can easily turn into the mob. He realizes that aesthetic judgements surf upon a tide of passion – that they express emotional responses as much as, perhaps more than, they express rationality. Furthermore, Bauman understands that postmodern experiments in living are *bricolage*, making use of bits and pieces of modernity lying around like hot metal after an explosion.

The postmodern habitat is not quite what it seems. It conveys the image of being a pleasure park, a consumer's playground, a place where you can pick-and-mix life-styles and beliefs according to taste. However, it is a pleasure park laid out on a demolition site that is still 'alive'. Beneath the surface lie the smouldering remains of modernity's attempt to plan a purposeful society, in which everybody played their part according to the commands of the elite.

Modernity played around with some very dangerous materials. According to Bauman, modern intellectuals were dissatisfied with the passivity of the populations they had learned to control. They dreamed of re-infusing their neatly planned societies with spontaneity and excitement – those very features that they had carefully drilled out of the masses. As he puts it, they wanted to combine the benefits of socialization – that is, the orderly training of the people – with the creative vigour of sociality: in other words, the fire and enthusiasm of the aroused crowd.

Bauman points out that sociality of this kind is 'an *aesthetic* phenomenon: disinterested, purposeless and autotelic (that is, its own end), a state in which feelings are shared before they are articulated' (1993: 130; emphasis in original). The challenge was how to harness this force, the energy of the crowd, and put it to use without the state losing control. Communist and fascist regimes both demonstrated the 'murderous potential' (p. 138) of this strategy when carried out effectively. Passions were systematically roused and put to deadly use. Morality was subordinated to politics.

The attempt to combine socialization with sociality was discredited by the defeat of Hitler and the demonization of Stalin. The postmodern state scaled down its ambitions on both counts. It stopped being a rabble-rouser and gave up trying to socialize its citizens. However, the discredited political technology has been difficult to dismantle rather in the same way that nuclear reactors are difficult to shut down.

Postmodernity witnesses repeated upsurges of sociality: the urge to assemble; the wish to feel the irresponsible joy of being part of a crowd. People feel safer, less empty and alone, when they wear the clothes and markings of a specific tribe or 'imagined community' (Anderson 1983). People like to identify with a style, a cause, a craze, a team, a theme or a fad – for as long as it lasts or as long as they feel like it.

These eruptions of sociality are temporary phenomena, not deeply rooted. They tend to focus on one dimension of existence – a single issue that unites its followers. They are not 'polysemic, multi-functional and multi-final' like 'classic tribes' (Bauman 1993: 143) – the kind that anthropologists seek out on the plains and in the forests.

The communities that people form in the postmodern habitat are often full of good intentions. They seek stability. They hunger for warmth and security. They want to do the 'right' thing, to implement 'humane' values. However, there are several counts against them, in Bauman's eyes. They are manufactured – put together deliberately – rather than having existed from time immemorial like real 'Tönnies-style inherited *Gemeinschaft*' (p. 186). As a result, their founders are always anxious and intolerant. They are hostile to outsiders. They oppress their followers.

Furthermore, when communitarians seek out 'natural communities of origin' to support, they home in on the highly localized entities that legislating intellectuals working for nation-states had once condemned '(not without reason) precisely because they were parochial, backwater, prejudice-ridden, oppressive and stultifying' (Bauman 1997: 192).

Finally, communitarianism thrives on the false hope that '*risk-free freedom*' (p. 193; emphasis in original) can be achieved by creating a planned community – a contrived togetherness of like minds. In fact, moral choices are no less risky when they are taken collectively than when taken alone. It only *seems* as if they are.[4]

The stranger

The postmodern habitat is shaped by the opportunities and threats that come with freedom. One source of opportunity and threat is irreducible. When the poor have been locked away, when communities have been imagined, when attractive identities have been purchased, when experts have been consulted, when public opinion has been sounded, when death and reality have been put in their place, then there still remains one challenge that cannot be dissolved: *the stranger*.

In the postmodern habitat, everyone is a stranger to most of the people he or she meets. This was true in the modern habitat also, but at least strangers were labelled reasonably clearly by a central bureaucratic authority. One knew what category they were in and therefore knew how to treat them. Postmodern strangers are a constant problem because it is never quite clear who they are or how one should feel about them or behave towards them. They are a cognitive, moral and aesthetic challenge.

The postmodern stranger is neither a familiar neighbour nor an alien. Instead, strangers have aspects of both. They remain at hand like neighbours, while remaining distant and unknown like aliens. One way to respond to strangers is to treat them as entertainment – as an aesthetic phenomenon. This is the approach of the *flâneur* or *stroller*, who roams along the avenues enjoying the human comedy. The *flâneur* is a stranger among strangers, who feels no particular moral responsibility for those providing the entertainment.

The stroller is one of a family of postmodern types who have replaced the modern pilgrim – that character who strides purposefully towards a clear destination, fulfilling a clearly defined vocation. The postmodern world is 'not hospitable to pilgrims any more' (Bauman 1995: 88). Instead, we meet, along with the stroller, the *tourist*, the *vagabond* and the *player*. The tourist is seeking new experiences in new places, while minimizing the risks that they bring. Tourists return home after each adventure, although, as they adopt the role more thoroughly, the sense of 'home' becomes eclipsed by the feeling of being perpetually on the move. Home sickness meets a strong challenge from 'fear of *home-boundedness*' (p. 97; emphasis in original).

The vagabond is a wanderer who has no home. Vagabonds do not wander out of choice, although in time they may come to cherish their capacity to move on when necessary. Such seasoned vagabonds would be tourists if they had the money. Finally, there is the player – the person who regards life as a series of games, each with its own rules. To avoid being permanently hurt, the player must be able to leave behind a game that is concluded, moving straight on to the next without grudges. The player has some kinship with the person who treats love as a relationship intended to produce joy without sacrifice – a sort of 'de-ethicized intimacy' (Bauman 1993: 106) that has no lasting consequences.

What do these four characters, with their different strategies for living, have in common? It is that they all

> tend to render human relations fragmentary . . . and discontinuous; they are all up in arms against 'strings attached' and long-lasting consequences, and militate against the construction of lasting networks of mutual duties and obligations. They all favour and promote a distance between the individual and the Other and cast the Other primarily as the object of aesthetic, not moral evaluation; as a matter of taste, not responsibility. (Bauman 1995: 100)

Bauman concludes that all four postmodern strategies for living 'cast individual autonomy in opposition to moral (as well as all the other) responsibilities and remove a huge area of human interaction, even the most intimate among them, from moral judgement (a process remarkably similar to bureaucratically promoted adaphiorization)' (p. 100).

I and the Other

In *Postmodern Ethics*, Bauman takes up the moral challenge posed by the solitary individual, the I, confronted with the stranger, the Other. What responsibility do I feel for the Other? This question cannot be answered by looking in a book of rules. No such book exists. Or, rather, there are several which contradict each other and no way to decide which is valid. In any case, mere rule following, obeying an imagined superior authority, does not entail an act of choice. One would be 'only following orders'.

When postmodernization undermines the authority of modern bureaucracies, when the rulebooks are shown to be useless, then each individual has to rely upon his or her sense of moral responsibility – a capacity weakened by modernity. In the postmodern habitat, it is no longer appropriate or possible to follow the 'modern' procedure of discovering what category the Other fits into, discovering the moral rule applying to that category, and then behaving accordingly. The question of how to respond to the Other, the stranger, cannot be decided by 'discovering the real situation'. It is not ontological.

Influenced by Emmanuel Lévinas,[5] Bauman plunges into a realm that we already inhabit before ontological issues break surface – before we are socialized into 'categories' and 'rules'. The self's original condition is to feel responsibility for the Other – for those others who occupy the world along with the self. This urge is not rooted in a sense of duty that challenges selfish inclinations. On the contrary, the moral urge is innate. It is rooted in the autonomy of the I, not imposed in a heteronomous way by society or the Other.

Each person experiences his or her being as a being-for the Other. The Other is a 'face' in close proximity, expressing a need. The Other has no force to impose a demand. The I has no right to claim that the Other should give something in return for any care received. There is nothing reciprocal or contractual in the relationship between I and the Other. However, the Other's proximity makes him or her the focus for the I's being-for. It stirs up moral anxiety – the urge to do something to meet the Other's needs. That is where the trouble starts.

The point is that, although we have a natural inclination to care for others, an inclination that postmodernity uncovers after centuries of deep burial, we rediscover this inclination at the same moment that all guidance about how to behave morally is taken away from us. We are like the released cage-dwellers stumbling about in the dark, whom I mentioned in the first chapter.

There are no moral rules, says Bauman, only moral standards, and these are so high that they can never be met. He adds: 'One recognizes morality by its gnawing sense of unfulfilledness, by its endemic dissatisfaction with itself. The moral self is a self always haunted by the suspicion that it is not moral enough.' He then quotes 'one of the most active and dedicated rescuers of Nazi victims', who said ' "Only those who died bringing help can say they have done enough" ' (Bauman 1993: 80). The function of rules is to give us the false feeling that, when we have complied in a minimal way, we can turn away. Rules are a mechanism for switching off our moral capacity, not a means of activating or fulfilling it.

Being-for the Other means trying to work out what the Other needs in the way of care. Bauman believes that this is a challenge we should not resist. However, danger confronts those who do not switch off their innate moral urges. Their behaviour towards the Other may create meanings and carry implications that do not become clear immediately and that are not completely within their control. They never know what they are 'getting into'.

Furthermore, once begun, moral responsibility is unending. It can become a burden. The Other's weakness becomes a drain upon the carer's strength. Care can turn to hatred. Alternatively, care can easily turn into domination. The carer may begin to define the Other's needs against the will of the Other.

Bauman does not provide solutions to these difficulties. In fact, he does not believe they are soluble. However, he much prefers a world in which the moral urge is active to one in which it is stifled. Indeed, one of the biggest challenges still facing us is how to activate our moral natures and apply them to global issues. The point is that, although we may be sensitive to the needs of the Other whose face is close at hand, the stranger next door or down the street, so to speak, we are much less likely to feel any responsibility for people on the other side of the world.

Distance is not the only problem. Complexity is another. Industry, finance and government rely on sociotechnical systems that are so complicated and interact at so many levels that it is impossible to say where responsibility and control lie. Every business, every national state, every organization tries to provide itself with an orderly local environment. However, these efforts do not add up to a coherent global order. On the contrary, each organization's attempts to maximize order and control for itself tend to undermine the order and control plans of its neighbours.

The fundamental problem is that our moral tools for handling these problems are quite inadequate. We are still facing up to the moral challenge of the stranger who is close at hand. How can we cope with the task of doing the right thing on a global scale? Bauman draws on Hans Jonas at this point.[6] Our primary purpose should be to develop an 'ethics of *self-limitation*' (Bauman 1993: 220; emphasis in original). In other words, before we take any action that feeds into the complex systems just mentioned, we have a responsibility to think through and visualize the effects of our actions upon third parties.

The fact that visualization of possible or likely consequences is an endemically uncertain activity is no reason not to carry it out to the best of our ability. It should involve detailed research, clear thinking and the exercise of empathy. Instead of saving our energies for crisis management – dealing with what-was-not-expected – we should be investing our energies in studying 'what-has-not-happened-yet' (p. 221) but might. So a person responsible for managing any kind of system (such as a chemical plant, a bank or a television channel) should be making two kinds of judgement.

The first kind of judgement relates to the efficient performance of the system. The second involves a '*second degree* evaluation' that examines the likely and possible consequences of the system's behaviour on third parties from a standpoint of moral responsibility. There is no way to reduce our irreducible uncertainty about the future consequences of our action. However, two principles should guide us: the '*Heuristics of Fear*' and the '*Principle of Uncertainty*' (p. 221; emphasis in original). In other words, we should pay more attention to prophecies of doom than promises of bliss, and make our goal the limitation of damage not the achievement of perfection.

The role of the sociologist

Finally, what is the role of the sociologist? The discipline of sociology came into being when intellectuals were still legislators. Now sociologists do their share of interpreting, operating at 'the interface between "language games" or "forms of life"' (Bauman 1992a: 42). However, they can do more than this. They should be developing 'a sociology of postmodernity' through 'the strategy of systematic, rational discourse' (p. 65). This means studying the nature of globalization, the consumer society, life without full employment and the other key features of postmodernization and the postmodern habitat.

Sociologists should stay close to ordinary people, engaging in a two-way transfer of knowledge, skills and experience. They should make available to them 'a "sense-making", a "world-mapping" knowledge' – one that contributes to 'a mental setting in which decisions are taken and freedom of choice is exercised' (p. 90). Sociology should be organized and systematic, but not insulated from the life it feeds on. Ideally, 'sociological knowledge is but a whirlpool in the incessant flow of human experience from which it draws and into which it discharges its material' (p. 74).

Sociologists who study postmodernity should accept the cognitive and moral uncertainties that postmodernity brings, but they should not abandon 'the Enlightenment dream of the meeting of rational minds' (p. 86). They should accept that History may not be on their (or anybody else's) side. They should stop talking about social-scientific laws and speak instead about human values, assumptions and purposes.

Sociologists can provide men and women with information and understanding that may help efface redundant fictions such as the British 'memories of class' (Bauman 1982), reawaken the citizen lurking inside the consumer, and remind people of their 'unsatisfied ambitions of autonomy and solidarity'. However, it has to be accepted that following this strategy is

> likely to annoy rather than entice the managers of law and order; it will appear incomprehensible to the seduced, and alluring yet nebulous to the repressed. A sociology determined to tread this path would have to brace itself for the uneasy plight of unpopularity. Yet the alternative is irrelevance. This seems to be the choice sociology is facing in the era of postmodernity. (p. 112)

Part III
Dialogue

10

Between Critical Theory and Poststructuralism

The ambivalence of criticism

'Modernity produces ambivalence' is one of Bauman's chief messages. In other words, it throws up phenomena that are difficult to categorize. Bauman himself is one such phenomenon. The critical response to his writings has been extremely ambivalent. The critics have not found it easy to pigeonhole him.[1]

For example, when *Modernity and the Holocaust* appeared, it was remarkable for Europeans to read a book on the Holocaust by a Polish Jew that did *not* describe it as an unparalleled crime stemming from the peculiar wickedness of the German people.[2] That was certainly against expectations; it commanded attention. As the critics began to tune in to what Bauman was saying, they heard a message that was clear, coherent and forcefully expressed, but nevertheless puzzling. Bauman was fusing together elements that people were used to thinking of as separate, even opposed.[3]

Two issues have been a particular source of perplexity. One is the question of where Bauman stands in the contest between German critical theory and French poststructuralism to define the human condition at the turn of the millennium.[4] The other is the question of whether Bauman is a 'modern' or a 'postmodern' sociologist. Commentators on Bauman cannot decide whether Bauman is a systematizing modern sociologist, building a grand theory, or a postmodern sociologist, experimenting with novel fragmentary forms.[5] They are unsure whether Bauman's interest in the postmodern means that he is a 'postmodern sociologist' or whether it simply means that he is an old-style modernist sociologist who happens to be interested in postmodernity.[6]

The journey from modernity to postmodernity

My own view is that Bauman has made an intellectual voyage from modernity to postmodernity and in doing this he has taken compass bearings from both critical theory and poststructuralism. He has borrowed what he needs from both these theoretical traditions, but belongs to neither. He has also been influenced by the broadly existentialist tradition that includes Arendt and Lévinas.

Bauman's analysis of postmodernity employs an intellectual apparatus that took shape at a time when he was committed to the methods and objectives of 'modern Marxism'. However, Bauman acknowledges that the objective conditions have become highly unfavourable to his earlier strategy of achieving social progress through dialogue and collective praxis.

As Bauman sees it, this change in objective conditions has produced the postmodern habitat in which he and the rest of us are forced to dwell. My interpretation is that, since he has no choice but to reside in this habitat, Bauman is very happy to join in the 'paralogical' game (to paraphrase Lyotard) that consists of experimenting with new forms and meanings, especially in the realm of art and literature.[7]

Although Bauman joins in these postmodern games in a highly creative way, he has not converted to a new 'postmodern' intellectual strategy. Instead, he has narrowed his ambitions, focusing his old weapons on a more delimited target. Bauman no longer pursues the idea of encouraging social groups to engage in open communication with each other, leading to creative action and bringing a 'good' society nearer. As he sees it, the postmodern public sphere is in no fit state to support such an enterprise and, in any case, Bauman has become deeply suspicious of 'manufactured' forms of group solidarity.

However, faced with a postmodern constituency of isolated strangers, Bauman turns his attention to them instead. His fundamental approach is the same: to encourage open communication and creative action. Individual action can be creative in the sense that, when 'I' enact care for the 'Other', I strengthen the tissue of interpersonal solidarity in which ethical behaviour resides.

Compared to the more optimistic programme of the 1970s, Bauman's ethical challenge to the inhabitants of the postmodern habitat is more diffident and presented in a less exhortatory manner ('the choice is yours'). He expects less. The impulse is conservatory, protecting the seed for a future sowing. It is a programme for the winter rather than the spring.

There is a very close connection between Zygmunt Bauman's life experiences and his developing theoretical approach. Bauman has made a long journey from his native 'modern habitat' in communist Poland to an increasingly 'postmodern habitat' – one initially located in the West, but gradually becoming global in extent. In this respect, there is an interesting parallel between Bauman and Alexis de Tocqueville, who made a similar journey from the aristocratic tradition in which he was reared as a child to the democratic social order to which he was forced to adapt as an adult.

I will explore the comparison with Tocqueville later in this chapter. However, my next task is to consider Bauman's intellectual relationship to two writers from the critical theory tradition, Theodor Adorno and Jürgen Habermas, and two from French poststructuralism, Michel Foucault and Jean-François Lyotard.

Adorno and Habermas

When Bauman received the Adorno prize in 1998, he described himself as Adorno's 'disciple'. He recalled the feeling of 'spiritual affinity, or temperamental kinship, which struck me many years ago when I first opened an Adorno book; that "this is it!" feeling' (Bauman 1998a: 1).[8]

Bauman's *Modernity and Ambivalence*, the last of his trilogy, was, as he put it, 'firmly rooted in the propositions first articulated by Adorno and Horkheimer in their critique of Enlightenment (and, through it, modern civilization)' and was an attempt 'to wrap historical and sociological flesh around the "dialectics of enlightenment" skeleton' (Bauman 1991: 17).

Anyone who glances through the chapters in *Dialectic of Enlightenment* (Adorno and Horkheimer 1979) on 'the concept of Enlightenment', 'the culture industry' and 'elements of antisemitism' will see many ideas developed later by Bauman. They will, for example, read about the 'mythic terror' (p. 29) or fear of violence, disorder and 'otherness' that fuelled the Enlightenment, and the Enlightenment's strong impulse towards totalitarian control over human beings and nature in the name of positivism.

Adorno and Horkheimer also write about the commodification of culture and its repackaging as entertainment and advertising. In addition, they analyse, as Bauman did later, the disciplinary power of the market, 'the illusion that expert knowledge is the only thing that counts' (p. 150), the widespread retailing of 'pseudo-individuality' (p. 154) and the exposed position of Jews as highly visible intermediaries in modernization processes.

During the 1990s, Bauman concluded, as Adorno did before him, that modern societies have lost their emancipatory potential; instead, they are dominated by instrumental reason and the market. Like Adorno, Bauman clings to the ideals of the early Enlightenment and tries 'to fight for "the redemption of the hopes of the past"' (Bauman 1998d: 14). Not least, Bauman has taken on board Adorno's conviction that the impulse to dominate humankind and nature that has ruled European society and politics since the seventeenth century leads towards fascism and the death camps.

Bauman freely acknowledges the debt that he owes to Adorno.[9] However, he is not a mere clone. In this context, it is legitimate to 'search for a peculiar biographical experience that was to be later reprocessed and sublimated' (Bauman 1991: 108) in the ideas of Bauman and Adorno. In fact, the backgrounds of the two men could hardly be more different.

Although they were both of Jewish descent, Adorno's father was assimilated and married a Catholic wife; by contrast, Bauman's parents considered making their future in Israel. Furthermore, Adorno came from wealth. Martin Jay writes that 'The young "Teddie's" early home life was comfortably sheltered, both economically and culturally, in the way that only an upper-bourgeois, European child's could be in the years before the First World War. From all accounts, his childhood provided him a model of happiness whose memory served as a standard against which he would measure all subsequent disappointments' (1984: 25).

Bauman's early life was more difficult: He was 'born and brought up in Poznan in a family of slender means. He . . . experienced much hardship and . . . suffered from anti-Semitism. At the start of the war he and his parents . . . fled to the Soviet Union where they . . . lived starving for many years' (J. Bauman 1988: 44–5). This was not a protected existence. I do not believe that

Bauman measured his subsequent disappointments against the standard of comfort and security provided by his home life as a child.

My guess is that in Bauman's case the key experience providing the backdrop for future disappointments was the tremendous excitement of the decade between 1943 and 1953. During these years he was part of a victorious army defeating fascism and installing a socialist system in Poland. He subsequently enjoyed rapid promotion up the military hierarchy and had increasingly important political work to do.

Alongside the image of Adorno's childhood idyll, we should set Janina Bauman's memory of her young Polish army captain: 'an honest Communist' who passionately believed he was part of a historic struggle for 'full equality between human beings' (p. 49). As a soldier, Bauman's goals and values were, we might well imagine, greatly influenced by authority figures such as his colonel. This man, Bauman's immediate superior, was 'Well into his forties, stiff and straight in his perfectly fitting uniform, with the balding head and piercing eyes of an intellectual' (p. 52). He commanded the 'total respect and admiration' of Janina's future husband.

The bourgeois drawing room in the 1900s and the officers' mess in the Polish army during the 1940s offer two very different perspectives on history. From the first vantage point, the upward curve of human progress culminates in the cultured life-style of Europe's upper middle class. For this class, the task ahead was to protect this privileged existence by gradually sharing it with the lower orders as their educational level increasingly prepared them to receive it. The danger was that the masses, manipulated by the state and the market, would degrade and destroy their cultural inheritance.

From the second vantage point, bourgeois individualism, however cultured, was the ideology of capitalist exploiters benefiting from an institutional order that denied freedom and equality to the majority of the population. The upward curve of human progress culminated not in the bourgeois drawing room, but in the people's republic. Under the guidance of the socialist vanguard, the people would construct a better society.

Adorno was deeply interested in avant-garde movements in art and music. His own work anticipated many aspects of deconstructionism. However, Adorno had inherited the tendency to shrink from political activism that characterized high bourgeois society in the German empire and the Weimar Republic. He deeply resented the advance of consumer capitalism and the increasingly interventionist state. As he saw it, the so-called spread of civilization was, in practice, the advance of barbarity – a process that led, ultimately, to Auschwitz.

From Adorno's point of view, 'enlightened' twentieth-century civilization was cutting down plants in full flower with more buds to come. By contrast, for a decade or more, Bauman had been in happy complicity with the 'gardening state', keen to wield the cutting shears. It was only when he lost his own confidence in the state's 'civilizing' mission that he found Adorno's analysis congenial.

Adorno's pessimism was stimulated by the observation that the sphere of relative freedom he had inherited from preceding generations, as a son of the bourgeoisie, was being eroded by the state and the market. By contrast, Bauman spent his early life following the Marxist credo, fighting to create a new sphere of freedom for those whom the bourgeoisie exploited. Creating that sphere was, for him, an active, military and then political struggle. Bauman has known the inside of the political world. He has smelled the corridors of power, and encountered the faces behind faceless bureaucracy.

Adorno is dismayed by the advance of both the state and the market. By contrast, Bauman's pessimism since the mid-1980s stems from his perception that the state bureaucracy and the public sphere are in full retreat before the market. In other words, the political arena, the arena of debate and manoeuvring where Bauman has a track record of exercising influence (in Poland, at least), has lost its importance. It has shrunk and given way before an expanding commercial arena where the intellectual counts for much less.

Unlike Adorno, Bauman's approach is interventionist rather than contemplative. He shares Adorno's deep interest in art, but he is nevertheless an activist rather than a student of aesthetics. This has remained true throughout Bauman's career. He has shifted the target of his activism as times have changed. For example, when the chance to magnify his action through the leverage of bureaucratic power passed away from Bauman early on in his career, he turned to the citizenry and concentrated on ways of building up his influence there.

Later, Bauman found that the people's interest in the opportunities of democratic citizenship was giving ground before the lure of consumption. So he began to approach his readers as human beings (rather than citizens or consumers) in books such as *Postmodern Ethics* and *Life in Fragments*. Bauman has worked hard to subvert the ideology of consumer choice. He has tried to confront people with the much more difficult existential challenge posed by the Other, the stranger.

In view of these differences between Adorno and Bauman, it would not be unreasonable to suppose that the latter might have more in common with Adorno's one-time pupil, Jürgen Habermas. Bauman (born 1925) and Habermas (born 1929) belong to the same generation. For several years Bauman found Habermas's model of 'ideal speech' and 'undistorted communication' a valuable intellectual support for his own utopian aspirations. However, at some point in the 1980s, Bauman made a decisive switch of loyalty away from Habermas towards Adorno. Why was this?

One reason may be the apparent decline in the practical viability of promoting dialogue between groups in a vigorous public sphere. Bauman has concluded that dialogue between interests within national societies is unlikely to produce significant progress towards a socialist utopia now that those societies are largely shaped, as he sees it, by the twists and turns of global capitalism.

However, the ferocity of Bauman's rejection of Habermas suggests that there is more to it than that. Bauman's changing attitude towards Habermas can be traced through his work between the 1970s and the 1990s. In 1973, in *Culture as Praxis*, Bauman explictly aligned himself with Habermas's argument in *Knowledge and Human Interests* (1971). He quoted with approval Habermas's view that 'An enticing natural force, present in the individual as libido ... urges towards utopian fulfilment ... What may appear as naked survival is always at its roots a historical phenomenon. For it is subject to the criterion of what society intends for itself as the good life' (Bauman 1973a: 170).

Three years later, in *Towards a Critical Sociology* (1976b), Bauman made the case that 'critical knowledge serving emancipatory interest differs from remaining types of knowledge'. He insisted that, although experts play a role in producing this kind of knowledge, their verdict may not be 'considered as final and conclusive unless "authenticated", i.e. confirmed in the act of rectification of communicative distortions'. He concluded that 'This realization sets Habermas apart from all previously considered sociologists who offered solutions to the problem of testing critical knowledge' (p. 104).

The high point of Bauman's approval of Habermas came with the publication of *Hermeneutics and Social Science* (Bauman 1978). He stated that 'Habermas's model of rational agreement . . . brings the methodology of understanding sciences as close to the ideal of truth-guided criticism as the rules of experimental practice brought empirical-practical sciences' (pp. 243–4).

By 1987 the tide had turned. In *Legislators and Interpreters* (1987), Bauman argued that postmodernity entails a fundamental 'redeployment of the intellectual world' (p. 140). However, he noted that 'Habermas can only perceive recent shifts in the intellectual worldview as a sort of aberration; a regrettable hardening of attitudes which in their benign form have been with us for a long, long time' (p. 128). Then, in an interview carried out in 1990, the following exchange took place:

> Q Your view of the main importance and function of sociology resembles that of the critical theory of the Frankfurt School . . . At one stage of your life you were a convinced advocate of the work of Jürgen Habermas, as a writer who attempted to combine the positivists' insistence on reliable knowledge with acknowledgement of the hermeneutic dimension of social life in a science with 'emancipatory' intent, in the Marxist tradition. Would you still regard yourself as a 'critical sociologist'?
>
> A Yes, I do. I don't like Habermas, however. (Bauman 1992a: 217)

Bauman added that he was attracted by Habermas's 'ideal of a society shaped after the pattern of a sociology seminar', but that 'once Habermas turned from there to a straightforward positivistic re-hashing of Parsons, then I lost my spiritual affinity with his project.' It is probably relevant that Bauman's discovery of postmodernity coincided with Habermas's attack on this concept: for example in *The Philosophical Discourse of Modernity* (1987) and *The New Conservatism* (1989).

Habermas was not convinced by suggestions that people were no longer motivated by the utopian aspirations contained in modernity. For example, in an essay entitled 'The new obscurity', published in *The New Conservatism*, he argued that

> [the] thesis of the onset of the postmodern period is unfounded. Neither the structure of the *Zeitgeist* nor the mode of debating future life possibilities has changed; utopian energies as such are not withdrawing from historical consciousness. Rather, what has come to an end is a particular

utopia that in the past crystallized around the potential of a society based on social labour. (Habermas 1989: 52)

If correct, this argument by Habermas undermines Bauman's assumption that the death of communism in the ex-Soviet bloc marked the final collapse of confidence in modernity itself. Bauman's case depended on the assertion that 'Communism was modernity in its most determined mood and most decisive posture; modernity streamlined, purified of the last shred of the chaotic, the irrational, the spontaneous, the unpredictable' (Bauman 1992a: 167).

Bauman's point was that, if the most pure and determined form of modernity had failed, then modernity as a whole had failed. Habermas disagrees: 'Of course, the utopian dimension of historical consciousness and political debate has by no means been completely closed off with the departure of the utopian contents of a labouring society' (1989: 68). As far as Habermas is concerned, modernity is not over. It is 'an unfinished project'.[10] For his part, Habermas believes that, in spite of the collapse of socialism, the spirit of the time continues to be informed by 'utopian thought', although this is checked by the more sceptical perspective contained in 'historical thought' (p. 49).[11]

At the end of 'The new obscurity', Habermas criticizes the suggestion that, if an 'ideal speech situation' were to be brought about in modern industrial societies, the probable outcome would be movement towards a socialist utopia. It was a 'methodological illusion' to imagine that a process of free and open dialogue would necessarily lead to the realization of any specific 'projections of a concrete totality of future life possibilities'.

All that could be 'outlined normatively' were 'the necessary but general conditions for the communicative practice of everyday life and for a procedure of discursive will-formation that would put participants *themselves* in a position to realize concrete possibilities for a better and less threatened life, on *their own* initiative and in accordance with *their own* needs and insights'.

Habermas concludes with the thought that 'it is utopian in the negative sense to confuse a highly developed communicative infrastructure of *possible* forms of life with a specific totality, in the singular, representing the successful life' (pp. 68–9; emphases in original). In these remarks, Habermas dismisses as misguided the idea that fostering creative dialogue is likely to lead towards the socialist utopia.

This analysis casts profound doubt upon the approach to which Bauman was committed for many years, frequently referring to Habermas in highly approving terms. At the same time, Habermas is refusing to allow socialists to translate the failure of a specific system (one in which they had a high 'psychic' investment) into the failure of modernity as a whole.

There is no obvious evidence to suggest that Bauman is intended as a particular target of this analysis by Habermas. However, Habermas's argument is deeply unsympathetic both to old-style Bauman, thinking through the preconditions of progress towards socialism, and to new-style Bauman, analysing the postmodern condition. It is, therefore, not surprising to find Bauman cooling towards Habermas in this later period.

By the time he wrote *Postmodernity and its Discontents* (1997), Bauman's view of Habermas was decidedly hostile. During a discussion of the subversive postmodern art, Bauman expressed his dislike of Habermas's 'modern, Thanatos-guided conception of progression as, essentially, the introduction of a higher-degree order, as an authoritative selection of possibilities and foreclosure of the others'. This approach reaches 'towards a state in which all further change is either frowned upon or illegal' (p. 107).

Foucault and Lyotard

Compared to Bauman's difficulties with Habermas, his intellectual relationship with Foucault has been less troubled. It is not possible here to go into the fascinating complexities of the overlaps between poststructuralism and critical theory.[12] However, Foucault has acknowledged that 'there are striking parallels between his own analysis of the disciplinary, carceral society of modernity and Adorno's "administered world"'.[13] This has made it easy for Bauman to incorporate Foucault's model of the Panopticon, borrowed originally from Jeremy Bentham.

Foucault recognized broad affinities between his own work and the Frankfurt School's concerns. However, he thought the School's 'conception of the "subject" was quite traditional' and 'noticeably impregnated with humanism of a Marxist type'. Their objective was to 'recover our "lost" identity, to free our imprisoned nature, our deepest truth'. However, as far as Foucault is concerned, 'the problem is to move towards something radically Other' (1991: 120–1). On the surface, Foucault's prescription of a move towards the Other seems to resemble Bauman's interest in coping with 'otherness'. However, their analyses are fundamentally different.

Bauman has always emphasized the capacity of men and women to 'make' society – to create the institutional order within which they live. In practice, he argues, for much of the time since the seventeenth century this capacity has been usurped and exercised as a virtual monopoly by the rationalizing state with the complicity of the intellectuals. Up to this point, his argument is compatible with Foucault's vision of human beings penetrated, shaped and confined by increasingly invasive discursive practices. Like Foucault, Bauman acknowledges the disciplinary power of the routines in which we are entrapped as pupils, patients, claimants and so on.

However, from this point on, Foucault and Bauman begin to differ. Foucault's unchanging objective was to break out of the atrocious confinement imposed by the straitjacket of the self – a self that is defined and prescribed by society. In his view, the bonds of inhibition and restraint could be radically loosened by vigorous and subtle action directed at the self, society or both. One avenue he took was sado-masochistic sexuality as a means of achieving psychic release. In fact, he believed, any kind of limit-experience, pushing to the extremes, led towards liberation.

Political resistance provided another route – one that Foucault followed in his campaigns to expose the conditions experienced by prisoners in French gaols. Another approach was the cultivation of alternative art forms such as the theatre of the absurd. The object in all cases, whichever approach was taken, was to subvert the discursive and non-discursive practices shaping 'normal' identity. By doing this, Foucault hoped to plunge into the dangerous and exciting maelstrom beyond human culture and language, leaving behind its obsession with subjectivity, merging instead with life itself and its infinite possibilities.

Bauman does not see things this way. He does not believe that people are faced with the choice between submitting to an oppressive centralized regime of discursive practices or escaping, Houdini-like, from its grip. During the 1970s and early 1980s, Bauman envisaged an alternative possibility, which is that the people might be able to reclaim control over discourse, purify it of distortions and make it work for them, so to speak. In other words, the disciplinary capacity exercised by centralized bureaucracies could be reclaimed by democratically organized groups within civil society, guided by skilled and sympathetic intellectuals.[14]

According to Foucault's view of things, the task of intellectuals in close touch with the people was to play a primarily destructive role, disrupting the ideological supply lines of the establishment. However, Bauman believes their mission is constructive, empowering ordinary men and women by making alternative perspectives available to them.

In *Freedom* (1988) and in his writing since then, Bauman has moved closer to Foucault's more pessimistic interpretation. Foucault stresses the resilience of centralized discursive practices and their tendency to guide human perception along narrow channels. For his part, Bauman acknowledges the seductive power of the discourses that advertisers deploy in order to lure customers into the shopping malls. The beneficiary of these practices is global capitalism and, as we have noticed, Bauman does not believe there is a viable strategy for controlling or directing this force.

Nevertheless, unlike Foucault, Bauman does see a chink of light – a point of leverage within the system. Consumer capitalism requires the commodification of human existence, but the market does not make rules for living. It sells the ingredients, but it does not dictate the recipe. Moreover, the market is unable to generate a social landscape with which individuals feel any deep resonance, sympathy or sense of belonging. Nor does the functioning of the market depend upon people having meaningful or even coherent selves.

On the contrary, postmodern consumer capitalism feeds ambivalence, making money out of every change of mood or fashion. Within the postmodern habitat, people feel rootless and estranged. They have a weak inner sense of self. They feel purposeless and ineffective. It is to this ever-enlarging constituency of the lost that Bauman speaks.

What is new in postmodernity is not the weakness or passivity of the self, but our *awareness* of this fact. Bauman argues that the self as an active moral agent was anaesthetized and weakened in the regime of high modernity. In the postmodern habitat, the anaesthetic is wearing off and people are confronted with the full force of unrestrained ambivalence. They feel the weakness of their 'choosing' selves. They are not used to making choices on their own authority.

For Bauman, the self is not a prison in which we are trapped, but an inner generator waiting to be re-ignited. Foucault wants to escape the self. Bauman wishes to invigorate it. Both reach towards otherness, but in different ways. For Foucault, otherness is the vast plenitude of life's possibilities made invisible to us by the ruling discursive practices. Otherness is a chaotic and exciting realm beyond reason, agency or morality. It can be reached only by slipping free of the self. In contrast, Bauman wishes to grasp hold of the self and to awaken it as an active moral agent disposed to care for the Other; a self that experiences a sense of obligation even before it grasps the Other's existence.

Foucault does not recognize 'postmodernity' as a distinct dimension of the human condition. However, if we turn to Jean-François Lyotard, we encounter a social theorist who does. Indeed, Lyotard's name is the one most commonly associated with this term. It is important to investigate how his approach differs from Bauman's and where their analyses converge.

Like both Foucault and Bauman, Lyotard is fascinated by the transformations affecting capitalism and bureaucratic-scientific rationality. According to Lyotard, the key change that ushered in postmodernity was the erosion of people's willingness to believe modernity's 'metanarratives' (1984: xxiv). These were the legitimating stories that justified modernity, especially the power of science, the state and capitalism. In particular, people stopped believing the metanarrative that declared scientific rationality would bring emanicipation and universal knowledge.

Lyotard thoroughly approves of postmodernity. He dislikes the fact that the oppressive structures of modern capitalism frustrate the free flow of desire. Lyotard is close to Foucault in his relish for the explosive power of unrestrained raw energy, the basis of creative art.[15] In his view, political economy crushed what he calls 'the libidinal economy' (Lyotard 1993).

In political terms, Lyotard's position is that the cause of human emancipation is best served by a climate of vigorous dissensus – a world in which a wide range of groups assert and argue for their own truths. In the postmodern world, he believes, there is a greater chance that the multitudinous forms of life experience will be properly respected and allowed to have their voice (Lyotard 1988).

Deprived of the 'covering fire' provided by metanarratives, scientists and others who claim to purvey knowledge have two

options. One is to claim legitimacy on the grounds of 'performativ-
ity' (Lyotard 1984: 46), which is a utilitarian principle stressing practical efficiency and 'the best input/output equation'. The other
approach is 'paralogy'. This means embracing a paradigm that
acknowledges 'undecidables, the limits of precise control, conflicts
characterized by incomplete information, "fracta", catastrophes,
and pragmatic paradoxes' (p. 60).

Lyotard aligns himself with paralogy and its conviction that
knowledge can only ever be uncertain, partial, local, pragmatic,
rooted in a specific context and tied to a particular perspective.
Bauman's approach to postmodern art overlaps with this. However,
Bauman adds a critical function. He argues that postmodern art not
only explores the unique vision of the artist, but also challenges
whatever consensus prevails. As Bauman puts it:

> postmodern art is a critical and emancipatory force in as far as it compels
> the artist, now bereaved of binding schemas and foolproof methods, and
> the viewer/listener, now left without canons of seeing and the comfort-
> ing uniformity of taste, to engage in the process of understanding/
> interpreting/meaning-making which inevitably brings together the
> questions of objective truth and the subjective grounds of reality.

In Bauman's view, postmodern art 'liberates the possibilities of life
from the tyranny of consensus'. It 'opens wide the gates of meaning'
(Bauman 1997: 111).

It is important to add that Bauman sees the artist as a lonely
figure, separated from both the comforts and the dangers that come
from being part of a like-minded community. This requires 'yet
more courage and determination on the part of the artist. The acts
of lonely dissent need to be undertaken without hope of being
rewarded by new collectivity' (p. 109).

Bauman sees more clearly than Lyotard the other side of
paralogy: the discomforts brought by ambivalence and oppression.
Lyotard ignores these aspects. His philosophy seems designed
for the cafés and common rooms of the Parisian Left Bank. We
can put it this way: if paralogy has a heaven, it must be an elite
university college where supporters of different intellectual
and aesthetic tendencies may pursue their interests in comfort,
untroubled by the need to justify themselves to each other.
However, if paralogy has a hell, it must be Bauman's postmodern
habitat in which confused wanderers try to make sense of the
contradictory signals beamed out by competing subcultures touting
for adherents.

Bauman has been alert to the debilitating effects of ambivalence in complex advanced societies ever since he first recognized the problem in Poland during the 1960s, well before his 'postmodern turn'. The adolescent trying to find his or her place in 'adult' society was, in effect, Bauman's first case study of 'the outsider' (Bauman 1966c) – one I briefly explored in an earlier chapter.[16]

Although he recognizes the difficulties of the outsider, Bauman is equally clear that being inside an aesthetic, intellectual or moral community may mean submitting to controls that reproduce the oppressions of modernity on a small scale. The community's freedom to choose its own 'language game' (to use the term that Lyotard borrows from Wittgenstein) may be accompanied by a readiness to impose that game upon potentially dissenting members of that same community.

This brings us to the central difference between Lyotard and Bauman. Lyotard sees the arrival of postmodernity in terms of increased freedom. Bauman observes the same sociocultural changes but sees that postmodernity is accompanied by disorientation and new threats to freedom. To be more specific, Lyotard celebrates the emancipation that postmodernity brings to a wide variety of different knowledge communities (scientific, artistic, religious and so on). Bauman emphasizes instead two things: the heavy burden of autonomous choice that postmodernity places on the shoulders of individual postmodern men and women, confronting ambivalence within themselves and in their social environment; and the oppressive nature of knowledge communities committed to maintaining their version of the 'truth'.

Finally, Bauman and Lyotard both face the problem of how to arrive at and apply standards of justice within a world where universalistic metanarratives have been abandoned. On what grounds would one decide that certain behaviour, such as terrorizing others by the use or threat of violence, was wrong? Both writers dismiss the approach taken by Habermas. As we have seen, Bauman for a while aligned himself with Habermas, but later condemned him as a 'positivist' intent on enforcing an authoritative closure of further experiment in the realm of life and meaning.

According to Lyotard, Habermas was wrong to make the 'assumption that the goal of dialogue is consensus', since 'consensus is only a particular state of the discussion, not its end'. Habermas made the error of believing, firstly, 'that humanity as a collective (universal) subject seeks its common emancipation through the regularization of the 'moves' permitted in all language games' and, secondly, 'that the legitimacy of any statement resides in its contributing to that emanicipation' (Lyotard 1984: 65–6). Lyotard argues that consensus as understood by Habermas asserts an imposed truth at the expense of individual freedom. For Lyotard, the proper end of dialogue is not consensus but paralogy.

Lyotard opposes Habermas's notion of humanity as a single universal subject speaking with one voice. Instead, he defends the idea that many different truths, inconsistent with each other, may be pursued side by side in separate knowledge communities. For his part, Bauman is wary of these localized knowledge communities, scientific, religious and otherwise. He sees totalitarian tendencies inherent in all community-building enterprises inspired by a 'dream of purity' (Bauman 1997: 5). Bauman finds the communitarian tendency as oppressive as Lyotard and himself both find Habermas's notion of universal consensus.

The comparison with Adorno, Habermas, Foucault and Lyotard carried out in the last two sections of the chapter has shown that Bauman has strong but partial affinities with all four writers. As we have seen, Bauman has distanced himself from Habermas who, during the 1980s, rejected the idea of postmodernity and criticized the suggestion that processes of discursive will formation would necessarily lead to any particular favoured vision of utopia.

Bauman is close to both Adorno and Foucault in his critique of modernity. However, in spite of this, neither Foucault with his views on the nature of discursive practices nor Adorno with his deconstructionist tendencies[17] has a perspective that is particularly sympathetic to Bauman's focus on the ethical self.

Bauman's analysis of the postmodern habitat and his resistance to the strategy for consensus proposed by Habermas both overlap to a significant extent with Lyotard's views. However, Bauman differs from Lyotard in his evaluation of the implications of postmodern cultural fragmentation for individual freedom and fulfilment. In conclusion, it is clear that Bauman cannot be unambiguously aligned with either the Frankfurt School or poststructuralism.

Enlightenment values

In concluding this chapter, I want to return briefly to the comparison with Tocqueville.[18] As I have argued, Bauman is best seen as a 'traveller' from modernity to postmodernity. He believes that the postmodern habitat is destined to be the basis of future society – something he accepts as being almost certain to happen rather than a scenario that he is particularly keen to promote. He is curious to work out how this habitat functions and 'hangs together'. He wants to know the costs and benefits of living there in terms of freedom, security, equality, happiness and justice.

In a similar way, the aristocrat Tocqueville visited the United States in the 1830s in order to see how democracy, which he took to be the pattern of the future, actually worked. In a similar vein to Bauman on postmodernity, Tocqueville regarded democracy as being inevitable rather than welcome. He investigated its culture, values, morality, politics and psychology – those very dimensions that Bauman has analysed in his studies of postmodernity.

However, there is an important difference between these two men. After he had carried out his research for *Democracy in America* (1968), Tocqueville was able to return from America to France, where he had a social and political base from which to fight for aristocratic values and principles, albeit unsuccessfully in the end.

Bauman did not get a similar chance to fight back. For a while in the early 1980s, the rise of Solidarity gave Bauman hope that the 'maturation of socialism' (Bauman 1981) might be finally under way in Poland. If that seed had flourished in the way Bauman wished, it might, perhaps, have been a modernity worth fighting for. However, things did not work out like that. By 1989 Bauman was marooned in postmodernity. In a way, *Modernity and the Holocaust*, his most bitter attack on modernity, was a ritual burning of the boats – ritual because by that time there was no socialist modernity to sail back to.

Bauman has not just been paying a temporary visit to the future, as Tocqueville did in his American trip. By necessity as much as by choice, Bauman has become one of postmodernity's pioneers, a frontiersman; not just a visiting sociologist, but an inhabitant of the postmodern habitat. However, as I have argued, he is an inhabitant whose ways of thinking, feeling and behaving were formed in the 'old world' of modernity.

It is worth recalling Tocqueville's description of the American pioneer recently arrived from Europe, building his new home in the depths of the forest: 'All his surroundings are primitive and wild, but he is the product of eighteen centuries of labour and experience. He wears the clothes and talks the language of a town; . . . he is a very civilised man . . . plunging into the wilderness of the New World with his Bible, axe and newspapers' (Tocqueville 1968: 375).

Bauman still carries his own equivalent of the American pioneer's 'Bible, axe and newspapers' brought from the Old World. From his own 'old world' of modernity, Bauman has brought a deep belief in the capacity and need of individuals to make autonomous life choices. He argues now, as he did then, that they should take personal responsibility for these choices in the knowledge that their effects can often not be predicted or controlled.[19] Bauman has also retained from the 'old world' his intense hatred of poverty and belief in freedom.

Bauman still holds the view, already well developed in the 1960s, that culture is the key arena in which the structure of society is determined. Equally long-standing is his conviction that intellectuals, especially sociologists, should stay close to ordinary men and women, injecting a critical perspective on the deeply conservative and potentially oppressive conventions of 'common sense'.

As I showed in chapter 5, Bauman's picture of the postmodern habitat, with its multitude of competing subcultures, was already part of his vision of modern Poland in the 1960s, although he used different terminology. He was already highly aware of the rootless and inconclusive existence that this type of urban habitat imposed upon its inhabitants.

Finally, Bauman's contempt for the authoritarian imposition of rules by central political authority assisted by legislating intellectuals is reproduced in his deep hostility to communitarian enterprises, which, in his view, are likely to follow a similar strategy of authoritarianism, again backed up by compliant intellectuals.

The standards that Zygmunt Bauman challenges his readers to meet in their personal behaviour at the turn of the millennium are the same as those he was espousing in the 1960s. They are standards of individual responsibility, equality and justice. According to his analysis, these standards were defined by modernity. They are 'western, Enlightenment values' (Bauman 1992a: 225).

Ironically, as Bauman shows, practical attempts to put those very same values into practice were frustrated and crushed by modernity itself. Modernity was unable to live up to its own ideals. As Bauman sees it, the onset of postmodernity removes the obstacles that modernity placed in the way of achieving a just, free and equal society. However, this certainly does not ensure that those values will be realized. In some ways it makes it harder, since global capitalism appears to be impossible to influence or control, in his view.

Nevertheless, as Bauman puts it, these Enlightenment values 'will haunt and pester us to the end of the world' (p. 225). He has made himself their agent and it is this mission that has turned him into a prophet of postmodernity. Bauman wishes the postmodern habitat to be as humane a place as it can possibly be. His strategy is to challenge its inhabitants to live up to the highest standards of the Enlightenment.

11

A Correspondence between Zygmunt Bauman and Dennis Smith

The letters were written in January–February 1997, before the book was completed

First letter

Dear Zygmunt,

Most of your work over the past few years has been exploring the contrast between modernity and postmodernity. These two conditions of existence (frames of mind, ways of looking at and being in the world) co-exist and interweave. So, presumably, a society or culture (and a person or group) can be both modern and post-modern at the same moment.

One of the conditions of postmodernity is stepping outside the promises and illusions of modernity, realizing that they are false even while, at the same time, continuing to participate in an institutional life – factories, offices, schools, surgeries, etc. – which has strong continuity with how it was when the self-images of modernity were more fully accepted. This continuity is expressed, for example, in the persistence of such key forms as bureaucracy and the market (although these are adapted to, for example, a greatly reduced workforce, an increased emphasis on flexibility, a shift of production to 'less developed' societies, etc.).

Were 'postmodern' responses to modernity present, albeit weak and often crushed, from the beginnings of modernity? If so, I suppose scepticism or disbelief on the part of Don Quixote-like old believers (shaped by pre-modern 'culture') has to be distinguished from disillusionment on the part of those who once responded positively to modernity's vision of the world but found through experience that things were not so. Do you have to have once believed in modernity to enter a postmodern frame of mind? Or, to put it another way, is that frame of mind – and the strategies associated with it – shaped by the experience of disillusionment (even though these are inherited by those, coming later, who were never 'illusioned' in the first place)?

There is, I think, a strong suggestion in your writings that the pervasiveness of postmodernity has increased over historical time, and this is associated with a number of things: the accumulation of ambivalences resulting from the tidying-up exercises of the gardening state; the shift away from the state (the ground-clearer) to market seduction as the principal source of regulation and discipline; a change in the intellectual's activity from 'legislator' to 'interpreter' (between cultures or subcultures); the associated transition from the producer/soldier to the consumer/sensation-experiencer as the primary figure; and the globalization of the market, putting many key levers of power and influence outside the grasp of the nation-state.

However, the institutions and practices of modernity remain important and active, for example in managing the 'slow holocaust' of 'flawed consumers' who don't fit in: the poor, the weak, the 'criminal'. (Incidentally, this reminds me of Barrington Moore's analysis of the enclosure movement in English society as a long drawn-out campaign of piecemeal violence against the peasantry.) Also, the temple of postmodernity, the shopping mall, depends upon complex and efficient (modern) bureaucratic systems to get the stuff on the shelves, properly priced, etc.

If the central contradictions of modernity revolve around the creation and handling of ambivalence, then there is, if I understand rightly, a basic tension within postmodernity between, on the one hand, the forms of identity ('who am I? how should I behave?' etc.) offered on the market and available within the kitbags of various psychosocial 'experts' and, on the other hand, the self-sourced moral capacity potentially released by the standing down of legislators ('ascetic priests', etc.) who previously imposed ethical codes and laws on the masses since the 'hoi polloi' could not, it was thought, be trusted to use their freedom wisely.

One issue is: is it possible to build a 'long-range' morality capable of handling the complex and uncontrollable chains of risky consequences flying from our actions, supercharged as these actions are by an ever more powerful technology? First, a side-issue. If I understand rightly, this moral capacity is not an exclusively postmodern phenomenon but can be found generally in zones outside the realm of modernity's predominance, including times and places before modernity has, so to speak, got to work (as is suggested, I think, in Moore's *Injustice*).

The weakening of modernity's hold, then, sees a re-emergence of moral capacity. I see some resemblance, not an identity, with the reassertion of the 'instinct of workmanship' in the latter days of business culture as described by Veblen. Veblen on consumer capitalism also overlaps with some of your themes, although he roots his analysis in the late nineteenth century. Just to continue that theme: I am intrigued by the echoes some of your recent writing has with early-twentieth-century Chicago thinking: the tourist/ vagabond/player/stroller figures, apart from the Benjamin– Simmel resonance, reminded me suddenly of Thomas and Zraniecki's references to bohemian/philistine/creative individuals, although they couch their 'typology' in terms of personality types rather than strategies.

Returning to moral capacity, being-for, etc: you suggest, I think, that a possible route from moral action in the primal 'moral party of two' to the institutionalization of the sort of long-range morality (macro-ethics?) envisaged by Hans Jonas is via political action. This is against the background of having decisively dismissed communitarian visions and enterprises, mainly for their fragmentary tendency, their focus on a few narrow dimensions of human existence in each instance, and in some cases their covert (or explicit) racism. In assessing possible forms of political action liable (or not) to institutionalise an acceptable macro-ethics (e.g. promoting social justice), you outline the deficiencies of 'campaign politics' as discussed by Rorty. Elsewhere (in *Postmodern Ethics*), you dismiss social movements as (again oversimplifying) too narrow and fragmentary in their purpose.

I just wonder whether you are too sweeping in this dismissal of social movements (as distinct from either communitarian enterprises or campaign politics). I recall that some of your earliest academic work, done in your twenties and thirties, was on the British labour movement. Does or did this count as a social movement of the kind you were criticizing? When I read *Between Class and Elite* I had the strong feeling that you greatly admired the leaders of this movement. You noted in that book that human history insidiously defied probabilities but also remarked that the labour movement never set itself targets it did not have the maturity and reserves to meet.

In general, your tone was positive, I thought. It could be argued (a) that the labour movement had some bearing on the emergence of a welfare state, and (b) that for a while at least some aspects of the welfare state institutionalized a macro-ethics of social justice.

Another case that comes to mind is the Polish Solidarity movement. Both the British labour movement and Polish Solidarity have been quite effective at creating myths for themselves – which might be taken as a negative comment except that one result of these myths may, perhaps, have been to nurture a popular demand/expectation that a macro-ethics of social justice should/could be institutionalized.

As far as I can see, social movements can at the very least have strong impacts at the level of micro-ethics in terms of 'I–Other' relations and also might have impacts at the macro level, even re-shaping the identities of whole societies in certain rare circumstances. They cannot do the latter 'alone'. The overall environment – political, economic, ecological, etc. – has to be destabilized in some way creating a general climate of uncertainty. Maybe there is a distinction between social movements in 'normal' times and movements that emerge in times of generalized crisis.

Yours, etc.
Dennis

Second letter

Dear Dennis,

You are surely a most serious contender for the next Olympics target-shooting; you hit all the targets and the bull's eye in each . . . To start with the first of your (and mine, I am pleased to say!) targets: Lyotard said once that one cannot be really modern without being postmodern first . . . What he had in mind, I suppose, was something like the Hegelian distinction between *an sich* and *für sich* – one can only be fully and truly modern, self-consciously modern, once the point has been reached from which one can take a cool long view of the things past, let the Owl of Minerva spread its wings while measuring words against flesh and summing up the gains and losses. In other words, what Lyotard meant was that 'the post-modern' is invisibly, sometimes *incognito*, present in every story of modernity – since the time the story of modernity started to be told ...

But there is another way of looking at that Siamese side of the modern–postmodern twinship: 'the postmodern' as a thorn inserted from the start in the modernity's body, resented most often as all pains are, but also reacted to the way a horse reacts to the spur ...Modern conditions – the more so the livelier is the pace of modernization – spread discontents lavishly and no wonder the search is going on all the time to find out what is wrong and how to heal the wounds or better still blunt the sword (and living in modernity means living in the state of permanent modernization – I think the habit of viewing modernization as 'a road to modernity', and modernity as an end-product of modernization is mistaken to the core: modernity *is* modernization, such social settings are modern which obsessively modernize – break customs before they freeze and produce the ambivalence in order to fight it, classify, differentiate, divide labour and expertise, set ever higher targets for rationality and all in all live-toward-future-while-instantly-forgetting-the-past; modernizing is modernity's mode of being). Inevitably, the search goes occasionally as far as questioning the wisdom of the way of life which breeds so much pain and discontent. It took the postmodern critique a couple of centuries to crystallize into a comprehensive world-view, but it was shadowing modernization from the start (a sort of shadow cabinet, indeed).

And yet it must be stressed that there is discontinuity in that continuity and that 'similar' does not necessarily mean 'the same'. One hears sometimes people pointing out the striking similarities between the Romantic critique of modernity and postmodern scepticism/irony towards the self-confidence and arrogance of the modern spirit – drawing the conclusion that postmodernity is but a 'Romanticism take two', if not just Romanticism resurrected. There is no denying the similarities – and yet there is an essential novelty which tends to be overlooked once the comparison is confined to the inventory of moods and values. Remember Marx's distinction between the 'utopian' and 'scientific' socialisms? Never mind the pretensions betrayed by the choice of names, but the distinction itself contains a sound idea of the essential difference between the criticism 'before' and 'after': 'utopian socialists' viewed the advancing capitalism as a monster which had to (and could!) be stopped so that it would not lie across the correct and righteous progress, while the 'scientific' socialists (that is, Marx himself) considered the shake-up perpetrated by capitalism irreversible and wished to pick up the job at the point where capitalism left it unfinished and build up from there. I guess we can make a similar distinction between early-modern romantic, and late-modern 'postmodern' critique. Post-modernity builds (whatever it builds) on the foundations set firmly in the modern era – it is, unlike the Romantics, not anti-modern, but indeed postmodern.

One can go further than that and point out that the troubles which besotted the denizens of the early modern era, the time of Romanticism, were of a different nature than those which torment postmodern men and women, and so the discontents of the two eras grow from different roots and shoot in different directions. I think one needs today to reverse the Freudian formula for *Das Unbehagen in der Kultur*: our ancestors bewailed the need to surrender a large chunk of their freedom in exchange of a modicum of security, while it has fallen upon us to sacrifice a good deal of our security in exchange for the robust expansion of freedoms. Hence, by the way, another Siamese tinge to the modernity/postmodernity twinship: if the discontents born of modernity glamorize postmodern living, the discontents born of postmodernity time and again restore lustre to modern ways and means. Each side adds vigour to the other one and keeps it alive!

And, of course, as you say so rightly, 'institutions and practices of modernity remain important and active'. Only that here, as elsewhere, there is a fine mesh of continuity and discontinuity. Basically unchanged actions with starkly different consequences. In my view by far the most seminal of such continuous/discontinuous modern procedures is in our times the manufacture of poverty, yet without the old recycling-of-the-poor corrective. The poor of today are no more a 'reserve army of labour'; they are neither exploited nor exploitable (already modernity put paid to their role of the Children of God on which to practise charity and earn spiritual salvation). The postmodern era is perhaps the first not to allocate a function to its poor – not a single redeeming feature which could prompt solidarity with the poor. Postmodern society produces its members as first and foremost consumers – and the poor are singularly unfit for that role; by no stretch of imagination can one hope that they would contribute to the 'consumer-led recovery'. For the first time in history the poor are totally un-functional and wholly useless; as such, they are, for all practical intents and purposes, 'outside society'. The Germans speak today of a *zwei-Drittel Gesellschaft*; it is no more fanciful to expect the coming of a one-third society . . .

I have no quarrel with Ulrich Beck when he says that the history of modernization is far from finished and that there is still a lot of it ahead. I disagree, though, that more modernizing is likely to cure the ailments of our time, as Beck seems to hope. If, for instance, ubiquitous risk is one of our daily pains and fears, modernizing will do precious little to alleviate them. I am afraid that given the non-functionality of the poor, rationalizing things would not come anywhere near solving their problem either. Claus Offe, using the terms in slighly different fashion than the one I apply, said in his *Modernity and the State* that 'the modernization of the parts comes at the cost of modernity of the whole' and we know of no other modernization but the modernization of the parts, an unredeemably partial modernization. Being partial, it cannot but increase the sum total of risk, of chaos, of contingency, of uncontrollability – all those banes on which modernity once declared a war of attrition.

You ask: 'is it possible to build a long-range morality capable of handling . . . etc.' Well, this is, it seems to me, the sixty-four thousand dollar question. Or, rather, the life-and-death issue for our type of human cohabitation. You have put your fingers on the sorest of spots on the face of humanity. In his latest book (*In Defence of Sociology*) Anthony Giddens suggested: 'Breaking away from the aporias of postmodernism, we can see the possibilities of "dialogic democracy", stretching from a "democracy of the emotions" in personal life to the outer limits of the global order.' Well, can we see such possibilities, or can't we? Here, as the Germans would say, *ist der Hund begraben*.

Personally, I find it difficult to 'see the possibilities' Giddens seems to have spotted; and not for the lack of trying on my part. Whether one takes 'democracy of emotions in personal life' (as Giddens does), or the 'moral party of two' (as I prefer, following Lévinas) for the greenhouse or testing site of moral impulse – beyond that relatively narrow territory stretches what looks uncannily as an anti-ethical conspiracy of institutions; it is as if the institutions swore to dash the best of ethical intentions and pushed the effects of human actions in a direction opposite to that which the moral ideas people openly and sincerely profess should have taken them. You know that Hans Jonas, worried by the sharp contrast between the notoriously short reach of our moral imagination and the ever more remote impact of technological capacity saw salvation in working out the principles of 'ethics of distance', one that is becoming imperative now but for which in more primitive stages of our history we had less need or no need at all. Contrary to Jonas, I believe that agreeing on ethical principles and values is by far the easiest part of the task, and one which would not solve anything by itself. On most important principles (avoid pollution, war, violence, hunger, persecution of minorities, etc.), we already agree; each of those principles could count on huge majorities in opinion polls . . . So what? All those widely, perhaps even universally condemned horrors go on unabated, prompted and exacerbated by what we do or what we desist doing. Ethical conscience presses one way, while the logic of daily life – most prominently of economics and politics – presses the other way, and the second gets the upper hand. The abdication or collapse of moral legislators (as far as the legislators themselves are concerned, they have lost little of their predecessors' zeal; but the rules they propound lack institutional grounding, while due to the proliferation and fragmentation of authorities they tend to cancel each other) left the 'primal moral scene' free to generate moral responsibility. This does not necessarily apply to justice, which is morality projected on the big screen of society – and in its essence a problem of politics, not ethics. Whatever bridge or at least gangplank we can imagine linking the always personal and focused moral impulse with necessarily abstract and diffuse rules of justice will need to be built with political means and using political action as its building material.

But what politics? I go one by one through the venerable, the well tested, and the yet untried 'talk of the town' political agencies, and find them all wanting under present circumstances. Of democracy we know from John Kenneth Galbraith that a 'contented majority' is perfectly capable of legally voting any noxious minority into prison or out of existence. Political parties, missing clear-cut class division and 'focal issues' which may serve as an axis around which to wrap disparate grievances and postulates of large divisions of society, tend to settle now for 'rainbow platforms' patched up incoherently of vote-gathering slogans and the latest vagaries of 'public opinion', that artefact of statistics and the obituary to the collective political actor RIP; the outcome of that is not just the disappearance of genuine political choices (Tony Blair, say, turning into John Major-in-waiting), but the incapacity of any non-suicidal politician to take up and even less to promote any issue meant for more than an instant consumption and trading off some immediate vote-sucking potential for some more distant and thus far less tangible benefits; none of the above mentioned bridge-building problems can be conceivably tackled by party politics. Social movements? They are now mostly 'opinion polls by other means', players in the vote-catching game; in such capacity their effectiveness is at its highest when it comes to pressing/blackmailing governmental agencies into concessions, that is to obtaining redistribution of preferential treatment (for instance, dumping toxic waste or toxic Gypsies in other people's backyards or sending a noisy by-pass around other people's houses); they fare much worse as the gathering points of broad interests, as transformers of 'classes *in sich*' into 'classes *für sich*' and the agencies of long-term and fundamental transformations; they also as a rule have a very brief life-span, remaining all along loose aggregates of individuals brought together momentarily by the contingency of single nuisance and falling apart again once the nuisance has been removed. And this is not the fault of their leaders and apostles, not the outcome of wrong-headed policies or the lack of imagination. Their plight reflects rather faithfully the essentially non-cumulative, non-integrative nature of the present-day individual sufferings and grievances; in terms of Barrington Moore Jr, whom you invoke, the virtual impossibility of congealing/translating the disperse and fleeting ('one-off'), thin ('single-issue') sentiments of injustice into a full-blooded, comprehensive and solid model of justice. The movements of today already are – not by choice, but by sheer necessity – phenomena from Rorty's 'campaign politics' realm, which has come to replace the domain of 'movement politics'. As the handling of 'big issues' demanding 'deep transformations' goes, they are poor substitutes for their predecessors and further exacerbate the selfsame fragmentation of the political scene which made the substitution inevitable. But here you are, they are the last soldiers on the battlefield; whatever you wish to do, you must start from here . . . It is not that I have lost my sympathy and respect for labour movements and the strides they made or enforced in the perpetual human war against injustices; it is just that the labour movement has its days of glory behind and now is no more than a (relatively weak, and weakening) player in the game of redistribution.

To rub salt in the wound: even if by some semi-miracle a popular movement emerged sufficiently integrated and long-lived to advance a cause more substantive than another shifting of another burden, where would you find the agency capable of 'getting the thing done'? For the last two centuries all politics held the state to be its plenipotentiary and executor, and ambitious politics demand ambitious and resourceful executors ... Most states of today are neither ambitious nor resourceful – they lack the military, the economic and the cultural sovereignty to decide and impose the rules of the game, let alone the game's outcome. The causes, particularly radical causes, have every chance of ending up in thin air once pressed in a tangible shape. The strings that move things on the ground rise far above the grasp of any single state; and the most important among them (deregulated capital, privatized 'public utilities', unbridled trade and finance) bypass the realm of politics altogether. There are the anonymous, unnamable, inscrutable, enigmatic 'global forces' on the top. The 'invisible hand' is now big enough to grip the globe; but it is more invisible than ever.

The 'global scene' reminds one of the Internet: everybody puts his/her finger in, but no one can squeeze the hand to hold the whole. The global chaos is the sum total of orderly parts; the more orderly the parts, the more chaotic the chaos ... From the perspective of the 'global scene', the states are local police stations, which use coercion to force their precincts into the placid acceptance of *laissez-faire*. The impotence of the states to influence the course of affairs on 'their own' territory seems but a minor irritant when juxtaposed with the complete absence of legislative, executive and judiciary powers entitled to as much, or rather as little, as to dream of effectively interfering with the vagaries of global trends; while conflicts and injustices internal to the states pale into insignificance when seen against the background of the global polarization of wealth, income and all the associated dimensions of humanity.

Now this is something to think about. I am doing my thinking for quite a few years by now, with nothing to show that I'd feel satisfied with. I am eager to hear your argument; one of your strengths I admired most over the years was your finely tuned sensitivity to the hidden links between the local and the global, the economic and the cultural, the political and everything else – and without taking proper heed of those links one cannot even begin to untangle the mesh.

Yours, etc.
Zygmunt

Third letter

Dear Zygmunt,

I was fascinated by your survey of the global scene. Let me pick up
from your conclusion which gave a bird's-eye view of our present
world. You saw it as a place in which states act as local police stations trying to maintain order (as opposed to justice) in their own
particular backyards; meanwhile, above their heads powerful
global trends are at work beyond their control, generating injustice
and suffering on a transcontinental scale.

Now, I suppose the general outlines of this picture are not peculiar to our own late modern/postmodern age and could apply at
pretty well any time during the past one (or even two) hundred
years. I would say there are three relatively new elements, however.
The first is the fact that we expect (or did expect until very recently)
'our' states to take responsibility for delivering substantial social
rights to us as citizens. The second is the fact that multinational
companies (successors of long-distance traders going back to the
Genoese, etc.) have greater capacity than ever before to store, access
and communicate information – so they can monitor and (perhaps)
control the different aspects of their operations to a much greater
extent than previously. The third new feature is the increased cost-
liness of the routine operations and unintended errors resulting
from the workings of global capitalism – which are not subject to
some benevolent master plan which takes all our interests into
account (instead there is, as you say, local rationality combined with
global irrationality).

The costs of global capitalism are inflicted upon our environment
(natural and social) in the form of a steady erosion of the conditions
which make for 'civilized' or 'decent' existence. Behind this lurks
the unsettling threat posed by the unholy mixture of increased
interdependence and more powerful technology. In other words,
failures in monitoring, control and prediction could and might
produce widely ramifying and ultimately disastrous consequences,

Let me go back to the first of those three 'new elements'. We are
losing our taken-for-granted assumption that a society in which the
state 'speaks for' the 'people' will normally be able to provide the
means for a coherent and satisfying life to be enjoyed by the vast
majority of the population. But where on earth did we get that
assumption from in the first place? I think it was the result of some
recent (and very unusual) conditions that lasted less than a quarter

of a century. When I say 'we' I am referring to the 'we' who experienced the period and social environment I know best, which is post-1945 Western Europe.

I think we can now see that stability from the mid-1940s to the mid-1960s was a result of the United States' international near-supremacy (with USSR playing the role of international enemy). America's military success and economic power helped implant 'capitalist democracy' as an ideal in Western Europe and other bits of the 'free world'. The capital (economic, social, cultural) accumulated in the colonial period throughout Western Europe cushioned the impact upon West Europeans of the USA's effective acquisition of the old European empires (EU and USA interests currently compete to insert themselves into the vacuum left by the 'liberation' of the last of these empires, i.e. the Russian empire in Eastern/Central Europe).

In 'undefeated' Britain, in particular, there was a strong feeling of historical continuity between the pre- and postwar periods. The loss of the British empire, a repressed trauma still not worked out, was a fairly drawn out process (twenty years?) compared to the sudden and intense shocks of defeat and invasion experienced on the continent. The British welfare-state reforms of the late 1940s seemed to be fulfilling a class-related ideal nurtured during the 1920s and 1930s. Meanwhile, in the United States, the post-1945 position was easy to interpret as the natural culmination of that society's rise to power in 'the American century'. This sort of thing conspired to conceal (from 'Anglo-Saxon' eyes even more than from 'continental' eyes) just how unusual the postwar period was.

What I am working towards saying is that just at the moment (in the 1990s) we are intensely aware of the state's inadequacies as an agent for steering us through danger towards security and fulfilment precisely because we are reacting to the pain of losing only recently (the key decade was, perhaps, the 1970s) some very special circumstances enjoyed in the 1950s and 1960s which allowed us to believe that this could indeed be the state's role in conjunction with a benevolent capitalism. There is more novelty in our shocked renewed awareness of the state's inadequacy than there is in the 'objective' situation.

In a sense this has happened before, earlier in this century. In the years between the first two world wars the propertied classes were dismayed at the fact that the 'bourgeois state' was unable to control the demographic tides and xenophobic hatreds swirling through

Europe. Instead, the waves were ridden by demagogues, bandits and generalissimos – such as Hitler, Mussolini and Stalin – who had expansionist, sometimes global ambitions reaching way beyond the bounds of existing national borders. There were some parallels in Asia (Japan? China?). Meanwhile, everywhere (e.g. India) colonial rule was under strain. In this earlier case the conventional bourgeois-liberal state failed to manage the people; more recently it has failed to manage capital.

Perhaps we could say that in Western Europe (I suspect the analysis might be different in part for USA) there have been two 'golden generations' in the past century or so; by that I mean generations of people who could feel that the world was delivering more or less what they hoped from it. Neither of these golden generations included the whole population. The first encompassed the professional, managerial and entrepreneurial upper middle class (and those 'above' them socially) in the two decades before World War I. Life was good for them. They had plenty of servants. They enjoyed the technological benefits of the second industrial revolution – gas, electricity, petrochemicals, improved medicine, etc. – as means to enjoying a world that technology had not yet transformed. They could travel more or less where they wanted. Popular unrest at home and in the colonies was being contained.

The irony of the period since 1914 is that the rest of the world has been demanding for themselves (in effect, demanding for everybody) something like the way of life this golden generation had – but which its members could only enjoy because they were a minority floating in a bubble belonging to a highly specific time and place, a bubble destined (as we now realize) to burst as the European upper bourgeoisie went over the rapids: 1914, 1917, 1933, etc.

Between the two world wars the spread of the franchise to all happened far more quickly than the extension downward of bourgeois comforts, resulting in the permeation of political life with intense class hatreds. However, after 1945 quite a lot of people enjoyed the newly available benefits of mass production technology combined with political stability and a feeling that the world was being run on their behalf and for their benefit. So, the second 'golden generation' encompasses the blue collar/white collar upper working/lower middle class (and upwards, socially) between the end of World War II and the mid-1960s. Capitalist democracy was, in effect, a mechanism for providing this part of society, for a while at least, with a mass-produced and scaled-down version of the urban life-styles enjoyed by the pre World War I bourgeoisie.

The largest single benefit the state provided in this remarkable and short-lived period (two decades out of five centuries of modernity) was a guarantee of full employment. The material benefits of capitalist democracy were largely delivered by capitalism; the role of the 'democratic' state was mainly to ensure that they were widely (not equally) distributed through the job market. (I wonder to what extent even the state's role in guaranteeing full employment may be less than it seems, given that the postwar period was one of economic growth and re-building after the four decades of war and political instability; in other words, demand for labour was bound to be high in those postwar decades.)

How should we react to the obvious imbalance between the global reach of late modern capitalism and the fragmented character and (increasingly) limited ambitions of late modern states? It seems to me that this situation parallels on a global scale the one that existed in Europe in the fifteenth and sixteenth centuries. It is quite conventional to argue that merchants in this period were free to develop their business operations in ways that were profitable and responsive to the growing market because – unlike in China – they were not confronted with a single mighty political authority able to regulate or tax them out of existence. In other words, political multipolarity was good for capitalist growth.

However, democratic national states did not exist so the question of what the labouring classes and the poor thought about the misery and damage produced by capitalism was kept off the political agenda except as a law-and-order issue. Furthermore, the prospect of inescapable pollution had not yet arisen: London was already 'the great wen' by Pepys's time but the countryside was readily available to the rich and, in any case, a risk-free existence was not envisaged in that age of plagues and dangerous travel. It is not too difficult to imagine (I obviously do not mean 'welcome') a return to some aspects of that social situation; perhaps there are elements of it at present in some parts of the ex-Soviet bloc.

More generally, if effective power is currently drifting into the hands of multinational companies and away from national states, this evokes an image of captains of industry at the helms of those large, expensive, complex craft, their corporations, weaving intricate passages through increasingly crowded shipping lanes, desperately trying to avoid collisions – with the state providing a law-and-order function, keeping the peace where necessary both on board and in harbour. This will involve (has already involved) some loss of citizenship rights – although some company employees may well find their job-related privileges increase. It won't be a new situation for the state to be mainly performing a specialist law-and-order function on behalf of property. That has, after all, been one of its main functions during modernity, including the relatively brief period of Keynesian welfarism during the mass-production/mass-consumption conditions of the second industrial revolution.

There at least two issues at stake. One is control. The other is rights. The loss of citizenship rights seems to me to follow (not inevitably but in practice) from the fact that the third industrial revolution has produced a capitalism that can get along with a much smaller labour force. The unemployed lack bargaining power and so cannot defend their rights. This brings disillusionment – which is grist to the mill of postmodern culture. The question of control (i.e. 'can we avoid environmental catastrophe through runaway technology?') seems to depend, in part at least, on the developing balance of power between businesspeople and professionals in the state/capital nexus. The elimination of all risk seems a utopian prospect. However, there is no reason to suppose that the desire for physical survival in decent circumstances should not be as powerful a motivation as balance-sheet profit in the ranks of the business community.

Almost by definition, the poor and weak will be unable to act directly on behalf of their own interests. The best hope for those who wish to act on behalf of the disadvantaged via the state may be that politicians do have a few points of leverage in their relationship with businesspeople. For example, during the next few decades Western business interests are going to look towards state agencies to help them manage the two major transitions in global power now under way: the assimilation of Eastern and Central Europe into wider European markets and institutions, and the increasing power of societies located in the Pacific Rim, notably China. (Hong Kong should make a nice case study.)

It is at least possible that some politicians may be able to use the leverage with business gained from their foreign policy activities to persuade capital to make investments which protect the environment and serve the interests of the poor and weak both at home and abroad. This is unlikely to happen without the backing of what

Galbraith calls the 'scientific and educational estate' and some recourse to the moral legacy of the Keynesian-welfarist period, now rapidly being eroded. In favourable circumstances, this 'social democratic' legacy could play the same role for the postmodernist era of the third ('Japanized') industrial revolution that the feudal Judeo-Christian legacy played for early industrial capitalism (to follow Schumpeter's argument here).

I am trying to find a way out of the pessimism implied by your perfectly accurate picture of our present condition. Are the hopes of moral re-engagement the soft imaginings produced by life inside the bubble of existence occupied by the British since 1945? Would substantial experience of a 'modern' existence outside the bubble produce a different point of view?

Yours, etc.
Dennis

Fourth letter

Dear Dennis,

One can rely on you to lay bare whatever seems to have been hidden safely beneath piles of words and to cross all the uncrossed t's and dot all the undotted i's; your letter proves this, if another proof was needed, beyond reasonable doubt. But you also want me to pronounce on yet unrealized future realities, and that I avoid with all my strength. One of my teachers, professor Lipinski, told me once: Zygmunt, never predict, and particularly never predict the future . . . How right he was. Everything of importance that occurred in our convoluted century came unannounced and unanticipated (so much so that people kept denying its happening well in the midst of it). None of the glittering tools we have acquired to dissect and examine living bodies allow us to surmise where the bodies would have turned next were they not deprived of life through our dissection. (Call it, if you wish, the *sozialwissenschaftliche* principle of indetermination. You can know human things only if you first dehumanize them – cutting the indefinite to the size of a definite, tapering possibilities to the stretch of the data and trimming the *autopoiesis* to norm-guided stochastics, and otherwise forcing the unembraceable into embrace.)

Historical precedents are notoriously misleading as tools of predicting the future (or, for that matter, of sheer understanding the present – the past of that future; my *Memories of Class* was intended as a case study of historical memories as blinkers rather than spy-glasses); they sharpen the focus on the similar, thereby exiling the different, and perhaps the decisive, to the background where it may be glossed over (the different is the most decisive almost by definition: after all, we look for 'historical precedents' precisely because we sense the novelty of the place from which we undertake our exploratory travels). In short, the historical-precedents device imposes upon realities an alien structure, which maims its true shape and prompts a derivative blindness to its own dynamics.

The difference I have in mind between the postmodern world of weak states and the premodern world of the dentist-like (the unforgettable metaphor of Ernest Gellner) kings' and princes' realms you so aptly, with great historic sense, describe, is not a difference of scale only (more traders, less troops; or faster movements, shorter border checks). Present-day supranationals are similar to East-Indian Companies in many a respect, but if we want to understand what is going on in the world of supranationals, we had better concentrate on what divides them from the East-lndian Company. Those traders were either path-finders for the troops or (more often, particularly from the eighteenth century on) following the armies *of occupation*. That variety of free trade, *laissez-faire*, open-the-ports pressure had military invasions and imposing a foreign rule for its principal instruments. Well, the present-day wisdom is that it is cheaper ('makes more economic sense') to keep the neighbour in debt rather than under military occupation. I guess that the spurt to take political power over the economically colonized territories was an oblique tribute to the modern might of the political, and above all of the state. Today's tribute to that cult is mainly a lip-service paid in electoral speeches. Who would bother now to invade and conquer and set garrisons in conquered lands when no border guards, however heavily armed, would as much as note the inflow or outflow of finances? How insignificant the governments of the day's intentions may be Carlsson of Sweden has learned recently the hard way, forced by that fleshless monster, 'the financial markets', to reverse the policies which won him the elections six months before. Tony Blair managed to learn that a lighter way, grooming and grimming himself into a lookalike of John Major well before knocking on 10 Downing Street . . .

The present-day 'New World Disorder' (the concept I borrowed from Kenneth Jowitt) cannot be explained away by pointing to the

morning-after semi-inebriated headache in the aftermath of the
Great Schism and the collapse of the power-block political routine.
It points, rather, to our sobering up – to our sudden awareness of
the essentially elemental and contingent nature of things – which
before was not so much non-existent, as barred from sight by the
all-energy-consuming day-to-day reproduction of balance between
the world powers. By dividing the world, power politics conjured
up *the apparition of totality*. That world was made whole by assigning to each nook and cranny of the globe its significance in the
'global order of things' – to wit, in the two power-camps' conflict
and equilibrium. The world was a totality in as far as there was
nothing in that world which could escape such significance and so
nothing could be indifferent from the point of view of the balance
between the two powers that appropriated a considerable part
of the world and cast the rest in the shadow of that appropriation.
Everything in the world had a meaning, and that meaning
emanated from a halved, yet single centre – from the two enormous
power blocks locked up, riveted and glued to each other in all-out
combat. With the Great Schism out of the way, the world does not
look a totality any more; it looks rather as a field of scattered and
disparate forces, sedimenting in places difficult to predict and
gathering momentum impossible to arrest.

To put it in a nutshell: *no one seems to be now in control*. Worse still
– it is not clear what 'being in control' could, under the circumstances, be like. Like before, all ordering is local and issue-oriented,
but there is no longer a locality which could pronounce for mankind
as a whole, or an issue which could stand up for the totality of
global affairs. It is this novel and uncomfortable perception which
has been articulated (with little benefit to intellectual clarity) in
the currently fashionable concept of *'globalization'*. The deepest
meaning conveyed by the idea of globalization is that of the indeterminate, unruly and self-propelled character of world affairs; the
absence of a centre, of a controlling desk, of a board of directors, of
a managerial office. Globalization is Jowitt's 'New World Disorder'
under another name. It stands for helplessness and surrender – not
ambition and self-confidence: in this the term 'globalization' *differs
radically* from another term, that of 'universalization' – once consti-
tutive of the modern discourse of global affairs, but by now fallen
into disuse and by and large forgotten.

Together with such concepts as civilization, development, convergence, consensus and many other terms of early- and classic-
modern debate, 'universalization' conveyed the hope, the intention,

and the determination of order-making. Those concepts were coined on the rising tide of modern powers and the modern intellect's ambitions. They announced the will to make the world different from what it was and better than it was, and expand the change and the improvement to global, species-wide dimensions. It also declared the intention to make life conditions of everyone everywhere, and so everybody's life chances, equal. Nothing of all that has been left in the meaning of globalization, as shaped up by the present discourse. The new term refers primarily to 'global effects', notoriously unintended and unanticipated, rather than 'global undertakings'. Yes, it says: our actions may have, and often do have, global effects; but no, we do not have nor are likely to obtain the means to plan and execute actions globally. 'Globalization' is not about what we all or at least the most resourceful and enterprising among us wish or hope *to do*. It is about what *is happening to us all*. It explicitly refers to the foggy and slushy 'no man's land' stretching beyond the reach of the design and action capacity of anybody in particular.

How come that this vast expanse of man-made wilderness (not the 'natural' wilderness which modernity set out to conquer and tame; but the post-domestication wilderness, which emerged *after* the conquest and *out of it*) has sprung into vision, and why it did it, with that formidable power of obstinacy which is taken to be the defining mark of 'hard reality'?

A plausible explanation is the growing experience of weakness, indeed of impotence, of the habitual, taken-for-granted ordering agencies. Among the latter, the pride of place throughout the modern era belonged to the state (one is tempted to say: the *territorial* state, but the ideas of the state and 'territorial sovereignty' have become in modern practice and theory synonymous, and thus the phrase 'territorial state' turned pleonastic). The meaning of 'the state' has been precisely that of an agency claiming the sole legitimate right and the adequate resources to set up and enforce the rules and the norms binding the run of affairs over certain territory; the rules and the norms hoped and expected to turn contingency into determination, ambivalence into *Eindeutigkeit*, randomness into predictability – in short, chaos into order. To order a certain section of the world meant to set up a state endowed with the sovereignty to do just that. And the ambition to enforce a certain model of preferred order at the expense of other, competitive, models could be implemented solely through acquiring the vehicle of the state or occupying the driving seat of the existing one. Max Weber defined the state as the agency claiming the monopoly of the means of coercion and their use.

Order-making requires huge and continuous effort, which in turn calls for considerable resources. The legislative and executive sovereignty of the state was accordingly perched on the 'tripod of sovereignties': military, economic and cultural. An effective order-making capacity was unthinkable unless supported by the ability to effectively defend the territory against challenges of other models of order, both from outside and inside the realm; by the ability to balance the books of the *Nazionalökonomie*; and by the ability to muster enough cultural resources to sustain the state's identity and distinctiveness. Only few populations aspiring to state sover-. eignty of their own were large and resourceful enough to pass such a demanding test. The times when the ordering job was undertaken and performed primarily, perhaps solely, through the agency of sovereign states were for that reason the times of relatively few states; and the establishment of any sovereign state required as a rule the suppression of state-formative ambitions of many lesser collectivities: undermining whatever they might possess of inchoate military capacity, economic self-sufficiency and cultural distinctiveness. Under the circumstances, the 'global scene' was the theatre of inter-state politics, which through armed conflicts or bargaining aimed first and foremost at the drawing and maintaining ('internationally guaranteeing') of the boundaries that set apart and enclosed the territory of each state's legislative and executive sovereignty. 'Global politics' concerned itself mostly with sustaining the principle of full and uncontested sovereignty of each state over its territory, with the effacing of the few 'blank spots' remaining on the world map, and with fighting off the danger of ambivalence arising from the overlapping of sovereignties. The meaning of the 'global order', consequently, boiled down to the sum-total of a number of local orders, each effectively maintained and efficiently policed by one, and one only, territorial state.

I anticipate you retorting: well, it only seems to those naive people to be like that – *we* now know better; with the benefit of retrospective wisdom we know that 'state sovereignty' was always to a large degree a sham. It was never so radical as the politicians and their court poets used to claim . . . You would be right, of course, but it makes a hell of a difference what people think when they act and even the falsest of pretences tends to become real in its consequences . . .

One way or the other, that genuine or imagined parcelled-out world of sovereign states was superimposed for almost half a century and until recently with two power blocks, each promoting a certain degree of coordination between state-managed orders within the territories of their respective 'meta-sovereignty', coupled with the assumption of each state's military, economic and cultural insufficiency. Gradually yet relentlessly, a new principle was promoted – in political practice faster than in political theory – of the supra-state integration, with the 'global scene' seen increasingly as the theatre of coexistence and competition between blocks of states, rather than states themselves. The Bandung initiative to establish the incongruous 'non-block block', and the recurrent efforts to align of non-aligned states, was an oblique acknowledgement of that new principle. It was, though, consistently and effectively sapped by the two super-blocks, which treated the rest of the world as the twentieth-century equivalent of the 'blank spots' of the nineteenth-century state-building and state-enclosure race. Non-alignment, refusal to join one or another of the super-blocks, sticking to the old-fashioned and increasingly obsolete principle of supreme sovereignty vested with the state, was the equivalent of that 'no man's land' ambivalence which was fought off tooth and nail, competitively yet in unison, by modern states at their formative stage.

The political super-structure of the Great Schism era barred from sight the deeper, and – as it has now transpired – more seminal and lasting transformations in the mechanism of order-making. The change affected above all the role of the state. All three legs of the 'sovereignty tripod', however rickety they might have been before, have now been broken beyond repair. The military, economic and cultural self-sufficiency, indeed self-sustainability, of the state – any state – ceased to be a viable prospect. In order to retain their law-and-order policing ability, the states had to seek alliances and voluntarily surrender ever larger chunks of their sovereignty.

When the curtain was eventually torn apart, it uncovered an unfamiliar scene, populated by bizarre characters: states which, far from being forced to give up their sovereign rights, actively and keenly sought the surrender and clamoured for their sovereignty to be taken away and dissolved in the super-state formations; long deceased yet born again, or never heard of but now duly invented 'ethnicities', much too small and inept to pass any of the traditional tests of sovereignty, but now demanding states of their own and the right to legislate and police order on their own territory; old nations escaping the federalist cages in which they had been incarcerated against their will, only to use their newly acquired decision-making freedom to pursue dissolution of their political, economic and military independence in the European market and NATO alliance. The new chance, contained in the ignoring of the stern and demanding conditions of statehood, has found its acknowledgement in the dozens of 'new nations' rushing to add new seats in the already overcrowded UN building, not designed to accommodate such numbers of 'equals'. Paradoxically, it is the demise of state sovereignty that made the idea of statehood so tremendously popular. In the caustic estimate of Eric Hobsbawm, once the Seychelles can have a vote in the UN as good as Japan's, 'the majority of the members of the UN are soon likely to consist of the late twentieth century (republican) equivalents to Saxe-Coburg-Gotha and Schwarzburg-Sonderhausen'.

To put it in a nutshell: today, *unlike* in the past, global finance, trade and the information industry depend for their liberty of movement and for their unconstrained freedom to pursue their ends on the political fragmentation, the *morcellement*, of the world scene. They have all, one may say, developed vested interests in 'weak states' – that is, in such states as are *weak* but nevertheless remain states. Deliberately or subconsciously, such inter-state institutions as there are exert coordinated pressures on all member or dependent states to destroy systematically everything which could stem or slow down the free movement of capital and limit market liberty. Throwing wide open the gates and abandoning any thought of autonomous economic policy is the preliminary, and meekly complied with, condition of eligibility for financial assistance from world banks and monetary funds. Weak states are precisely what the New World Order, all too often mistaken for the world disorder, needs to sustain and reproduce itself. 'Quasi-states' can be easily reduced to the (useful) role of local police precincts, securing a modicum of order required for the conduct of business, but need not be feared as effective brakes on the global companies' freedom; it is as if the borderposts have been manned mainly to make sure that no one stops the free passage of capital and trade . . . As Michel Crozier pointed out many years ago, domination always consists in leaving as much leeway and freedom of manoeuvre as possible to oneself, while imposing as close as possible a constraint on the decision making of the dominated side; to rule, said Crozier, is to be close to the 'source of uncertainty'. This strategy was successfully applied once by state powers, which now find themselves on its receiving end – it is now world capital and money which are the focus and the source of uncertainty. It is not difficult to see that the replacement of territorial 'weak states' by some sort of global legislative and policing powers would be detrimental to the interests of the extra-territorial companies. And so it is easy to suspect that far from acting at cross-purposes and being at war with each other, political 'tribalization' and economic 'globalization' are close allies and fellow conspirators.

Integration and fragmentation, globalization and territorialization are mutually complementary processes; more precisely still, two sides of the same process, that of the worldwide redistribution of sovereignty, power and freedom to act. It is for this reason that – following Roland Robertson's suggestion – it is advisable to speak of *glocalization* rather than 'globalization', of a process inside which the coincidence and intertwining of synthesis and dissipation, integration and decomposition are anything but accidental and even less rectifiable.

As to the 'loss of citizen rights': the notion of the 'citizen' makes sense only together with the 'polis', and the crux of our problem is where to locate the 'polis'; or how to make it fat enough to support the 'citizen'. One by one, the contemporary states cede the domains once under their control to the market game. 'Privatization' affects the economics of things, but it also changes beyond recognition the meaning of the political – the more thorough it is, the more toothless is the 'polis' and the thinner the contents of 'citizenship'. The demise of the welfare state is not just the outcome of a change of mood or the 'great compromise' going out of fashion; there are simply not enough resources left in the public domain (as measured by the scope of state administration) to sustain such a vast distributive operation. Galbraith wrote of the 'contented majority' which tends for the first time in the history of electoral democracy to vote the deprived out of state-managed remedies; but would even a 'discontented majority', were it somehow to come about once more, be capable to arrest the trend which, as I suspect, has already passed a point of no return? Emaciation of citizenship is not a by-product of political mistakes and neglect – it seems rather such a corollary of the postmodern quasi-state as strong citizenship used to be of the boisterous and resourceful modern state. There is less and less flesh and substance and attraction and stakes at the level occupied half a century ago by the 'nation states'.

You juxtapose the 'desire of physical survival in decent circumstances' with 'balance sheet profit' and ask which may be a stronger motivation. I would dearly wish to share your hope that the first would prevail over the second. But to be put on the same table and compared in size by forces stronger than academic imagery, where are they to meet, recognize each other as competitors and cross the swords? One aspect of 'late modernity' is (despite the 'globalization of information flow', widely cherished and applauded by the chattering classes) the polarization of experience: the same sea is lived by some as surfing beach or marina, by others as Bermuda Triangle. To anticipate your justified counter-argument from historical precedents, I would like to quote from my recent ICA speech (on the occasion of the new Giddens publication) in which I elaborate a bit on the *new* (new!) 'non-functionality' of the poor, which I briefly mentioned in my last letter to you:

> The poor will be always with us; and so will the rich – according to the age-old popular wisdom, now intensely dug up from the oblivion in which it was kept during the brief romance with the 'welfare state' and the sponsored/assisted 'development'. Yes, indeed, the rich/poor split is neither a novelty nor a temporary irritant which, with due effort, will go away tomorrow or some time later. The point is, however, that hardly ever before was this split so unambiguously, unequivocally, a *split*; a division unredeemed and unrelieved by mutual services or reciprocal dependency; a division with no more underlying unity than that between the clean typescript and the waste-paper bin. The rich, who happen to be at the same time the resourceful and the powerful ones among the actors of the political scene, do not need the poor either for the salvation of their souls (which they do not believe they have and which at any rate they would not consider worthy of care) or for staying rich or getting richer (which they gather would be easier if not for the calls to share some of the riches with the poor). The poor are not God's children on which to practise the redeeming charity. They are not the 'reserve army of labour' which needs to be groomed back into wealth-production. Neither they are the consumers which must be tempted and cajoled into 'giving lead to recovery'. Whichever way you look at them, the poor *are of no use*. This is a real novelty in a world undergoing perhaps the deepest transformation in the long history of mankind.
>
> The unity/dependency which underlay most historical forms of the rich/poor division used to be in all times the necessary condition of that – however residual – solidarity with the poor, which inspired the efforts, however half-hearted and incomplete, to relieve the poor's plight. It is that unity/dependency which is now missing. No wonder the pollsters of both competing camps informed their respective candidates for the US presidency that the voters want the benefits of the poor to be cut together with the taxes of the rich. No wonder both rivals did their best to outspit each other in their proposals to cut down welfare assistance and to lavish the saved funds on building new prisons and employing more police [. . .]

In his recent witty account of *The Struggle for Cultural Identity and Intellectual Porkbarrelling*, Jonathan Freedman restated a seldom recalled, though for that reason no less obvious truth: that 'the logics that develop in underclass neighbourhoods are likely to be of a different nature than those that develop among the highly educated world travellers of the culture industries'. The emergent, postmodern division is, according to Freedman, one between the new free-roaming cosmopolitan, thoroughly modern yet without modernism (that is, without a unifying, universalizing, rationalizing project) and the increasingly fixed and rapidly 'ethnicizing' masses. Hence 'the hybridity experienced by the cultural elite' 'opposed to the balkanization and tribalization experienced at the bottom of the system'.

Two worlds, two experiences; how to build a bridge – a gangplank at least reaching, as Giddens suggests is possible, from the 'democracy of emotions' of the first to the 'outer limits' of the second? This is, I suggest, *the postmodern question*. And also a quandary which goes some way towards explaining why it is so easy to list the postmodern discontents and so damn difficult to heal them.

We seem to have divided our roles; you stress continuity, I obsessively trace discontinuities . . . Is this a matter of temperament? Or rather the logic of our discussion? Perhaps a little bit of both. I do want to round up this letter with restating what I said in the beginning: while searching the precedents/continuities supplies the frames to intellectually domesticate the strange and unfamiliar, it also easily misleads into mistaking the wild beast for a pet yet untrained or getting awry . . . And this may be a very costly mistake – just how costly, one would not *live* to appreciate. The most important consideration to me, however, is that no amount of repetition is, contrary to our regularity-loving reason, a valid cause to assume that the future will be 'more of the same' or that history will go on running in circles or that people in 'the same' circumstances will reach for 'the same' weapons and take 'the same' positions (even logically thinking in terms of the 'sameness' is seriously flawed – remember Wittgenstein's incisive critique of the idea). What we both seem to assert in unison is that, as far as the solution to the present troubles is concerned, we have a fight on our hands; we only differ as to the degree of probability with which the outcome of that fight, and the very way in which it is going to be conducted, is predictable; and on what intellectual resources it is advisable to draw when playing the game of the prediction. Looking forward to another display of your exquisite non-sequitur-spotting skills.

Yours, etc.
Zygmunt

Fifth letter

Dear Zygmunt,

Thanks for your last letter which prompted me to go back to Wittgenstein. I returned from him with a warning ringing in my ears about the danger of indulging our 'craving for generality' when instead we should be staring long and hard at the unique, the particular (e.g. in this case, our unprecedented postmodern existence). Going to Wittgenstein, I find a philosopher with a deep moral and spiritual sense who is burning to say the unsaid or unsayable about what the world is, what it consists of. Coming back to Zygmunt Bauman, I reckon I find a not dissimilar determination to capture and convey what is new, different and disturbing about our present condition.

Wittgenstein insists that what we cannot speak about we must pass over in silence. In a similar vein, though not in the same context, you point out, quite fairly, that we cannot predict the future. But I was not asking for any predictions. I was, rather, thinking about some possible strategies – those I suggested were broadly Galbraithian – for trying to stop the most horrible possibilities of our present and immediate future from turning into fact. I was suggesting there might be some mileage in identifying specific contexts in which politicians, public officials and 'experts' could exercise leverage over corporations in the medium-term future. This was on the assumption that business networks, at least, spanned the globe and so we should try to influence them for 'good', if possible.

In exploring this avenue, I was no doubt letting myself be seduced by the oversimplifying idea that 'global control' had fallen into the hands of an 'international technostructure'. You replied by showing me that, just because we are being tossed about helplessly by devastating whirlwinds, that does not mean there is a Wizard of Oz or some Wicked Witch directing them.

So I reorient myself by remembering your suggestion (I am paraphrasing) that we postmoderns are now sadder and wiser spectators, observing modernity as, like an ocean liner, lights blazing and band playing, it passes by and slips away into the distance, leaving mess and turbulence in its wake. We have been deprived of the illusion of security and happiness enjoyed by the liner's partying passengers, especially those travelling first class. We ourselves used to be those very passengers but now, instead, we are just as likely to find ourselves tipped unceremoniously into the ocean itself.

As we splash about looking for a barrel to scramble into or a piece of driftwood to cling to, we might well be persuaded that our lot is no more than to be acted on, unpredictably, uncontrollably, by a globalized (or 'glocalized') system of forces. No wonder we admire round-the-world yachtspersons and balloonists – postmodern heroes all – whose success depends on the skill or luck to nudge themselves into the midst of powerful currents at just the right point so they are swept along in the direction they want to go.

However, what I find really disturbing about our situation now is not the current lack of a dominant or controlling locality, nor the difficulty of seeing any obvious successor to the Pax Britannica and Pax Americana (though I suppose the Chinese equivalent may yet arrive). We (humankind, that is) have survived disorderly and 'acephalous' periods before: for example, 'forward planning' must have been a bit tricky in ninth-century France. What is more, we have had 'world-systems' (à la Wallerstein – but without buying the whole argument) on and off for centuries. What is unprecedented about the present is not the unpredictability of twists and turns within the particular supralocal cosmos acting upon us – that was always the case for those at the 'bottom' of the system – but the perceptible disappearance of any margin for error 'around' the system.

The early capitalist 'world-economies' were supranational but not global. They were surrounded by a large hinterland of unincorporated humankind, organized in a range of social orders from imperial bureaucracies as in China to chiefdoms, tribes and hunter-gatherer groups as in Africa. This hinterland was a sort of blotting paper, absorbing a lot of the mess produced by capitalism as it expanded. I'm thinking, for example, of the way people and other resources were wrenched out of tribal societies in the tropics by greedy risk-takers working the 'triangular trade' between Europe, Africa and America in the eighteenth century.

Heavy costs could be imposed on 'outsider' societies that functioned as a sort of handy global rubbish bin. Africa could be laid to waste because it was not part of the capitalist world-economy. However, this continent was drawn into that expanding system during the nineteenth century. As a consequence, the massively disruptive slave trade that undermined African social cohesion was abolished: a minimal degree of 'care' for the cohesion of African societies became necessary. By the end of the twentieth century we find that there are no more handy wastebins on earth. The oceans are heaving with muck. The ozone layer is fraying badly. The margin for error is fast disappearing.

In my last letter I was trying to find a pattern of historical change within the 'postmodern' present and look for points where political action might make a difference. I was trying to break away from the picture of us crouching near-helplessly inside barrels swirling around within turbulent maelstroms and instead get some notion of the changing continental formations around which the oceans (and barrels) rush. I thought it might be possible to identify some of the tectonic shifts now occurring: for example, the re-engagement of East and West within Europe, the changing balance of power between the Atlantic and the Pacific, and the crumbling of the old familiar landscape of the second industrial revolution (leaving its vast factory workforce now largely redundant). I would also add to this list the widespread abandonment of universalism, the assertiveness of movements grounded in 'particularistic' characteristics (such as feminism or the various ethnic/national movements), the violent emergence of Islamic fundamentalism, the dazzling advances in communication technology, the astonishing disinvestment of state influence through privatization and the dismantling of the welfare state, and so on.

Now, these transformations involve people acting as well as being acted upon. We are not all inside ocean-tossed barrels, even if Mr Carlsson of Sweden cannot get his way in the face of the financial markets. (Can a medium-sized company get its way, either? Don't both Bill Clinton and the head of British Petroleum have more say in the world than their little brothers and sisters?) It is common ground between us that there has been a shift in power balances away from the state and towards capital in recent decades. We can also both see the 'functionality' for capital of there being many relatively weak states that maintain order without being able to impose comprehensive regulation. I argued that this state of affairs (this aspect of the present) had obtained in Western Europe in the early modern period with 'positive' results for capitalist growth.

On further reflection, might there not be a rhythm to all this? Perhaps it was the accumulation and mobilization of new resources by an aggressively expansive capitalism only loosely contained by weak states in the fifteenth and sixteenth centuries that provided the materials used for European state building between the seventeenth and early nineteenth centuries. In other words, a period of 'strong' capitalism helped to make possible a period of 'strong' states. Against this background, could we see the nineteenth and early twentieth centuries as a long war between 'strong' capitalism

and 'strong' states (with the United States and Germany representing different – and competing – outcomes)? Crucially, America won.
We are now once more in a period of 'strong' capital and 'weak'
states. (Why this has happened is an interesting question that I
have not yet seen a convincing comprehensive answer to . . . It is
not simply a matter of the outcome of World War II.) Perhaps this
will provide the materials for a later period of strong states: again,
the example of Hong Kong's take-over by (reintegration into) China
is a fascinating instance.

One key issue, it seems to me, is how we manage the current
phase of 'strong' capitalism (and all successive phases, if there
are any) without losing too many of the advantages secured for
'ordinary' people during the past half-century or so. I am not
optimistic and agree with your assessment of the dire situation
of the poor, although I think you are overplaying the supposed
lack of connection currently between rich and poor. You are too
readily assuming away the culturally-induced sympathies of the
past couple of centuries – in spite of the contrary precedent provided by the feudal culture which permeated successive ages for a
very long time.

The novelty of our current situation is the erosion of the 'margin'
– although we can't rule out the possibility that science and technology might re-establish this margin in some way in the course
of the next century. A lot of postmodernity's perceived 'newness',
apart from technological innovation, is, I would guess, the spread
of old experiences to new groups. On the one hand, consumer
capacity has been extended down the social order (not a recent
change but a steady 'achievement' of the whole past century). On
the other hand, the de-construction of the Keynesian welfare state
has imposed upon intellectuals a level of insecurity and a feeling of
insignificance they have not known for a couple of centuries.
However, insecurity and insignificance have been the common lot
during modernity of most of humankind apart from those lucky
enough to belong to the two 'golden generations' I mentioned
before. Is it a coincidence that the onset of the interest in 'postmodernity' (in Britain at least) more or less coincided with the loss
of tenure in the universities?

You warned me against the danger of coming to postmodernity
in a history-soaked frame of mind and finding too much comforting familiarity in the present. I have got three defences. First, it is
by recognizing *similarities* between present and past that the *differences* between present and past can be most clearly seen. Second,

being 'similar in some important respects' is different from being 'the same in all respects' – and I usually intend the former. Third, historical 'continuity' does not mean unremitting sameness through time but 'connectedness': the past shapes what comes after but in ways that are by no means fully understood or controlled either at the time or later.

I am not sure whether you are saying that the onset of post-modernity (could one say the clear establishment of postmodernity's dominance in the modernity/postmodernity relationship?) is an occurrence of equal, or even greater, magnitude than the emergence of capitalism, and perhaps equally difficult to 'read' when you are living through it? If so, the pictures of postmodernity you are painting would perhaps be the functional equivalent (not the same but similar!) of Hobbes' model of human beings and their social order as presented in *Leviathan*. As Arendt (among others) would have it, Hobbes depicted the essentials of the inner and outer world of the capitalist bourgeoisie centuries before these came into full florescence.

There are (would you agree?) two equal dangers. One is to misread the extraordinary as the normal, as denoting 'business as usual'. You are currently fighting against this attitude in others by your remarkable evocation of postmodernity's discontents. The other pitfall is to misread the normal as extraordinary. For my part, I have been testing out the extent to which we are falling into exactly this trap in our understanding of postmodernity: in other words, I have been trying to locate it as emerging out of previous historical phases and as being in tune with a pre-existing logic. By contrast, you have been emphasizing the extent to which a new logic is taking shape.

You have issued the warning that we should not treat the normal as being extraordinary in your analysis of the Holocaust. As I understand it, a central point of your argument was that genocide was a procedure inscribed in the bureaucratic routines and rationalizing intentions of the modern state from the beginning and so should not be treated as a monstrous aberration undertaken by assorted lunatics in control of a renegade political movement.

So, there are opposite dangers. One danger is that a normal possibility (e.g. the Holocaust) might be mistaken for a radical realignment of human possibilities and prospects. The other danger is that a profound reordering of the fundamental conditions of human existence (e.g. postmodernity?) might be mistaken for a continuation of a pre-existing normality. I suppose it is possible that there may be normal *and* extraordinary characteristics in *both* the Holocaust and postmodernity.

I was intrigued by your analysis of the state in late modernity, especially the notion that the popularity and pervasiveness of the state has increased at the same time as the capacity of most states to get their own way has diminished. As I argued (or at least, I hope, implied) before, nowadays states are in the business of channelling as many of the benefits of capitalism as possible to their 'own' people. However, the way they do this has changed. In particular, it is not feasible to legislate for full employment, which I reckon was the main device for providing the 'good times' of the postwar boom.

Since the 1970s the favoured technique has been to tout for investment by 'footloose' capitalists, trying to seduce the seducer into setting up his dream factory in your backyard rather than someone else's. To do this you need an 'independent' state that has the right to issue the appropriate licences and offer tasty tax advantages. Added to that, most states have the added job of symbolically (and sometimes militarily) promoting the interests of a specific ethnicity (or, perhaps, a mix of ethnicities) – in other words, the state has the (impossible?) task of realizing the dreams of national groups.

There is a fascinating parallel between the fate of the (would-be?) nation-state and that of the modern family. Like the state, marriage is both a much weaker institution and a more popular institution than ever before. Marriage is so popular that many people get married more than once, even several times. The hopes of millions are vested in the possibility of fulfilment within the bond of the couple. This collective experiment flows outside the bounds of state-sanctioned 'legal' coupledom to encompass a growing variety of household arrangements, same sex and mixed sex, official and informal. If the dream of happy coupledom cannot be turned into reality, then the arrangement can be ditched and the ex-partners can begin their search for a soul-mate anew.

Does this sound over-cynical? Perhaps, however, it is the way some ethnic groups behave in their search, first, for a state apparatus to attach their name to, and second, for alliances with other states to keep them warm in a blustery world. Even more prominent at the moment are some of the 'divorce settlements' being sought: for example, by nationalists in Scotland, Quebec and so on. In the case of marriage and the state, the strategic flexibility which potential partners enjoy is due to the fact that neither the nation-state nor the domestic household any longer bears a decisive burden in maintaining the structure and functioning of the world we live in.

Obviously, there was a time when lordly dynasties and peasant households formed the backbone of human social orders. Also, as you point out, the territorial state on its military/economic/cultural tripod played this role for a while. The growth of the welfare state released the household into this fluid games-playing world. Now globalization and the enhanced significance of transnational capital have done the same for nations and ethnic groups.

I suspect that one source of differences in our initial approaches is that I want to colour in different parts of the postmodern map in different shades – e.g. distinguishing the American experience from that of the Soviet bloc, balancing the Pacific Rim against the Atlantic arena – whereas you are keener to grasp at 'core' concepts that, you believe, underlie these 'secondary' disparities.

Another difference is that I have tended to treat the postwar period of the mid/late 1940s to mid/late 1960s, especially as it registered in the hopes and experiences of the worker in employment, as being the 'high point' of modernity, whereas I suspect you may be more inclined to see the curve as rising to a high point (or low point) represented by the experience and extreme claims of the legislators during the 1930s.

In other words, my perceptions have been grounded more in the trajectory of the bourgeois-democratic nation-state, whereas you make stronger implicit reference to the non-democratic Soviet-or-fascist state. In this context, I felt able to refer to the Hitler/Stalin episodes as 'extraordinary' instances of the bourgeois state failing to manage the people, thus allowing demagogic mass organizers to seduce and dominate the *Volk* and then overawe the state apparatus – whereas perhaps you would see this more as a 'normal' development of the potential inscribed in modernity.

I just wonder whether the extreme state domination of the 1930s and 1940s (and beyond in Eastern Europe) and the widespread material comfort extending far down the class hierarchy enjoyed during the postwar boom were *both* highly unusual and temporary phenomena, disturbances on a trajectory which looks much smoother if we jump straight from 1914 to 1989. If we imagine away the intervening decades, then the break-up of the Russian empire appears as the 'natural' complement to the end of the Hapsburg and

Ottoman megaliths. The recent disenfranchisement of the poor then seems quite expected, a restoration of the status quo. The tumbling career of postmodern capital around the globe seems quite familiar to a reader of Hobson's analysis: not the same but in some respects similar, an understandable further development. If World War I and the Russian Revolution had not occurred, would we be talking about postmodernity now?

Yours, etc.
Dennis

Notes

Chapter 1 Living Without a Guidebook

1 Compare Veblen, who took history by the scruff of the neck and rewrote it as a morality tale illustrating the parts played by force, fraud, wishful thinking and self-deception in human affairs. He traced the career of the 'predatory' tendency – the urge to seize and control property. He showed how it stifled the expression of the deep-rooted 'instinct of workmanship' (Veblen 1970: 30, 75): in other words, the inclination to engage in purposeful activity for the benefit of the whole community. Veblen anticipated that the collapse of capitalism would make it possible for groups of working people to engage in healthy and constructive cooperation for the common good. In other words, once the pressure of false needs and destructive drives was lifted, the instinct of workmanship would resurrect and open up a new panorama of human possibilities. There is some similarity between Veblen's idea of a natural inclination to cooperate constructively with others and Bauman's notion of an innate human propensity to care for others. Both function as a kind of buried treasure, hidden deep in the psyche, ready for excavation when the time is ripe.
2 For my own approach to these issues, see Smith (1990).
3 See Rose (1991).
4 See Smith and Wright (forthcoming).
5 On these themes, see Smith (1988).
6 See, for example, Burgin (1986), Fekete (1988), Fuller (1988), Hassan (1987), Jameson (1984), Jencks (1986) and Lyotard (1984). Readers unfamiliar with the modernity/postmodernity debate might start by looking at Wagner (1994), Seidman (1998), Lash (1990), Harvey (1989) and Calhoun (1995) as well as the texts by Lemert, Smart and Rose already mentioned. That is only the beginning of a vast literature.

Chapter 2 No Easy Choices

1 Bauman's main works in English fall into three groups. Firstly, there are six books written in the 1970s and early 1980s with his gaze firmly fixed on the horizon of a socialist utopia: *Between Class and Elite* (1972), *Culture as Praxis* (1973a), *Socialism: the active utopia* (1976a), *Towards a Critical Sociology* (1976b), *Hermeneutics and Social Science* (1978) and *Memories of Class* (1982). Secondly, there are four books from a transitional period in the late 1980s and early 1990s when Bauman is reorienting himself, allowing his hopes of a socialist utopia to fade, and turning towards the postmodern horizon. During this period, Bauman discovered a new persona as a Jewish intellectual as distinct from being a socialist intellectual. He published his trilogy on the historical experience of Europe's intellectuals and Europe's Jews: *Legislators and Interpreters* (1987), *Modernity and the Holocaust* (1989) and *Modernity and Ambivalence* (1991). He also wrote *Thinking Sociologically* (1990b) in this period. Thirdly, there are the books written by Bauman during the 1990s which survey the postmodern world that he believes is coming into existence. These are: *Intimations of Postmodernity* (1992a), *Mortality, Immortality and Other Life Strategies* (1992b), *Postmodern Ethics* (1993), *Life in Fragments* (1995), *Postmodernity and its Discontents* (1997), *Work, Consumerism and the New Poor* (1998e) and *Globalization: the human consequences* (1998b).

Chapter 3 Who is Zygmunt Bauman?

1 For a discussion of the way legal professionals try to keep the postmodern disturbance of such concepts as 'truth' and 'reality' at bay, see Fiske and Glynn (1995).
2 The original text uses the name 'Konrad', which is the pseudonym that Janina Bauman employs for her husband in this book.
3 The book is Jaff Schatz's *The Generation: the rise and fall of Jewish communists in Poland* (1991), originally published in 1989 by University of Lund Press. Schatz interviewed a number of Jewish communists who had emigrated to Sweden. An interview that Ulrich Bielefeld conducted with Zygmunt and Janina Bauman in 1993 gives useful background (see Bauman and Bauman 1993).
4 Not surprisingly, one of Bauman's earliest interests as a sociologist was the idea of the 'career'. In 1960 he published a book on the subject (see Bauman 1960).
5 The Polish editions appeared in 1964 and 1966, the Serb in 1969 and the Italian in 1971 (Bauman 1971a). For details, see the bibliography in Kilminster and Varcoe (1996: 248–9).
6 Some details in this paragraph come from *The Polish Sociological Bulletin*, 1961, 1(1–2), 123, 141 and 1996, 6, 2 (14), 185–6.
7 According to Morawski, who was there at the time, 'Bauman, as much as his nearest colleagues at the University of Warsaw, objected by thought and action to the Stalin–Zhdanov slogan of the creative intelligentsia as the "engineers of the soul". The slogan meant: "You will realize what the party headquarters recommend as the best spiritual nourishment for the masses." The opposition consisted in an adamant refutation of this recommendation

because it was fraudulent and enslaving' (1998: 32–3). Zhdanov, who died in 1948, had been Party boss of Leningrad and a close associate of Stalin. He implemented Stalin's policy of eliminating Western or cosmopolitan influences in Soviet life.

8 The range of Bauman's interests during his years in Poland can be seen from the titles of those papers, both empirical and theoretical, which appeared in English. They concern aspects of state socialism, culture, sociology and Marxism: for example, 'Social structure of the party organization in industrial works' (1962a), 'Values and standards of success of the Polish youth' (1962c), 'Economic growth, social structure, elite formation: the case of Poland' (1964), 'Social structure and innovational personality' (1965), 'The limitations of perfect planning' (1966b), 'Three remarks on contemporary educational problems' (1966c), 'Two notes on mass culture' (1966d), 'Image of man in modern sociology' (1967a), 'Modern times, modern Marxism' (1967b), 'Polish youth and politics' (1967c), 'Some problems in contemporary education' (1967d), 'Marx and the contemporary theory of culture' (1968a), 'Semiotics and the function of culture' (1968b) and 'Macrosociology and the contemporary theory of culture' (1968c).

9 See Bauman and Bauman (1993).

10 One example is Norbert Elias. In his book *The Germans* (1996), Norbert Elias pays remarkably little attention to the plight of the Jews at the hands of the Nazis. He is much more interested in the decivilizing processes within German society that facilitated the rise of Hitler. Elias was a German at least as much as he was a Jew. What disturbed him most, I believe, was the fact that it was the Germans who committed the horrors of Auschwitz. On Elias, see Smith (forthcoming).

11 At least one of Bauman's early works was translated into Hebrew (see Bauman 1962b; Kilminster and Varcoe 1996: 248).

12 Cf. Pirsig (1979).

Chapter 4 The Power of the Past

1 In 1939 Arnold Toynbee used the phrase 'post-modern' to describe the period from 1914 onwards (Toynbee 1954; Rose 1991: 171).

2 See, for example, Bauman (1973a: 134–5; 1978: 197–201; 1982: 40–8; 1987: 40–4; 1989: 45–6).

3 The quotation comes from an interview with Zygmunt Bauman by Richard Kilminster and Ian Varcoe, published as an appendix to *Intimations of Postmodernity* (Bauman 1992a).

4 A hint of Bauman's feelings comes at the end of 'Social dissent in East European polities' (1971b), where he describes the paradigm he had both fought for and served as a communist activist: 'the ever increasing satisfaction of the ever increasing needs of the ever increasing number of people, striven for by the ever increasing power and competence of the state'. He adds in a note that this paradigm had been rejected by 'those who call themselves, with a remarkable degree of ignorance, the "new left"; the most important departures preached by some consist in rejecting the value of technical improvement, of the accumulation of knowledge, and of intellectual prowess – and in simultaneously ascribing an autotelic value to violence. A similar lack of a novel, alternative paradigm, coupled with an

almost total (vociferously activist by some, passively escapist by others) rejection of the existing one, was typical of classical Medieval civilization in the time of the Great Crisis of the IVth Century, rather than of any branch of the modern Left.' Bauman argues that the features of that earlier period, such as 'a drive to voluntary servitude, escape from military and administrative service, fascination by Oriental mystics and proliferation of weird fanatical sects, sexual laxity, etc., all bear a striking resemblance indeed to what goes now sometimes for the "new left"' (1971b: 51).

Chapter 5 The Road to the West

1 On Mill and Galbraith, see my *Capitalist Democracy on Trial* (Smith 1990: esp. 17–36, 151–61).
2 Bauman's paper was originally published in 1967 (in *Social Research* 34, 3, 399–415).
3 Bauman comments that '"unified" is not the proper word in this context; the word implies something which is brought together after having been divided; what we have in mind however is the kind of unity existing before any division took place' (1969: 1). He wants to overcome the fragmenting effect of concepts such as 'economic man', 'social man', 'cultural man' and 'political man'.
4 Following C. Wright Mills, Bauman observes that Talcott Parsons has moulded a 'global world-image' (1969: 10) out of the everyday pragmatics of the managerial role. He adds that Marx has done the same with the everyday experience of those who are managed and manipulated.
5 'An average peasant now consumes three times more sugar and twice as much meat, animal fat, and eggs than before the war' (Bauman 1971b: 36).
6 Their situation was contradictory because bureaucracy and the market were in constant tension. To be efficient, the market needed to be as free as possible from bureaucratic constraints. To be equal, socialism needed to subject the market to a great deal of bureaucratic regulation. See also 'Twenty years after: the crisis of Soviet-type systems' (Bauman 1971c) and 'Officialdom and class: bases of inequality in socialist society' (Bauman 1974).

Chapter 6 The Road to Utopia

1 Bauman was sceptical of the claims of some structuralists that the logic of culture was an expression of 'the generative grammar of language' or some other specific feature of language. His main counter-argument is that 'the role played in linguistic analysis by the semiotic field is assumed, in the world of human relations, by social structure' (1973b: 80; 1973a: 106).
2 Bauman had already developed some of these ideas in *Kultura i spoleczenstwo: preliminaria* (Culture and Society: preliminaries) (1966a).
3 Bauman quotes from Marcuse's *An Essay on Liberation* (1972).
4 As Bauman puts it, 'Articulating the Gramscian tradition of Marxism in the vernacular of modern social science, Habermas stands the chance of getting the message through' (1976b: 102).

5 I sense a conflict running through Bauman's work in this fascinating period of his career. It is a conflict between, on the one hand, a desire to be active, to participate in struggle, to impress his ideas upon the minds of others, and, on the other hand, a desire to learn new things, both empirically and theoretically, by engaging in open-ended and open-minded exploration and dialogue. Although action and dialogue/exploration can be reconciled and can actually feed upon each other, there remains a basic conflict. Activists who allow themselves to be overwhelmed by new information and ideas, or who are constantly reconsidering their fundamental strategy of action, may act too late, indecisively or not at all.

6 Here, as in other places, the echoes of Veblen in Bauman's work are fascinating.

7 See Bauman (1971b).

8 In the early 1970s, Bauman stressed a number of key differences between East and West. For example, the pattern of historical development in the capitalist West had provided a social basis for intellectual freedom, but a different pattern had been followed in Eastern Europe, with the result that the demand for security was much higher on the agenda. By implication, Bauman preferred a society that mixed 'Eastern' and 'Western' characteristics, and that followed 'an alternative way, leading to bread, security and freedom at the same time' (1971b: 50). The Czech experience of socialism seems to have been of special interest to Bauman. Many of his early books were translated into Czechoslovakian (see Kilminister and Varcoe 1996: 248–9).

Chapter 7 The Road to the Berlin Wall

1 Crawford (1996: 42–3).

2 *Memories of Class* is also influenced by the work of Barrington Moore, Jürgen Habermas, James O'Connor, Claus Offe, John Rule, John Foster, Bob Jessop, Keith Middlemas, Alain Touraine and others.

3 In a key passage, Bauman states that 'pride of place among the new problems belongs to the self-assertion of the Third World. It is truly impossible to exaggerate the impact exerted by this by far the most seminal of the postwar developments upon the totality of Western mentality. It amounts to the general collapse of self-confidence and has manifold manifestations.' Bauman argues that the West has an unspoken, underlying fear of devastating 'global wars of redistribution', possibly pursued with nuclear weaponry. However, despite this fear, the West tries to curry favour with the 'up-and-coming world powers' by supplying them with arms. He concludes that 'The bewildering inconsistency of reactions on all levels is symptomatic of the situation of acute uncertainty and ambiguity' (1982: 172).

4 Bauman adds: 'from *manumittere*, to send forth from one's hand' (1988: 30).

5 Bauman (1988: 10–12); Bentham (1843).

6 The full title of Bentham's book, cited by Bauman (1988, 10–11), is *Panopticon, or, the Inspection House, containing the idea of a new Principle of Construction applicable to any Sort of Establishment, in which persons of any description are to be kept under Inspection and in particular to Penitentiary-House, Prisons, Houses of Industry, Work-Houses, poor-Houses and Manufactories, Mad-houses, Lazarettos, Hospitals, and Schools; with a Plan of Management adapted to the Principle.*

7 See Albert Hirschman's discussion of 'exit, voice and loyalty' (Hirschman 1970; Bauman 1988: 82–5).

Chapter 8 The Trilogy

1 See Bauman and Bauman (1993: 20).
2 On *Kristallnacht*, see Bauman (1989: 75).
3 Compare the interpretation of the Migram experiments given by Barrington Moore in *Injustice*: 'The facts, insofar as they are revealed by the experiment, may be interpreted as follows: pure moral autonomy in the form of lone resistance to an apparently benign authority is very rare. With support from peers, on the other hand, the same kind of resistance increases enormously. These facts correspond to what it is possible to observe in the real world and shed much light on why it happens. What the data reveal is the significance of social support for correct moral reasoning. Even with social support, on the other hand, the individual has to recognize the correct nature of the reasoning and to act on it' (Moore 1978: 97). For a discussion of the Milgram experiments, see the articles by Baumrind and by Orne and Holland in Miller (1972). I am grateful to Lee Ross for this last reference.
4 Bauman treats Norbert Elias's work *The Civilizing Process* as, in effect, giving support to an 'etiological myth deeply entrenched in the self-consciousness of our Western society', which is 'the morally elevating story of humanity emerging from pre-social barbarity' (Bauman 1987: 12). According to Bauman, however, the civilizing process was 'a conscious proselytizing crusade waged by men of knowledge and aimed at extirpating the vestiges of wild cultures – local, tradition-bound ways of life and patterns of cohabitation'. The trend was towards functional centralization. The experts would be in charge. It was to be 'a knowledge-led management . . . aimed above all at the administration of individual minds and bodies' (p. 93). Bauman and Elias differ in two fundamental ways. Firstly, they see European history in dissimilar ways. Unlike Bauman, Elias anchors his account in a Hobbesian medieval world where power balances are radically unstable, allegiances shift constantly, violence perpetually threatens and the boundaries between one lord's territory and another are forever changing. The ambiguity and flux of medieval life was life-threatening, but posed no threat to people's sense of reality. The mentality and emotional life of participants in this form of life were well adjusted to it. Only later, when stable power monopolies were established at the royal court and elsewhere, were courtiers constrained gradually to abandon their old habits and adapt to new forms of control. They adopted more 'civilized' modes of behaviour and, in so doing, developed more 'civilized' personalities. Secondly, Elias and Bauman have very different approaches to the sociality of human beings. Elias argues that we acquire our sense of who we are and the appropriate way to behave as social beings in the course of early experience within the figurations (families, social classes, ethnic groups, nations and so on) into which we are born. For Bauman, the key process is the imposition of rules of conduct 'from above' by bureaucrats, experts and other agents of oppressive modernity. In his view, socialization is not so much the 'filling out' or creation of a person as the 'smothering'

of their essential humanity. Bauman argues that we are all born with innate moral dispositions, including an aversion to causing suffering in others and a desire to exercise care for them. In modernity, people are systematically deprived of the chance to exercise their capacity to act morally, to make ethical choices. Instead, they are forced to follow rules about how to behave. I explore these issues further in my forthcoming book on Elias. Norbert Elias's key works are *The Court Society* (1983), *The Civilizing Process* (1994) and *The Germans* (1996). Also relevant are Elias (1956, 1971, 1974, 1978, 1982, 1984, 1987a, 1991). In 1929 Elias wrote an article on the sociology of German anti-Semitism (Elias 1929). This is summarized by Klaudia Meyer in *Figurations* (1998). See also Birkitt (1996), Dunning and Mennell (1998), O'Kane (1997), Freeman (1995) and Wagner (1994: 44).

5 Bauman's argument overlaps at several points with that made by Hannah Arendt in *The Origins of Totalitarianism* (Arendt 1958b) and *Eichmann in Jerusalem* (Arendt 1963a). Also relevant are *The Human Condition* (Arendt 1958a) and *On Revolution* (Arendt 1963b). Bauman is much more sympathetic to Arendt's approach, which reflects her existentialist background, than he is to Elias.

6 In part, this section draws upon ideas developed in Smith (1992). See this article also for a comparison between the approaches taken by Zygmunt Bauman and Anthony Giddens. See also Shilling and Mellor (1998).

Chapter 9 Bauman's Vision of Modernity and Postmodernity

1 In 1992 *Intimations of Postmodernity* (Bauman 1992a) appeared – a collection of essays whose overriding theme was sociology's response to the postmodern condition. In the same year, Bauman also published *Mortality, Immortality and Other Life Strategies* (1992b), exploring modern and postmodern approaches to dealing with the awareness of death. Two years later, Bauman brought out *Postmodern Ethics* (Bauman 1993), to be followed by *Life in Fragments* (1995). Both these books examined questions surrounding moral responsibility and our ethical nature. In *Postmodernity and its Discontents* (1997), Bauman explored a multitude of anxieties that flowed from the removal of security. In 1998 Bauman turned his attention to changing economic, political and class structures in *Work, Consumerism and the New Poor* (1998e) and *Globalization: the human consequences* (Bauman 1998).

2 This image occurred to me when reading Peter Beilharz's insightful article entitled 'Reading Zygmunt Bauman: looking for clues'. Beilharz reports: 'As the house guest of the Baumans, one morning in Leeds I descended the staircase to catch the sociologist sweeping up. He looked at me knowingly, and said it was like our situation: every day we sweep, every day the dirt returns and we repeat the ritual, only now, in postmodern times, without illusion' (Beilharz 1998: 35).

3 Bauman has a tendency to present social development as a series of rather abrupt transformations, rather like a tram going over a set of points and switching from one line to another. For example, the seductive power of the consumer market place is introduced into his analysis to

fill the gap left by the weakening influence of disciplinary power exercised by state bureaucrats and employers. However, this pays too little regard to the fact that one of the reasons why workers were lured into factories and offices during the late nineteenth century was the wide range of consumer delights coming on stream for those with wage packets in their pocket. Disciplinary power and consumer seduction ran side by side for the best part of a century.

4 For a defence of communitarian ethics registering 'qualified disagreement with Bauman', see Lash (1996).

5 See, for example, Lévinas (1979; 1985; 1991).

6 See, for example, Jonas (1974; 1984).

Chapter 10 Between Critical Theory and Poststructuralism

1 An issue of *Theory, Culture and Society* that appeared in 1998 is devoted to critiques of Bauman's work. It includes articles by Stefan Morawski, Hans Joas, Ian Varcoe, Richard Kilminster, Douglas Kellner, Pieter Nijhoff and Dennis Smith as well as a piece by Bauman.

2 On the reception of Bauman's work in Germany, see Joas (1998) and Varcoe (1998).

3 For example, on the one hand Bauman made clear his intellectual kinship with Adorno and writers close to him such as Walter Benjamin. On the other hand, however, Bauman embraced the idea of postmodernity, to which Adorno's pupil, Jürgen Habermas, was deeply unsympathetic. To take another example, Bauman aligned himself not only with Adorno but also with Hannah Arendt, who was much closer to existentialism (criticized by Adorno in *The Jargon of Authenticity* (1986)) than she was to critical theory. When she lived in Frankfurt during the early 1930s, Arendt is reported to have said of Adorno: '"Der kommt uns nicht ins Haus!" (That one's not coming into our house!).' Arendt was instrumental in passing Walter Benjamin's manuscript later published as *Theses on the Philosophy of History* on to Adorno, his executor, after Benjamin's suicide in 1941. However, according to her biographer, she was reluctant to do so (Young-Bruehl 1982: 80, 166–7). Finally, although Bauman incorporated certain elements from poststructuralism – citing Lyotard on occasion, for example – he drew most freely upon Foucault, a writer who did not find the concept of postmodernity useful.

4 David Held neatly summarizes the aim of critical theory, both pre- and postwar, as being 'to lay the foundations for an exploration, in an interdisciplinary research context, of questions concerning the conditions which make possible the reproduction and transformation of society, the meaning of culture, and the relation between the individual, society and nature' (1980: 16). Some central aspects of poststructuralism are: a rejection of the notion that language is transparent or that texts represent anything beyond themselves; an interest in 'deconstructing' texts to demonstrate their self-reflexivity; and a thematic focus upon the body and desire as constituted by discourse.

5 For Peter Beilharz, Bauman is 'the greatest sociologist writing in English today', a man whose sociology 'eschews the systemic [and] . . . pursues the fragment' (Beilharz 1998: 25). Steven Seidman is almost as laudatory: 'Bauman has provided perhaps the most compelling sociological analysis

of postmodernity.' However, on one point Seidman takes a tack diametrically opposite to Beilharz. He does not see Bauman as a pursuer of the fragment. On the contrary, Seidman criticizes Bauman for failing to escape 'the seductive charms of grand theory', and for continuing to adhere to 'the generalizing and normative standpoint of modernity' (Seidman 1998: 338–9). Pieter Nijhoff leans towards Beilharz's side of this argument. He finds that 'Bauman's argumentation does not follow the clearly marked and narrow road of connected concepts. His discourse combines terminology from different contexts; by transferring expressions – concrete and abstract, colloquial and esoteric, narrative and analytical – he dovetails, in fact, all sorts of separate spheres and sectors' (Nijhoff 1988: 96). Bauman's style expresses his 'sympathy for the re-enchanted world' of postmodernity – a 'sympathy with a sad undertone' (p. 98). In Nijhoff's view, a discourse like Bauman's 'with so many lateral suggestions and sideward steps is rather suspicious in modern eyes' (p. 96). However, in fact, Bauman's mission is a 'time-honoured' one with its origins in the era of modernity: to provide men and women with ' "sociological imagination" ' (p. 111; Bauman 1992a: 110).

6 Both Seidman and Nijhoff see 'modernist' aspirations in Bauman's work, though Nijhoff sees them being pursued with some of the stylist devices made available by postmodern sensibility. Steven Seidman's response to Bauman may be contrasted with Douglas Kellner's. Seidman, it will be recalled, thought Bauman had produced a 'modernist' sociology of postmodernity. Kellner takes the opposite view. He argues that Bauman has 'not really developed a sociology of postmodernity', but instead 'provides an impressive effort to develop a postmodern sociology' (Kellner 1998: 85). As a third variant, Shaun Best is not at all impressed by Bauman's attempts 'to devise a distinctly postmodern sociology' and asserts that Bauman's analyses are actually 'built upon a modernist notion of the social' (Best 1998: 320). Finally, George Ritzer claims that Bauman 'is generally opposed to the development of what he calls "postmodern sociology" ' (Ritzer 1997: 158).

7 See, for example, his chapters on postmodern art, fiction and the 'consumer cooperative' in *Postmodernity and its Discontents* (Bauman 1997: 95–140).

8 On Adorno, see Jay (1984). For the Frankfurt School, see Bottomore (1984), Held (1980), Jay (1996) and Wiggershaus (1994).

9 Bauman's view of how sociologists should contribute to social change has echoes of Adorno's 'negative dialectics'. He believes sociologists should get closely involved in the processes of self-reflexivity within society, helping people monitor their actions as they engage in 're-evaluation of the original purposes and adequacy of the originally selected means' (Bauman 1992a: 90). David Held summarizes 'negative dialectics' as follows: 'It starts with the conceptual principles and standards of an object, and unfolds their implications and consequences. Then it re-examines and reassesses the object (the object's function, for instance) in the light of these implications and consequences . . . As a result, a new understanding of the object is generated – a new comprehension of contradictions and possibilities' (Held 1980: 184). See also Adorno (1973).

10 'Modernity – an unfinished project' was the title of the speech Habermas gave when accepting the Adorno prize in 1980 (see Habermas 1981). For a recent discussion of Habermas and Foucault, see Flyvbjerg (1998).

11 By 'utopian thought', Habermas means thought that has 'the function of opening up alternatives for action and margins of possibility that push beyond historical continuities'. 'Historical thought', which is 'saturated with actual experience, seems destined to criticize utopian schemes' (Habermas 1989: 49).

12 See, for example, Jay (1996: xviii–xix), Lash (1990: 114ff) and Bertens (1995: 111–37).

13 As reported by Martin Jay, based on a conversation with Foucault (Jay 1984: 22). See also Foucault (1991: 115–29).

14 Foucault did not think this was possible in modern societies. However, he believed that adult male citizens in classical times were dominated by disciplinary power and centralized discursive practices to a much lesser extent. See the second and third volumes of his *History of Sexuality* (Foucault 1987; 1990). For a discussion of this work, see Smith (1999).

15 *The Libidinal Economy* (Lyotard 1993) was originally published in 1974 and Lyotard has modified his position since then. For a discussion, see Bertens (1995: 134–6).

16 See chapter 5.

17 See Jay (1984: 21).

18 On Tocqueville, see Smith (1990: 17–36).

19 I broadly agree with Varcoe and Kilminster's view that Bauman's work during the 1990s represents 'an exploration of his original theme of the human way of being-in-the-world, practised under what he sees as new conditions of cultural and moral fragmentation' (Varcoe and Kilminster 1996: 242).

Bibliography

Adorno, T. 1967: *Prisms*, translated by Samuel and Shierry Weber. London: Neville Spearman.

Adorno, T. 1973: *Negative Dialectics*. New York: Seabury Press.

Adorno, T. 1986: *The Jargon of Authenticity*. London: Routledge; originally published in 1964.

Adorno, T. and Horkheimer, M. 1979: *Dialectic of Enlightenment*. London: Verso; originally published in 1944.

Anderson, B. 1983: *Imagined Communities*. London: Verso.

Arendt, H. 1958a: *The Human Condition*. Chicago: University of Chicago Press.

Arendt, H. 1958b: *The Origins of Totalitarianism*. San Diego, Calif.: Harcourt Brace and Co.

Arendt, H. 1963a: *Eichmann in Jerusalem: a report on the banality of evil*. Harmondsworth: Penguin.

Arendt, H. 1963b: *On Revolution*. Harmondsworth: Penguin.

Bauman, J. 1985: *Winter in the Morning: a young girl's life in the Warsaw Ghetto and beyond, 1939–1945*. London: Virago.

Bauman, J. 1988: *A Dream of Belonging: my years in postwar Poland*. London: Virago.

Bauman, J. and Bauman, Z. 1993: Gespräch mit Janina Bauman und Zygmunt Bauman (by Ulrich Bielefeld). *Mittelweg 36*. August/September, 17–22.

Bauman, Z. 1959: *Socjalizm brytyski*. Warsaw: Państwowe Wydawnictwo Naukowe.

Bauman, Z. 1960: *Kariera: cztery szkice socjologiczne* (Career: four sociological essays), Warsaw: Iskry.

Bauman, Z. 1962a: Social structure of the party organization in industrial works. *Polish Sociological Bulletin*, 2, 1–2 (3–4), 50–64.

Bauman, Z. 1962b: *Sotsyologyah shel yahase enosh*. Merhavya, Jerusalem.

Bauman, Z. 1962c: Values and standards of success of the Polish youth. *Polish Sociological Bulletin*, 2, 1–2 (3–4), 77–90.

Bauman, Z. 1964: Economic growth, social structure, elite formation: the case of Poland. *International Social Science Journal*, 16, 2, 203–16.

Bauman, Z. 1965: Social structure and innovational personality. *Polish Sociological Bulletin*, 5, 1 (11), 54–9.
Bauman, Z. 1966a: *Kultura a spoleczeństwo: preliminaria* (Culture and Society: preliminaries). Warsaw: Państwowe Wydawnictwo Naukowe.
Bauman, Z. 1966b: The limitations of perfect planning. *Co-existence*, 3, 2, 145–62.
Bauman, Z. 1966c: Three remarks on contemporary educational problems. *Polish Sociological Bulletin*, 6, 1 (13), 77–89.
Bauman, Z. 1966d: Two notes on mass culture. *Polish Sociological Bulletin*. 6, 1 (14), 58–74.
Bauman, Z. 1967a: Image of man in modern sociology. *Polish Sociological Bulletin*, 7, 1 (15), 12–21.
Bauman, Z. 1967b: Modern times, modern Marxism. *Social Research*, 34, 3, 399–415.
Bauman, Z. 1967c: Polish youth and politics. *Polish Round Table*, 1, 69–77.
Bauman, Z. 1967d: Some problems in contemporary education. *International Social Science Journal*, 19, 3, 325–7.
Bauman, Z. 1968a: Marx and the contemporary theory of culture. *Social Science Information*, 7, 3, 19–34.
Bauman, Z. 1968b: Semiotics and the function of culture. *Social Science Information*, 7, 5, 69–80.
Bauman, Z. 1969: Modern times, modern Marxism. In P. Berger (ed.), *Marxism and Sociology: views from Easten Europe*, New York: Appleton-Century Crofts, 1–17.
Bauman, Z. 1971a: *Lineamenti di una sociologia marxista* (Nuova biblioteca di cultura 101). Rome: Editori Riuniti.
Bauman, Z. 1971b: Social dissent in the East European political system. *European Journal of Sociology*, 12, 25–51.
Bauman, Z. 1971c: Twenty years after: the crisis of Soviet-type systems. *Problems of Communism*, 20, 6, 45–53.
Bauman, Z. 1972: *Between Class and Elite*: the evolution of the British labour movement – a sociological survey. Manchester: Manchester University Press; originally published in 1960.
Bauman, Z. 1973a: *Culture as Praxis*. London: Routledge.
Bauman, Z. 1973b: The structuralist promise. *British Journal of Sociology*. 24, 1, 67–83.
Bauman, Z. 1974: Officialdom and class: bases of inequality in socialist society. In F. Parkin (ed.), *The Social Analysis of Class Structure*, London: Tavistock, 129–48.
Bauman, Z. 1976a: *Socialism: the active utopia*. London: Allen and Unwin.
Bauman, Z. 1976b: *Towards a Critical Sociology: an essay on common sense and emancipation*. London: Routledge.
Bauman, Z. 1978: *Hermeneutics and Social Science: approaches to understanding*. London: Hutchinson.
Bauman, Z. 1981: On the maturation of socialism. *Telos*, 47, 48–54.
Bauman, Z. 1982: *Memories of Class: the pre-history and after-life of class*. London: Routledge.
Bauman, Z. 1987: *Legislators and Interpreters*. Cambridge: Polity Press.
Bauman, Z. 1988: *Freedom*. Milton Keynes: Open University Press.
Bauman, Z. 1989: *Modernity and the Holocaust*. Cambridge: Polity Press.
Bauman, Z. 1990a: Review of J. Schatz, *The Generation: the rise and fall of the generation of Jewish communists of Poland*. *Acta Sociologica*, 33, 2, 175–7.

Bauman, Z. 1990b: *Thinking Sociologically*. Oxford: Blackwell.

Bauman, Z. 1991: *Modernity and Ambivalence*. Cambridge: Polity Press.

Bauman, Z. 1992a: *Intimations of Postmodernity*. London: Routledge.

Bauman, Z. 1992b: *Mortality, Immortality and Other Life Strategies*. Cambridge: Polity Press.

Bauman, Z. 1993: *Postmodern Ethics*. Cambridge: Polity Press.

Bauman, Z. 1994a: After the patronage state. In P. Bardham, Symposium on democracy and development, *Journal of Economic Perspectives*, 7, 3, 45–9.

Bauman, Z. 1994b: *Alone Again: ethics after certainty*. London: Demos.

Bauman, Z. 1995: *Life in Fragments*. Cambridge: Polity Press.

Bauman, Z. 1997: *Postmodernity and its Discontents*. Cambridge: Polity Press.

Bauman, Z. 1998a: Adorno prize address, July (manuscript supplied by author).

Bauman, Z. 1998b: *Globalization: the human consequences*. Cambridge: Polity Press.

Bauman, Z. 1998c: The spectre still haunts us. *Enlightenment 2*, 28.03.98 on website www.e2-herald.com/280398/n5.html and n6.html.

Bauman, Z. 1998d: What prospects of morality in times of uncertainty? *Theory, Culture and Society*, 15, 1, 11–22.

Bauman, Z. 1998e: *Work, Consumerism and the New Poor*. Buckingham: Open University Press.

Baumrind, D. 1972: Some thoughts on ethics of research: after reading Milgram's 'Behavioral Study of Obedience'. In A. G. Miller (ed.), *The Social Psychology of Psychological Research*, London: Collier-Macmillan, 106–11.

Beilharz, P. 1998: Reading Zygmunt Bauman: looking for clues. *Thesis Eleven*, 54, August, 25–36.

Beilharz, P. forthcoming: McFascism? Reading Ritzer, Bauman and the Holocaust. In B. Smart (ed.), *Resisting McDonaldization*, London: Sage.

Bendix, R. 1964: *Nation-Building and Citizenship*. New York: Wiley.

Bendix, R. 1974: *Work and Authority in Industry*. Berkeley, Calif: University of California Press.

Bendix, R. 1984: *Force, Fate and Freedom: on historical sociology*. Berkeley, Calif. University of California Press.

Bentham, J. 1843: *The Works of Jeremy Bentham*. Edinburgh: William Tait.

Berger, P. (ed.) 1969: *Marxism and Sociology: views from Eastern Europe*. New York: Appleton-Century Crofts.

Berger, P. and Luckman, T. 1967: *The Social Construction of Reality*. Harmondsworth: Penguin.

Bernesconi, A. and Wood, T. (eds) 1988: *The Provocation of Lévinas: Rethinking the Other*. London: Routledge.

Bertens, H. 1995: *The Idea of the Postmodern: a history*. London: Routledge.

Best, S. 1998: Zygmunt Bauman: personal reflections within the mainstream of modernity. *British Journal of Sociology*, 49, 2, 311–20.

Birkitt, I. 1996: Civilization and ambivalence. *British Journal of Sociology*, 47, 1, 135–50.

Bottomore, T. 1984: *The Frankfurt School*. London: Tavistock.

Burgin, V. 1986: *The End of Art Theory: criticism and postmodernity*. London: Macmillan.

Calhoun, C. 1995: *Critical Social Theory: culture, history and the challenge of difference*. Oxford: Blackwell.

Connor, S. 1992: *Theory and Cultural Value*. Oxford: Blackwell.

Crawford, K. 1996: *East Central European Politics Today*. Manchester: Manchester University Press.

Dunning, E. and Mennell, S. 1998: Elias on Germany, Nazism and the Holocaust: on the balance between 'civilizing' and 'decivilizing' trends in the social development of Western Europe. *British Journal of Sociology*, 49, 3, 339–57.

Elias, N. 1929: Zur Soziologie des deutschen Antisemitismus. *Israelitisches Gemeindeblatt: offizielles Organ des israelitischen Mannheim und Ludwigshafen*, 12, 3–6.

Elias, N. 1956: Problems on involvement and detachment. *British Journal of Sociology*, 7, 3, 226–52.

Elias, N. 1971: Sociology of knowledge: new perspectives. *Sociology*, 2, 149–68; 3, 355–70.

Elias, N. 1974: The sciences: towards a theory. In R. Whitley (ed.), *Social Processes of Scientific Development*, London: Routledge, 21–42.

Elias, N. 1978: *What is Sociology?*, translated by Stephen Mennall and Grace Morrissey. London: Hutchinson; originally published in 1970.

Elias, N. 1982: Scientific establishments. In N. Elias, H. Martins and R. Whitley, *Scientific Establishments and Hierarchies*, London: Reidel, 3–69.

Elias, N. 1983: *The Court Society*, translated by Edmund Jephcott. Oxford: Blackwell; originally published in 1969.

Elias, N. 1984: On the sociogenesis of sociology. *Sociologisch Tijdschrift*, 11, 1, 1452; originally published in 1962.

Elias, N. 1986: The genesis of sport as a sociological problem. In N. Elias and E. Dunning, *Quest for Excitement: sport and leisure in the civilizing process*, Oxford: Blackwell, 126–49.

Elias, N. 1987a: *Involvement and Detachment* (part III originally published in 1983, translated by Edmund Jephcott). Oxford: Blackwell.

Elias, N. 1987b: The changing balance of power between the sexes – a process-sociological study: the example of the ancient Roman state. *Theory, Culture and Society*, 4, 287–316.

Elias, N. 1988: Violence and civilization: the state monopoly of physical violence and its infringement. In J. Keane (ed.), *Civil Society and the State: new European perspectives*, London: Verso, 177–98.

Elias, N. 1991: *The Society of Individuals*, edited by Michael Schroter, translated by Edmund Jephcott. Oxford: Blackwell; originally published in 1987.

Elias, N. 1994: *The Civilizing Process*. Oxford: Blackwell.

Elias, N. 1996: *The Germans: power struggles and the development of habitus in the nineteenth and twentieth centuries*, edited by Michael Schroeter, translated with a preface by Eric Dunning and Stephen Mennell. Cambridge: Polity Press.

Elias, N. and Dunning, E. 1986: *Quest for Excitement: sport and leisure in the civilizing process*. Oxford: Blackwell.

Elias, N., Martins, H. and Whitley, R. (eds) 1982: *Scientific Establishments and Hierarchies*. London: Reidel.

Fekete, J. (ed.) 1988: *Life after Postmodernism*. London: Macmillan.

Fiske, J. and Glynn, K. 1995: Trials of the postmodern. *Cultural Studies*, 9, 3, 505–21.

Flyvbjerg, B. 1998: Habermas and Foucault: thinkers for civil society? *British Journal of Sociology*, 49, 2, 210–33.

Foucault, M. 1977: *Discipline and Punish: the birth of the prison*, translated by Alan Sheridan. Harmondsworth: Penguin.

Foucault, M. 1987: *The History of Sexuality, Vol. 2: The Use of Pleasure*. Harmondsworth: Penguin.

Foucault, M. 1990: *The History of Sexuality, Vol. 3: The Care of the Self*. Harmondsworth: Penguin.

Foucault, M. 1991: *Remarks on Marx*. New York: Semiotext(e).

Freeman, M. 1995: Genocide, civilization and modernity. *British Journal of Sociology*, 46, 2, 207–23.

Fuller, P. 1988: *Theoria: art and the absence of grace*. London: Chatto and Windus.

Galbraith, J.K. 1974: *The New Industrial Estate*. Harmondsworth: Penguin.

Galbraith, J.K. 1992: *The Culture of Contentment*. Harmondsworth: Penguin.

Gellner, E. 1979: *Words and Things*. London: Routledge.

Giddens, A. 1976: *New Rules of Sociological Method: a positive critique of interpretative sociologies*. London: Hutchinson.

Giddens, A. 1991: *Modernity and Self-identity: self and society in the late modern age*. Cambridge: Polity Press.

Habermas, J. 1971: *Knowledge and Human Interests*. London: Heinemann.

Habermas, J. 1981: Modernity versus postmodernity. *New German Critique*, 22, 3–14.

Habermas, J. 1987: *The Philosophical Discourse of Modernity*. Cambridge: Polity Press.

Habermas, J. 1989: *The New Conservatism*. Cambridge: Polity Press.

Harvey, D. 1989: *The Condition of Postmodernity: an enquiry into the origins of cultural change*. Oxford: Blackwell.

Hassan, I. 1987: *The Postmodern Turn: essays in postmodern theory and culture*. Columbus, Ohio: Ohio State University.

Held, D. 1980: *Introduction to Critical Theory: Horkheimer to Habermas*. London: Hutchinson.

Hillberg, R. 1983: *The Destruction of the European Jews*. New York: Holmes and Meyer.

Hirschman, A. 1970: *Exit, Voice and Loyalty*. Cambridge, Mass.: Harvard University Press.

Jameson, F. 1984: Postmodernism, or the cultural logic of late capitalism. *New Left Review*, 146, July–August, 53–92.

Jardin, A. 1988: *Tocqueville: a biography*, London: Peter Halban.

Jay, M. 1984: *Adorno*. London: Fontana.

Jay, M. 1996: *The Dialectical Imagination: a history of the Frankfurt School and the Institute of Social Research 1923–1950*. Berkeley, Calif.: University of California Press.

Jencks, C. 1986: *What is Postmodernism?* London: Academy Editions.

Joas, H. 1998: Bauman in Germany: modern violence and the problems of German self-understanding. *Theory, Culture and Society*, 15, 1, 47–56.

Jonas, H. 1974: *Philosophical Essays: from ancient creed to technological man*. Englewood Cliffs, NJ: Prentice Hall.

Jonas, H. 1984: *The Imperative of Responsibility: in search of an ethics for the technological age*. Chicago, IU.: University of Chicago Press.

Keane, J. (ed.) 1978: *Civil Society and the State: new European perspectives*. London: Verso.

Kellner, D. 1998: Zygmunt Bauman's postmodern turn. *Theory, Culture and Society*, 15, 1, 73–86.

Kilminster, R. and Varcoe, I. (eds) 1996: *Culture, Modernity and Revolution: essays in honour of Zygmunt Bauman*. London: Routledge.

Koestler, A. 1964: *The Act of Creation*. London: Pan.

Lash, S. 1990: *Sociology of Postmodernism*. London: Routledge.

Lash, S. 1996: Postmodern ethics: the missing ground. *Theory, Culture and Society*, 13, 2, 91–104.

Lemert, C. 1997: *Postmodernism Is Not What You Think*. Oxford: Blackwell.

Lévinas, E. 1979: *Le temps et l'autre*. Paris: Presses Universitaires de France.

Lévinas, E. 1985: *Ethics and Infinity: conversations with Philippe Nemo*, translated by Richard A. Cohen. Pittsburgh: Duquesne University Press.

Lévinas, E. 1988: The paradox of morality: an interview with Emmanuel Lévinas by Tamara Wright, Peter Hayes and Alison Ainley. In A. Bernesconi and T. Wood (eds), *The Provocation of Lévinas: rethinking the Other*, London: Routledge, 168–80.

Lévinas, E. 1991: *Entre Nous: essais sur le penser-à-l'autre*. Paris: Grasset.

Lévi-Strauss, C. 1966: *The Savage Mind*. Harmondsworth: Penguin.

Lyotard, J.-F. 1984: *The Postmodern Condition: a report on knowledge*. Manchester: Manchester University Press.

Lyotard, J.-F. 1988: *The Differend*. Minneapolis, Minn: University of Minnesota Press.

Lyotard J.-F. 1993: *The Libidinal Economy*. Bloomington, Ind: Indiana University Press.

Marcuse, H. 1964: *One-Dimensional Man*. London: Routledge.

Marcuse, H. 1972: *An Essay on Liberation*. Harmondsworth: Penguin.

Marx, K. 1954: *Capital: a critique of political economy*, vol. I. London: Lawrence and Wishart; originally published in 1867.

Marx, K. and Engels, F. 1935: *The Communist Manifesto*. In *Selected Works*, vol. 1, London: Lawrence and Wishart.

Mathiesen, T. 1997: The viewer society: Michel Foucault's 'Panopticon' revisited. *Theoretical Criminology*, 215–34.

Meyer, K. 1998: On the sociology of German anti-Semitism: Norbert Elias embarks on the sociology of knowledge. *Figurations*, 9, 1–2.

Mill, J.S. 1964a: On liberty. In J.S. Mill, *Utilitarianism, Liberty, Representative Government*, London: Dent, 65–170; originally published in 1859.

Mill, J.S. 1964b: *Utilitarianism, Liberty, Representative Government*, with an introduction by A.D. Lindsay. London: Dent.

Miller, A.G. (ed.) 1972: *The Social Psychology of Psychological Research*. London: Collier-Macmillan.

Misztal, B.A. 1996: Postcommunist ambivalence: becoming of a new formation? *Archives Européennes de Sociologie*, 37, 1, 104–40.

Moore, B. 1969: *Social Origins of Dictatorship and Democracy: lord and peasant in the making of the modern world*. Harmondsworth: Penguin.

Moore, B. 1972: *Reflections on the Causes of Human Misery and on Certain Proposals to Eliminate Them*. Harmondsworth: Penguin.

Moore, B. 1978: *Injustice: the social bases of obedience and revolt*. London: Macmillan.

Morawski, S. 1998: Bauman's way of seeing the world. *Theory, Culture and Society*, 15, 1, 29–38.

Nijhoff, P. 1998: The right to consistency. *Theory, Culture and Society*, 15, 1, 87–112.

Offe, C. 1996: *Modernity and the State: East, West*. Cambridge: Polity Press.

O'Kane, R.H.T. 1997: Modernity, the Holocaust and politics. *Economy and Society*, 26, 1, 43–61.

Orne, M.T. and Holland, C.H. 1972: On the ecological validity of laboratory deceptions. In A.G. Miller (ed.), *The Social Psychology of Psychological Research*, London: Collier-Macmillan, 122–37.

Parkin, F. (ed.) 1984: *The Social Analysis of Class Structure*. London: Tavistock.

Pirsig, R.M. 1979: *Zen and the Art of Motorcycle Maintenance: an inquiry into values*. London: Bantam.

Popper, K.R. 1972: *Objective Knowledge: an evolutionary approach*. Oxford: Clarendon Press.

Rex, J. 1991: Race, ethnicity and the rational organization of evil. *Theory, Culture and Society*, 8, 1, 167–74.

Ritzer, G. 1997: *Postmodern Social Theory*. New York: McGraw-Hill.

Rose, M.A. 1991: *The Post-modern and the Post-industrial: a critical analysis*. Cambridge: Cambridge University Press.

Schatz, J. 1991: *The Generation: the rise and fall of Jewish communists in Poland*. Berkeley, Calif.: University of California Press.

Schumpeter, J.A. 1986: *History of Economic Analysis*, edited by Elizabeth Boody Schumpeter. London: Allen and Unwin; originally published in 1954.

Seidman, S. 1998: *Contested Knowledge: social theory in the postmodern era*. Oxford: Blackwell.

Seidman, S. and Wagner, D.G. (eds) 1992: *Postmodernism and Social Theory*. Oxford: Blackwell.

Sennett, R. 1992: *The Conscience of the Eye*. New York: W.W. Norton.

Shilling, C. and Mellor, P.A. 1998: Durkheim, morality and modernity: collective effervescence, *homo duplex* and the sources of moral action. *British Journal of Sociology*, 49, 2, 193–209.

Skocpol, T. (ed.) 1984: *Vision and Method in Historical Sociology*. Cambridge: Cambridge University Press.

Smart, B. (ed.) forthcoming: *Resisting McDonaldization*. London: Sage.

Smelser, N.J. 1959: *Social Change and Industrial Revolution*. London: Routledge.

Smith, D. 1981: *Conflict and Compromise: class formation in English society 1830–1914 – a comparative study of Birmingham and Sheffield*. London: Routledge.

Smith, D. 1983: *Barrington Moore: violence, morality and political change*. London: Macmillan.

Smith, D. 1984a: Discovering facts and values: the historical sociology of Barrington Moore. In T. Skocpol (ed.), *Vision and Method in Historical Sociology*, Cambridge: Cambridge University Press, 313–55.

Smith, D. 1984b: Morality and method in the work of Barrington Moore. *Theory and Society*, 13, 151–76.

Smith, D. 1988: *The Chicago School: a liberal critique of capitalism*. London: Macmillan.

Smith, D. 1990: *Capitalist Democracy on Trial: the transatlantic debate from Tocqueville to the present*. London: Routledge.

Smith, D. 1991: *The Rise of Historical Sociology*. Cambridge: Polity Press.

Smith, D. 1992: Modernity, postmodernity and the new Middle Ages. *Sociological Review*, 40, 4, 754–71.

Smith, D. 1997: Civilization and totalitarianism in the work of Norbert Elias and Hannah Arendt. American Sociological Association Annual Conference, Toronto, August.

Smith, D. 1998a: How to be a successful outsider. *Theory, Culture and Society*, 15, 1, 39–45.

Smith, D. 1998b: Norbert Elias and the New Europe. World Congress of Sociology, Montreal, July/August.

Smith, D. 1999: 'The Civilizing Process' and 'The History of Sexuality': comparing Foucault and Elias. *Theory and Society* (US), 28, 79–100.

Smith, D. and Wright, S. (eds) forthcoming: *Whose Europe?* Oxford: Blackwell.

Smith, D. forthcoming: *Norbert Elias*. London: Sage.

Sobel, D. 1996: *Longitude*. London: Fourth Estate.

ten Bos, R. 1997: Business ethics and Bauman ethics. *Organization Studies*, 18, 6, 997–1014.

Thomas, W.I. and Znaniecki, F. 1918–20: *The Polish Peasant in Europe and America*, 5 volumes. Boston, Mass.: Richard G. Badger (vols 1 and 2 originally published by University of Chicago Press).

Tocqueville, A. 1958: *Journeys to England and Ireland*, translated by George Lawrence and J.-P. Mayer. New Haven, Conn: Yale University Press.

Tocqueville, A. 1968: *Democracy in America*, translated by George Lawrence, edited by J.-P. Mayer and Max Lerner. New York: Collins.

Toynbee, A.J. 1954: *A Study of History*, 6 volumes. London: Oxford University Press; originally published in 1939.

Varcoe, I. 1998: Identity and the limits of comparison: Bauman's reception in Germany. *Theory, Culture and Society*, 15, 1, 57–72.

Varcoe, I. and Kilminster, R. 1996: Addendum: culture and power in the writings of Zygmunt Bauman. In R. Kilminster and I. Varcoe (eds), *Culture, Modernity and Revolution: essays in honour of Zygmunt Bauman*, London: Routledge, 215–47.

Veblen, T. 1918: *The Higher Learning in America: a memorandum on the conduct of universities by businessmen*. New York: August M. Kelley.

Veblen, T. 1970: *The Theory of the Leisure Class*. London: Allen and Unwin; originally published in 1899.

Wagner, P. 1994: *A Sociology of Modernity: liberty and discipline*. London: Routledge.

Whitley, R. (ed.) 1974: *Social Processes of Scientific Development*. London: Routledge.

Wiggershaus, R. 1994: *The Frankfurt School: its history, theories and political significance*. Cambridge: Polity Press.

Woodiwiss, A. 1997: Against 'modernity': a dissident rant. *Economy and Society*, 26, 1, 1–21.

Young-Bruehl, E. 1982: *Hannah Arendt: for love of the world*. New Haven, Conn.: Princeton University Press.

Index